ANTON LaVEY AND THE CHURCH OF SATAN

"In *Anton LaVey and the Church of Satan,* the 'Black Pope' of modern Satanism finds his most able interpreter and biographer. Carl Abrahamsson, the doyen of occulture, has studied LaVey's life and influence for years, focusing his peculiar instinct for the esoteric and transgressive on a character who brought the two into a piquant and appealing blend. Part showman, part huckster, part prophet, and all devil, LaVey's shaved head, Fu Manchu moustache, kitschy horns, and buxom coven brought a comic touch to a heresy that is more often taken all too seriously. Abrahamsson captures the smoky, saucy flavor of LaVey's devilish humor with gusto. Tempted? You should be."

GARY LACHMAN, AUTHOR OF
TURN OFF YOUR MIND AND *THE RETURN OF HOLY RUSSIA*

"A rich, engaging, and insightful exploration of one of the most influential and misunderstood thinkers of late twentieth-century occultism. . . . an invaluable resource for anyone interested in the history of Satanism and late-modern occulture."

MANON HEDENBORG WHITE, SENIOR LECTURER OF RELIGIOUS STUDIES
AT KARLSTAD UNIVERSITY AND AUTHOR OF *THE ELOQUENT BLOOD*

"Unique insights into the myth and man that was Anton LaVey—a must-read for anyone interested in the history and future of Satanism."

PER FAXNELD, PH.D., SENIOR LECTURER
AT SÖDERTÖRN UNIVERSITY AND AUTHOR OF *SATANIC FEMINISM*

"*Anton LaVey and the Church of Satan* is an act of magic, for it takes you to the Black House at 6114 California Street where you are invited to a party in the honor of Doktor LaVey. Carl Abrahamsson is the ideal host of the party—not only has he invited all the right people, but he will introduce them to you as he takes you by the arm and leads you through the house, making sure that you are having fun while generously sharing his profound knowledge about the Doktor. If you're lucky, Doktor LaVey will show you a movie or play on one of his many synthesizers. Enjoy the party!"

HENRIK BOGDAN, PROFESSOR OF RELIGIOUS STUDIES
AT THE UNIVERSITY OF GOTHENBURG AND EDITOR OF
THE OXFORD STUDIES IN WESTERN ESOTERICISM BOOK SERIES

"At a moment when there is increased academic interest in the history of Satanism and the gamut of Satanic religion has fanned out from the radical left to the alt-right, there is great value in revisiting Anton LaVey. With fresh analysis and precious interviews with friends and family, Carl Abrahamsson sheds new light on this controversial and enigmatic figure. The more we learn about LaVey, the more he appears as a node, linking diverse streams of culture from magic to art to politics."

JOSEPH P. LAYCOCK, ASSOCIATE PROFESSOR OF RELIGIOUS STUDIES
AT TEXAS STATE UNIVERSITY AND AUTHOR OF SPEAK OF THE DEVIL

"Abrahamson's work is a personal, sympathetic, yet nuanced portrait of one of the most enigmatic and fascinating figures of the twentieth century. Anton LaVey was a mercurial figure who contained within him paradoxes that continue to defy any simplistic interpretation of him. The diversity of his influence is clearly felt in this work. With several unique interviews and recollections of LaVey, this book will be essential reading for all future studies on Satanism."

FREDRIK GREGORIUS, ASSOCIATE PROFESSOR OF
THE HISTORY OF RELIGION AT LINKÖPING UNIVERSITY AND COEDITOR
OF THE INTERNATIONAL JOURNAL OF THE STUDY OF NEW RELIGIONS

"Through a vivid examination of LaVey's insistence on paving his own road through the pop-cultural landscape of the mid-twentieth century United States, Abrahamsson illuminates a thought-provoking, occultural individual and his circle, ready to shake up any beliefs set in stone to make you think for yourself. Read, and shake!"

KASPER OPSTRUP, AUTHOR OF THE WAY OUT

"As a whole, Abrahamsson's personal and scholarly reflections and the unique assembly of interviews form an archive useful for the newly curious, the jaded occultist, the brazen scholar, and the mostly antagonistic. An impressive work."

JESPER AAGAARD PETERSEN, VICE DEAN OF RESEARCH
AT THE NORWEGIAN UNIVERSITY OF SCIENCE AND TECHNOLOGY

ANTON LaVEY
AND THE
CHURCH OF
SATAN

INFERNAL WISDOM FROM THE
DEVIL'S DEN

CARL ABRAHAMSSON

Inner Traditions
Rochester, Vermont

Inner Traditions
One Park Street
Rochester, Vermont 05767
www.InnerTraditions.com

Text stock is SFI certified

Cataloging-in-Publication Data for this title is available from the Library of Congress

ISBN 978-1-64411-241-0 (print)
ISBN 978-1-64411-242-7 (ebook)

Printed and bound in the United States by Lake Book Manufacturing, Inc.
The text stock is SFI certified. The Sustainable Forestry Initiative® program
promotes sustainable forest management.

10 9 8 7 6 5 4 3 2 1

Text design and layout by Debbie Glogover
This book was typeset in Garamond Premier Pro with Bodoni Std, Gill Sans
MT Pro, ITC Legacy Sans Std, Portia, and WTC used as display typefaces

To send correspondence to the author of this book, mail a first-class letter to the
author c/o Inner Traditions • Bear & Company, One Park Street, Rochester, VT
05767, and we will forward the communication, or contact the author directly at
www.carlabrahamsson.com.

This book is dedicated to
Anton LaVey (1930–1997),
Adam Parfrey (1957–2018), and
Genesis P-Orridge (1950–2020).

Mortui vivos docent!

Contents

"No More Mr. Nice Guy"

IN CELEBRATION OF ANTON LAVEY

By Mitch Horowitz

If you're picking up this book, chances are that you, like me, are rediscovering an artist and a magician with whom neither the mainstream nor the counterculture has ever fully come to terms: Anton LaVey.

With his founding of the Church of Satan in 1966, Anton became the first spiritual rebel to attain superstar status since British occultist Aleister Crowley (1875–1947) more than a generation earlier. And in some respects, no one since Anton's death in 1997 has filled the same role. New Agers and self-helpers have hit best-seller lists, run for president, and attracted millions of television viewers. But no outsider occult figure—one unfit for weekend seminars or headset-wearing TED talks—has upended our cultural assumptions, exposed moral hypocrisies, and embraced outcast iconography as Anton did.

The price of notoriety is misunderstanding. And Anton attracted misperception in unprecedented amounts. Was he evil incarnate? (Spare me.) A usurper of pretense? (Getting warmer.) An artist who wielded outsider themes to reflect back to us our own foibles, failed assumptions, and untapped potential? (Pitchforks up!) Even those who love Anton's work, as I do, differ about his legacy. My act of loosely referencing him as "spiritual" or "occult" will attract the umbrage of some who see him, not without reason, as shattering even those conventionally overused terms. Anton LaVey, a generation following his death, still makes complacency impossible.

Into this wonderfully chaotic and unclassifiable cultural space steps artist, social critic, and filmmaker Carl Abrahamsson. Carl's work, both in this book and his previous *Occulture* (2018), does so much to contextualize Anton LaVey as the Promethean, boundary-breaking provocateur and artist that he was. Literally just as I was writing these words, I hit a wrong key on my laptop and started playing the 1973 Alice Cooper song, "No More Mr. Nice Guy." What a delightful "mistake." As unclassifiable as his subject, Carl Abrahamsson is, in fact, an accurately self-described nice guy—a warm, loving, and ethical man. Yet Carl also reflects what he discovered in Anton and what he has helped others to see in him: the embodied imperative to seek out and define your own road-tested values of honor, loyalty, questioning, and aesthetic integrity, no matter who the hell it offends.

When I first discovered Carl's writing on Anton LaVey in fall of 2017, twenty years after the magician's death, I was close to being lost. A corporate takeover eliminated my long-held position at the helm of a New Age publishing imprint. Cut loose, I felt a sense of adventure but also nervousness about the future—about who I was with my job title gone and a redefinition thrust on me. Although I was already successful as a writer and speaker on alternative spirituality, I felt that my search was getting a little stale. I caught myself repeating certain themes and phrases. I suspected that I was over-relying on insights that were already a few years old. I didn't like it.

One day, Carl's publisher sent me an advance copy of *Occulture* with the request for an endorsement. I opened the table of contents and spotted a chapter title that shot electricity through me: "Anton LaVey, Magical Innovator." I cannot say quite what it was, but the moment that I eyed that chapter I knew I was poised for a change in my life. I already knew of Anton and held a half-formed opinion of him as a goad to mainline culture and, in my view then, as a showman. But I hadn't regarded him with sufficient seriousness—a mistake on my part—and I neglected to include him in my 2009 book *Occult America*. As I held Carl's book in my hands, however, I intuited that his chapter and its reassessment held what I was looking for. My instinct proved right. I read that chapter first, and then the whole book, and I felt moved to do more than just endorse Carl's work. I delved deeply into the ideas of the man who had inspired him and soon produced my own article reassessing a figure whose output I had previously neglected and to which Carl had shaken me awake. Anton's heterodoxy also spurred my own self-defined experiments—literary, intellectual, and spiritual—into Satanism, which have formed a vibrant (and at times also misunderstood) aspect of my current career and search, which are one and the same.

I am writing this introduction in tribute to these figures—Anton, whom I never knew, and Carl, whom I am happy to call a friend—who rescued me when I was starting to trace the arc of a circle in my search. Life may be cyclical, but truth arrives in schisms. Anton was a master at creating schisms.

In this book Carl calls Anton "America's own pop Nietzsche." There is more to that designation than may first appear. I believe that people often require novelty to enter new ideas. Most people who are searching for practical philosophies will not find their way to Nietzsche; they will recall him only as the guy who wrote, "God is dead," and some may even repeat uninformed tropes about the German philosopher and Nazism. Within Anton's work, however, you will discover what I consider a reasonable iteration of the philosophy of self-verification and the rejection of handed-down meaning. You will find this outlook framed within the iconography of revolt against domesticated and often unfulfilled Judeo-Christian values. Yes, it is pop Nietzscheanism, and a sturdy variant of it.

In a 2018 article, "The Devil's Reading List," I reconsidered Anton's iconic and perennial seller, *The Satanic Bible* (1969): "Critics dismissed LaVey's mass-market paperback as a bastardization of Nietzsche and

Ayn Rand, with occult frosting—to which I argue: So what? Much religious and philosophical writing is syncretic, and I see LaVey's work as an effective popularization of those writers combined with his own shrewd insights into human nature. Some readers called the book a catalyst in their lives."

I would no more dismiss a popularization of modern philosophy than I would Shakespeare's reckoning of the machinations of Ancient Rome because it's secondhand history. Artists not only provoke but also mediate. Anton successfully brought decades of readers, including Goth teens at mall bookstores and later online, to the ideals of self-determination when they might otherwise have had no accessible outlet to discover them. The best medicine is the kind that actually lands in your mouth and not on the kitchen floor. That is what Anton offers.

Detractors assert that Anton's celebration of self-attainment lacks ethics. That misperception gets repeated by those who haven't read him or have read him only in an act of prejudicial skimming. Reciprocity, loyalty, respect, and rejection of nonprovoked violence form the code of Anton's outlook. His core ethic could be defined as: *Thou shalt leave another alone*—unless intruded on. If humanity, or even 10 percent of it, could learn the actual lesson of what it means to *leave people alone,* it could revolutionize the world.

Earlier I mentioned the ultraindividualist and utopian capitalist Ayn Rand, a street-fighting philosopher who, like Anton, often inspires umbrage. My reference requires clarification, as does my earlier mention of Aleister Crowley. In a 2017 article inspired by Carl's work, "Good, Clean Satanism," I noted:

> To clarify Anton's belief system, he neither believed in nor worshipped Satan as a literal entity. Rather, he defined Satanism as the instinct and ethic of radical nonconformity. To him, Satanism existed as the countercurrent to crowd mentality, and the pushback against the human mass of group-thinkers who, historically, are responsible for most earthly catastrophes. In Anton's eyes,

the Satanist, rather than being a force of malevolence, is history's rebel, romantic, and freethinker—but with a razor's edge of self-determination, which might be best summarized in the statement famously (if loosely) attributed to Ayn Rand: "The question isn't who is going to let me; it's who is going to stop me."

But Anton could not be called a Randian Objectivist, since he also believed in the power of rite and ritual, practices that were anathema to the hyper-rational capitalist Rand. Nor was Anton in line with the mystical outlook of his aesthetic antecedent Aleister Crowley, whose ceremonial magick and philosophy of living from the True Self is captured in the occultist's celebrated maxim: "Do what thou wilt shall be the whole of the Law. Love is the law, love under will."

Rather than comparing Anton to past or contemporaneous figures, I would describe his outlook more as Positive Thinking Weaponized. He took the creative ethic of America's positive-mind philosophy—specifically the idea that *thoughts are causative*—and married it to a sense of thoughtful hedonism and unfettered creativity, augmented by the power of ritual, pageantry, and self-invention.

My personal philosophy has differences with Anton's, but mostly in emphasis and degree and not in foundation. I believe that our ancient ancestors were on to something very real when they personified and sought relationships with metaphysical energies, which they named Jupiter, Minerva, Set, and so on. I take a spiritual—which is to say extraphysical—view of life. We live under many laws and forces, not all of them, in my view, matters of ordinary cognition, motor skills, and mass. For his part, Anton saw ritual not as a means of reaching out to some unseen dimension of existence but as a way of heightening and sharpening the aims of your individual psyche. Does this present an unbridgeable gap in viewpoint? Not really.

Here, again, I honor the tone and perspective of Carl Abrahamsson. In a manner that I consider historically and biographically accurate,

Carl captures the subtleties of Anton's approach. We live in an interconnected world; when you alter one thing you alter everything. "As above, so below," goes the Hermetic dictum. An act of ritual, use of symbol, or performance of self-expression is "magical" insofar as one altered element necessarily reorders all other elements, including the workings of your psyche, sense of possibility, and perspective. Successful rituals beget change. That was the approach of Anton's magical work, and it is one of several ways in which his actions as an artist and experimenter elude static definition.

This book is not for you if you like life easy and safe. People will judge you—and sometimes seek to penalize you—for exploring Satanism, a term that most people have no interest in probing or reconsidering beyond what they hear from entertainment, friends, or exoteric religion.

A New Age organization with whom I enjoyed years of fruitful collaboration publicly expunged me when rumors got afoot of my exploration of LaVeyan and other forms of Satanism. A Freemasonic lodge cancelled a contracted talk. A popular astrologer threatened to quit a metaphysical venue if I spoke there on the topic. (I spoke anyway.) I have no way of knowing how many people or places have removed me from their invite list or withheld "likes" on social media because of my associations. And ultimately, I do not care.

I write that not in some maudlin or self-glorifying way. I do not crave controversy. And in fact, I am sympathetic to people who run membership-based venues or organizations. At the same time, I refuse to compromise my search, however easily misconstrued. Otherwise, who am I? Some politician or pitchman delivering a sales talk for whatever book I have coming out? My search and my work are the same. Or both are dead.

I cannot pinpoint precisely what attracts me, or maybe you, to the aesthetics and sledgehammer philosophy of Anton LaVey. (He did note that Satanists are born and not made. Ralph Waldo Emerson said something very similar.) I can relate this much: When I was a young editor I was befriended by a much older and highly successful publisher named Peter Mayer. Although I did not know it then, Peter was the one who first approached Anton with the idea of writing *The Satanic Bible*. When I met him in 1989, Peter bravely published novelist Salman Rushdie's *The Satanic Verses* in the United States, attracting some of the same death threats that drove its author into hiding. Beyond what I've noted, the two books, Rushdie's and Anton's, have nothing in common. Or do they? The willingness to embrace and discerningly pursue a radical line of thought—through any medium and without apology—is the one thing that makes free inquiry a practice and not a slogan. It divides thought from habit.

If the classical Satan is, as I argue, the disembodied but not quite metaphorical impulse of usurpation, rebellion, and nonconformity, then that, in itself, suggests why, after centuries upon centuries, thinking people continue returning to Satanic themes, iconography, and aesthetics.

This book and your participation in it reflect a renewal of the questions and challenges that arise from the adversarial impulse. Exploring Satanism on the terms offered here may not win you praise. But doing so may help you—and those who think like you—to succeed in a contest that each of us, in every generation, must face, flee from, or ignore: the elevation of questioning above ease; of verification above recitation; and of choosing to rule in one's choice rather than serve in another's designation.

Good luck in your fight. And remember: "No More Mr. Nice Guy."

Mitch Horowitz is a PEN Award–winning historian and a widely known voice of esoteric ideas with bylines in the *New York Times*, *Time*, *Politico*, *Salon*, and the *Wall Street Journal*. He is the author of several books, including *Occult America*, *One Simple Idea*, *The Miracle Club*, and *The Man Who Destroyed Skepticism*. His book *Awakened Mind* is the first work of New Thought published in Arabic. His work is censored in China.

PART I
INTO THE DEVIL'S DEN

1
STEP RIGHT UP!

Oh, these aren't tricks, madam. Tricks are things that fool people. In the last analysis tricks are lies. But these are real flowers, and that was real wine, and that was a real pig. I don't do tricks. I do magic. I create; I transpose; I color; I transubstantiate; I break up; I recombine; but I never trick. Would you like to see a turtle? I can create a very superior turtle.

CHARLES G. FINNEY, *THE CIRCUS OF DR. LAO*

In 2016, the controversial and eclectic organization called the Church of Satan celebrated its fiftieth anniversary. Its founder, Anton Szandor LaVey, had by then been dead for nineteen years. When strong leaders disappear, it often leaves any organization on shaky ground. What was clear in this case, though, was that the Church of Satan (or "CoS") seemed to have pulled out of these first decades as a very stable and solid group of more or less like-minded individuals who are willing and enthusiastic to be visible and transparent and to eloquently express what's what and what's not in terms of Satanism.

Parallel to this, or perhaps even owing to it, the legacy of the man Anton LaVey has become more visible, accepted, and even honored in other environments than that of the "infernally faithful." One example of this would be his increased presence within academia, most notably in the fields of the history of religions, the history of ideas, and anthropology. It's simply not possible to study and write about Satanism as a phenomenon without passing through LaVey and his Church. This makes perfect sense in many ways, and especially in an America plagued by conflict and dispute that very much still seems rooted in a monotheistic culture of extreme dualisms (good/evil, friend/enemy, etc.). Options are needed, and alternate perspectives are often ushered in through healthy controversy and shock tactics.

LaVey had adopted and adapted a Nietzschean philosophy of life enhancement, personal freedom, and ecstatic epicureanism for the American "market" of the 1960s, but our present time has seen a reaction from all sides of society to the perceived threats of too much freedom in the hands of someone else. In the years since the formation of the Church of Satan, what could have been a well-paved road to more individual freedom has turned slippery at the hands of bitter amateur demagogues with vague theories, always pointing the finger at those happier than themselves. For every hot-button issue, the conflicting sides nowadays usually can't even agree on the fact that they all basically just want more freedom. Instead, they focus the discourse on simplified arguments of why the other side is "wrong" rather than of why one's own perspective is "right."

To me, it's a no-brainer why someone like Anton LaVey appears today as the level-headed voice of reason in a culture so aggressively divided and diametrical in its outlook. Not only did he thrash monotheistic pipe dreams belonging to a mythical past, but rather advocated common sense and a rationalist approach to the most feral and ferocious beast of all: the human being. LaVey also advocated a healthy integration of "responsibility to the responsible" as an absolute prerequisite for organizing a society that *actually functions*.

Just like the proverbial Devil in many cultures, Anton LaVey has popped up in an assortment of manifestations to reflect, pinpoint, and heckle. Sometimes he has been used for cheap thrills or chills and sometimes to concretely promote a philosophy that makes more sense than ever before in human history. The increasing cultural presence of this proto-American iconoclast has also created an interest in the actual philosophy of Satanism. Whereas kids in the past might have used the dreaded "S word" to shock their parents, today it's almost as if the meaning has changed: in an angst-ridden collectivist culture, Satanism has in many ways become a very tangible cluster of creativity, self-empowerment, and constructive approaches to organizing one's own life. It's no longer just a shocking paperback book and symbol in disgruntled teenage rebellions.

For me, this has been very interesting to watch as the years go by. My own reasons for seeking out Anton LaVey and his philosophy back in the 1980s may have been the same as for young people today, but the overall culture is very different. Culture has undoubtedly caught up with the LaVeyan philosophy to a greater extent, and I can certainly see this continuing as both the man himself and his philosophy (as well as the Church of Satan) are regarded with more respect than ever before.

The "Satanic Panic" hysteria of the 1980s, expressed through trashy TV talk shows, ranting radio shows, scandalous (and libelous) books, articles, and fake sensationalist histories, all of which pointed the finger at some dreamed-up devil worshippers, is now but a darkly laughable enigma. Today, any similar kinds of expression can only be found online in the most ridiculous conspiracy theories, designed solely to milk gullible cretins of their hard-earned money and votes.

It is undoubtedly a great time to watch the world go by. As mentioned by several people included in this book, Anton LaVey would have loved so much of what is going on today. Not necessarily to gleefully gloat but just to reaffirm that the human animal would do a whole lot better if the focus lay on pleasure and egotism rather than on endless preaching of compensatory moralisms and self-destructive collective escapisms. The song remains the same: a more balanced and nuanced worldview is necessary in order to make any progress whatsoever. Anton LaVey was indeed a brave man to present his kind of solution the way he did, and at the time he did.

In the year of 2019, I released a documentary film called *Anton LaVey: Into the Devil's Den.* The premise was quite simply to talk to people who had been the notorious Satanist's friends and collaborators at his world-infamous Black House at 6114 California Street in San Francisco, during the last decade of his life (LaVey was born in 1930, and died in 1997).

The reason was simple: I had been one of those people myself, and the experience was in equal parts overwhelmingly mind-boggling and infernally empowering. Some people I got to know early on, in the late 1980s; others were added to this Devil's Den bouquet as the years, and even decades, progressed.

Slightly before the filmmaking was set in motion, there was another project that had got me thinking along similar lines: the book *California Infernal: Anton LaVey and Jayne Mansfield as Portrayed by Walter Fischer.* It was a lavish volume of photographs I had published on my own Trapart Books imprint in 2016, and that really stirred things up inside me. The sometimes candid and sometimes blatantly strategized photos by master paparazzo Walter Fischer became little gateways into the dusty vaults of my memory.

Growing up during the 1970s in Stockholm, Sweden, I led a very stable, safe, and secure life. No wonder then that I gravitated to the realms of underground comics, weird science fiction, and dark occult-isms. Many unconventional strains of culture inspired my prurient youth, and they all merged into substantial parts of my being, most of which are in fact very much alive still.

American pop culture was one seminal part of this imprint cluster. My parents had friends in the United States, and they regularly sent comics, candy, and clothes to me that all became parts of my identity.

A delightful bookstore called Hörnan ("the Corner") in central Stockholm sold weird books, magazines, and comics. I was often in there, being willingly enchanted before I could even fully figure out what was being said on the pages in question.

Occultism was exciting (and it still is!). I drifted into intuitive excursions and eventually came across Anton LaVey's *The Satanic Bible* from 1969. What healthy teenager can resist such an alluring title and tome? And I was thrilled to discover that he had actually founded the Church of Satan in 1966—the very year I was born!

In the Swedish men's magazines at the time, there were often picture stories about scandalous magicians from the ages—frequently using sexually extravagant escapades as "magical" techniques. Anton LaVey was one of these recurring favorites. The photos were titillating, to say the least: LaVey looked so sinister in his black cape and devil horns, and there were always nude ladies serving as altars; smiling seductively at the cameras.

All of these things definitely made an impact on my malleable teenage boy mind. I was pleasantly surprised when I was offered the use of the Walter Fischer images for the *California Infernal* project—some thirty years later! These were basically the same images as in the Swedish men's magazines; only a lot more of them. Were they coming back to haunt me, or what?

Writing the intro for that book had me roaming my memory as well as my diaries. One question surfaced over and over: If I had had these wonderful experiences at the Black House, then surely others had, too? This became the "pre-premise" of the project, gradually crystallizing into the full premise: "Why do you think LaVey showed you what he showed you?" Because I had always had that feeling when I was leaving his house early in the morning (and had ruminated over it throughout the decades): "What the hell just happened?"

I set to work in my already existing network of friends, which then bloomed to include others as well and turned into a real, tangible, and very contemporary bouquet of Satanic flowers. I traveled with my wife, Vanessa Sinclair, to New York, Miami, Los Angeles, San Diego, and San Francisco to conduct filmed interviews. This mosaic of stories from long ago created a pattern that tilted and jolted my mind and opened up far more than mere memories or details. It was a pattern mainly consisting of warm and positive emotions for this unique and creative individual who inspired us so much, and in so many different ways. I followed up with further interviews and questions, and dug up archival documents that had languished for years. These combinations revealed or synthesized an image or crystallization that in most ways confirmed what I had intuited as I set out: that Anton LaVey had shared his time and space (and his many interests) with specific people he liked, in order to not only enjoy himself but to also secure a legacy in the flesh, so to speak. Books are obviously one very important aspect of a legacy, but active memories in other people are something completely different.

The most striking thing about Anton LaVey in this kind of rearview mirror is that he has made a real impact on culture. There was always a prescience there that not only reshaped the past—in terms of his lauding his favorite movies, books, music, occultisms, and the like—but that at the same time also looked deeply into the wells of the future. LaVey's insistence on the importance of phenomena such as the "total environment," the "third side," and "artificial human companions" didn't only turn out to be real; they could in fact have helped spawn and inspire these phenomena.

The similarities with good science fiction are obvious: by writing about the future and thereby inspiring the young in their life choices, and—even more importantly, according to LaVey—their aesthetics, science fiction also helps define the future beyond the mere fictional aspects. LaVey's intuitive assumptions became obsessions, and when he eventually divulged these, they became little spells that affected the big picture in various ways: infernal memes, if you will.

When working on this book, I one evening watched a Q&A with Bavarian film director Werner Herzog, apropos his strangely entertaining 2019 film *Family Romance, LLC*. It's a weird story about warped emotional relationships in contemporary Japanese culture; one in which not only household robots and robot hotels are common, but also one in which "relational" humanoids are on the rise. When Werner Herzog claimed in the Q&A that "they are coming, big time!" I realized that

LaVey's prophecy had manifested. When something moves from the sphere of the prurient, secret, and sexual (or, in a way, from the occult) to the public domain of general acceptance, it's a real paradigm shift that can never be revoked. And some people can see it happening before it's even happening.

> We feel as Nietzsche felt when he wrote in *Zarathustra* that men can no longer fall back on established religion as a sort of identity, a collective identity. Occultism is a sort of do-it-yourself god kit in whatever form it takes. Those who could be accepted collectively simply by being Christians at one time, for example, now find that with automation and with advances in technology, their roles as human beings are much less than ever before. As a result of this, they have set themselves up in a sort of minor godhead role—a god role or goddess role in an, at times, illogical form of importance, or sense of importance. I honestly feel that occultism gives many people a chance to be big fish in little ponds. Man must learn his animal nature by studying the nature of the beast, and from the children— this childlike sense of wonder!—and be able to relate to these things within himself, and the animal within him, in order to develop into the higher man, the man who is ultimately going to succeed, or to survive, on this planet. [1]

Before Anton LaVey became America's own pop Nietzsche, he had a colorful career in many fields. From the late 1940s and onward, the musically skilled LaVey played keyboards in many different settings: at nightclubs, events, bars, circuses, and sideshows. The accumulated experiences of seeing how people behaved in various states of successful (and quite often not so successful) states of lustful inebriation became the cornerstones of his philosophy of life. This also included wisdoms from other animals than the human one—mainly large cats, such as lions and tigers—as he learned how to interact with them at the circus. For many years, he even kept a Nubian lion called Togare as a pet inside the Black

House—until it became too big and noisy, and the neighbors petitioned to have it removed to the San Francisco Zoo.

Over the years, this feral philosophy gravitated toward an inclusion of occult symbols and thoughts, mostly of the "dark" kind that every kid was warned about, but therefore sought out first. The symbol of Satan was in many ways perfect for Anton LaVey, as he cultivated his Mephisthophelean look and his reputation of being a magician—and not only of the kind on stage. Satan was without a doubt the most feared symbol around, and therefore the most attractive.

In the early 1960s, Anton LaVey's interest in magic grew. He was established in his Black House and held lectures and classes. Topics could range from vampires, werewolves, freaks, the Black Mass, death, ghosts, and gothic culture to many other things. The "Great Szandor" (as he had been called as a dramatic organ player at the circus) spellbound his visitors. As his magic circle of friends and allies grew, what happened then seemed inevitable: in 1966 he founded the Church of Satan, and in 1969 *The Satanic Bible* was published. Media attention was massive: from men's magazines focusing on the nude ladies and the sexual rituals to mainstream magazines focusing on the alarming resurgence of non-Christian allegiances.

Satan may not mean so much in a cultivated, secular society, but talk to most any Christian and he or she will react as if Satan actually exists as some kind of anthropomorphic monster. LaVey knew how easily provoked his fellow Americans could be and decided to press that button, thereby getting negative attention from reactive, monotheistic simpletons, but also positive attention from people who could see beyond the jolt, and who used the very word as a provocative bullshit detector. Anton LaVey had found a method that worked: mixing showbiz shock tactics with clever demagogic strategies.

LaVey basked in the attention and wrote the books *The Compleat Witch, or What to do When Virtue Fails* (1970, later reissued as *The Satanic Witch* in 1989) and *The Satanic Rituals* (1972). Beneath all the scandalous exposure was also a serious magician who wanted to break away from dusty, arcane, esoteric systems basically stemming from medieval times. LaVey came up with new magical concepts based on psychological insights, gained as much from the carnival as from Sigmund Freud, as much from playing the organ at dive bars as from Friedrich Nietzsche. Active psychodrama, the use of sex, creating your own temple space by indulging in whatever gives you most pleasure, creating artificial human companions instead of wasting time on dull acquaintances, and definitely integrating a dark sense of humor—all of these things he now presented as "Satanism."

LaVey's Satanism is a cluster, not only of philosophy, but also of aesthetics. It's an aesthetic not only dimly lit in gothic horror gaslight or garish circus light bulbs. The evocative shadow world of German expressionist cinema and early Hollywood horror films—not forgetting the stark contrasts of film noir—deeply influenced the young LaVey. The lighting and composition theories of American photographer William Mortensen became almost an obsession, and LaVey integrated many of Mortensen's ideas into the designs and performances of various Church of Satan rituals.

Throughout his books, LaVey generously name-dropped his inspirations and influences, and it is indeed an interesting cultural archaeology to journey in the trails of his philosophical explorations. Aesthetically minded precursors such as Max Reinhardt, Fritz Lang, and Reginald Marsh got their acknowledgments on the very first pages of *The Satanic Bible;* as did Wilhelm Reich, Basil Zaharoff, P. T. Barnum, Mark Twain, George Orwell, and H. G. Wells. It's a veritable who's who of dangerous (in the sense of revolutionary) ideas, hidden keys, cabals, and pragmatic approaches.

But it's also interesting to see those he left out in these printed sources, although their influence was massive. I'm thinking specifically of British author W. Somerset Maugham and British inventor and eccentric Dr. Cecil Nixon. Although certainly acknowledged at times, they weren't included in the same way as many others. I have often wondered if that was perhaps another clue in itself, or perhaps simply examples of "omission by obsession." Their stature and status in the LaVeyan universe cannot be overstated, so I will dedicate one whole separate chapter to influences like theirs.

The same goes for the ladies. . . . In times like ours, when identity politics have morphed with the LaVeyan "good guy badge" concept on steroids, and the self-appointed spokesperson virus is raging beyond pandemic level—and thereby inducing the worst possible censorship of all: self-censorship—it is appropriate that I also focus on the radical ideas that LaVey summarized in his still provocative grimoire of carnal wisdom: *The Satanic Witch*.

In this book, I have tried to give a better and fuller insight into a man and magician who has morphed from a media savvy enigma to a genuine American icon. And I hope also an insight into, and a vivid picture of, the structure that was the exquisite total environment that attracted us all: the Black House. After LaVey's death in 1997, and ensuing turns of events that led to his partner Blanche Barton and son Xerxes LaVey having to move out, the actual house at 6114 California Street was demolished on October 17, 2001, a mere month after "9/11." In many ways, the violent end of an American era of optimism was symbolized by these powerful buildings in rubble—one heap on each American coast.

2

WELCOME TO THE HOTEL CALIFORNIA!

Within a sideshow tent are people dealing with mysteries as old as the human race—and dealing with them in the same cool professional manner that pharaoh's magicians must have shown when they duplicated Moses's feat of turning his rod into a serpent. But I realized that whatever secrets they knew would always be hidden from me unless I joined a sideshow.

DAN MANNIX, *STEP RIGHT UP!*

Late 1989, I entered the Devil's Den for the first time. The building itself was a typical Victorian San Francisco lady, yet untypically painted black. Being let into a dimly lit corridor, I almost tripped on a box by the door. I was being led into a purple room, with bookshelves, a nice couch, two easy chairs, a coffee table made out of a tombstone, some decorative peacock feathers, a TV set. . . .

I was welcomed by Blanche Barton, who offered me a drink and told me that "the Doktor" would be with us shortly. She was elegantly dressed, as if she had just stepped up from a 1940s movie, looking every bit the part of a femme fatale in cahoots with the toughest player in town (which was undoubtedly true). A real moll doll, and definitely a swell dame with nice "stems."

I looked around, curiously. Yes, it was indeed the same Purple Parlor I had seen so, so many times in Ray Laurent's great 1969 documentary, *Satanis,* which I had at home on a third generation VHS dupe.

Suddenly Anton LaVey came in—Doktor LaVey to his friends—and we greeted each other enthusiastically. I was definitely flabbergasted. Although I had plenty of experience in dealing with celebrities from having been a fanzine editor for so many years, this was probably the first time I felt completely starstruck and genuinely nervous. The good Doktor, however, immediately set me at ease.

LaVey is usually described as having styled himself on Emperor Ming the Merciless in the great *Flash Gordon* serial from 1936 (with Ming superbly played by Charles Middleton), and there was definitely some of that in the man who now greeted me. But there was also simply a self-confident American man, suavely dressed in all black, who had a lifetime of absolutely unique experiences, and the captivating ability to tell the stories that fit the moment . . . and the guest.

LaVey told me that he had heard that I had already met up with Boyd Rice—the infamous noise musician and prankish provocateur—which was true. On the day before, I had visited Boyd at his apartment on Jones Street together with my friend Tim O'Neill. Boyd was kind enough to lend me his copy of the very rare Burton Wolfe paperback, *The Devil's Avenger* (the first Anton LaVey biography). Boyd was happy that I was going over to Anton's and said that we'd probably meet up there at some point—he was at this time a regular at the Black House.

Both LaVey and Blanche complimented me on the first issue of my occultural journal *The Fenris Wolf,* which had been published recently and contained not only my infatuated article "Jayne Mansfield—Satanist!" but also LaVey's own "Evangelists vs the New God." I was very proud of this new publishing endeavor and was of course very happy that LaVey had let me use one of his many great pieces from the Church of Satan newsletter, the *Cloven Hoof.*

Late in the evening, we boarded LaVey's exquisite black Jaguar XJ-16 (license plate: "Szandor") and ended up at the MacArthur Park restaurant, where we indulged to the fullest.

We returned to the Black House, and with the help of coffee I got into a second gear. But it wasn't as if I needed it; as soon as we got inside the kitchen, I was boosted with new energy. As I looked at the black walls, decorated with colorful and cartoonish demons—one of them even swallowing a kitchen pipe—and a beautiful vintage poster of LaVey's favorite film (*Nightmare Alley,* Edmund Goulding, 1947), LaVey sat down by his many synthesizers, arranged on convenient racks. He had a very particular smile when he was seated there: the very epitome of gleeful. Like a mischievous boy ready to have some fun, LaVey looked at Blanche and me, and then threw himself headfirst into a medley that contained Wagner's "Ride of the Valkyries" and the "Horst-Wessel-Lied," but also many melodies unknown to me. It was a wild, wild ride, orchestrated by a real dark side impresario.

When he took a little break, basking in our applause, I asked whether he knew some music from Scandinavia, and if so, if I could record it for the upcoming White Stains album (my band at the time). He nodded and seemed almost happy to have been given a sacred mission. I immediately got out my Sony cassette recorder and pressed record.

Sure enough, LaVey joyfully embarked on something that definitely sounded like an old folk song, but arranged and performed as if it had been included in some 1960s science fiction film. He even hollered at the right place, and in my mind I could almost see a young couple, dancing, dressed in old, traditional Swedish clothes. It was a remarkable experience. One year later, the recording was included on the White Stains album, *Dreams Shall Flesh.* I called the piece "The Satanic Hambo."

(Much, much later someone told me that it was actually some kind of Danish Christmas song, and I wondered where the hell LaVey had first not only heard but also memorized this peculiar little tune.)

Back in the Purple Parlor, we talked about anthologizing his essays from the *Cloven Hoof,* and also, at my suggestion, a Swedish translation of *The Satanic Bible.* I planned to start a company called Psychick Release upon my return to Sweden, to act both as a record and book publishing company. I had already translated Aleister Crowley's *The Book of the Law* and the main Temple Ov Psychick Youth text, *Thee Grey Book,* into Swedish, so I felt it was high time to move on with a new and powerful project. LaVey, of course, happily agreed.

On the next evening we watched the wonderful film *The Falcon's Alibi* (Ray McCarey, 1946). It was one of a series of light detective films about the womanizing sleuth, The Falcon, but the main thing here seems to have been LaVey's admiration for the actor Elisha Cook Jr. He told me to always keep an eye out for movies with Cook, which I have since diligently done.

LaVey also took out a book from his shelf and read to me. It was Ben Hecht's *Fantazius Mallare: A Mysterious Oath,* originally published in 1922. It's a sublime piece of evocative writing, relaying darkly disturbed free associations from a delirious protagonist; much in the same vein as Lautréamont's *The Songs of Maldoror.* He then went on to pick another book from the shelf. It was Hecht's *A Guide for the Bedevilled* (1944). I can't remember the exact passage, but it was read with weight and declamation, instilling in me the feeling that it was important.

I was not aware of this book at the time. LaVey explained that Hecht had been a staunch anti-anti-Semite and had been active in trying to awaken the powerful Jews of Hollywood to become not only enraged but also engaged in the critical situation in Europe. Alas, to no avail. After the war, Hecht was a rogue Zionist, trying to facilitate the establishment of the State of Israel in every way he could. I knew of Hecht mainly as an author of dark 1920s fiction, and as an Academy Award–winning scriptwriter. Now, LaVey had brought out a wider reflection of this obvious hero of his.

Not long after this, Boyd Rice dropped by, and we all had a great night together. The talks were focused solely on movies. To tie in with Ben Hecht, we watched the Marx Brothers in *At the Circus* (Edward Buzzell, 1939). Both Hecht and Buster Keaton were uncredited writers of this amazing film. We also watched clips from the macabre anthology film *Death Scenes* that LaVey had narrated in his dramatic voice. He also told us that he had been instrumental in the revival of Tod Browning's *Freaks* from 1932, as well as in promoting Herschell Gordon Lewis's classics *Blood Feast, Two Thousand Maniacs!,* and *Color Me Blood Red,* as well as Tobe Hooper's *The Texas Chainsaw Massacre.*

On that gory note, LaVey also showed clips from a low-key film about the murderer Ed Gein, which was the same film I had watched in 1988 at a great film show in Gothenburg, curated and introduced by (literally) explosive performance artist and painter Joe Coleman, *Ed Gein: A Nice, Quiet Man.*

Sometime during the late night, LaVey's daughter Karla dropped by together with her friend Leonard from the San Francisco band The Dickies, and the conversations kept on flowing.

On my way out of the Black House at 8 a.m. the following morning, I almost tripped over that same box in the corridor by the front door again. As LaVey waved goodbye, he explained that the box in question had been used by Skippy, the dog who played the chipper Asta in the successful *Thin Man* series of films between 1934 and 1947. Before I left, LaVey also told me that he had been on the phone with Kenneth Anger earlier, who had relayed that there were no problems at all in regard to my visiting him: all I had to do was take a taxi straight from the airport to his house in Hollywood. A new and mythic world was opening up to me, and needless to say, I liked it.

After visiting Kenneth Anger in Hollywood—a tale for another time—I traveled on to Palm Springs and stayed with friends of Anger's who were involved in arranging film festivals. We also went to have lunch with the surrealist sculptor Sésame Thanz-Buckner and her husband, who in turn were friends of Samson De Brier (half of whose house Anger was living in, the very same house where Anger's masterpiece *Inauguration of the Pleasure Dome* had been filmed in 1954).

To cut a long story short, Sésame made beautiful sculptures that enchanted many a Palm Springs garden. She mentioned in passing that she also sold used, collectible books. Although I was practically penniless at the time, heading back to Sweden with an overweight suitcase and an equally full mind, I asked her—just for the hell of it—if she perhaps had some Ben Hecht books for sale. Sésame said she didn't but wanted to check with a friend close by who also sold books. After having called her friend, she came back and told me, "Yes, there's one Hecht book we can pick up later. It's called *A Guide for the Bedevilled*. Would that be something for you, Carl?" In that moment, my acknowledgment of synchronicities was thoroughly and irrevocably cemented.

One full year later, I returned to the Black House in the company of my girlfriend at the time: Swedish filmmaker Beatrice Eggers. Tony, the seemingly ever-present majordomo, let us into the house, and very soon I was back in the timeless zone of the Purple Parlor.

It had been a very good year for me, and LaVey and Blanche poured praise over the second issue of *The Fenris Wolf,* and White Stains' first album, *At Stockholm,* a collaboration with Genesis and Paula P-Orridge of Psychic TV.

We had dinner at Joe's in Daly City—a snazzy diner with wonderful American food. I specifically remember our talking about the future of humanity. LaVey was definitely a real misanthrope, and of a kind that could be easily riled up when something extra idiotic had happened in the world. I believed then, and still do, that there can be potential disadvantages if you have the good fortune, which LaVey had, to be too wholly immersed in a beloved total environment. Despite the fact that it brings on an increase in joy and harmony, it can also potentially make you more sensitive to *la comedie humaine* outside, which could then disturb you even more than perhaps necessary.

Back at the Black House, I asked LaVey if he would officiate a wedding for Beatrice and me. We both felt humbled and honored when he agreed to this.

Two evenings later, on New Year's Day 1991, we were back at the Black House. We were brought into the ritual chamber, the very same room I had fantasized about since I was a teenager. There it all was: Rasputin's rocking chair, Francis Dashwood's chair from the Hellfire Club, a Knights Templar sword, the skull of a pope, Bram Stoker's ashes inside an Egyptian statue, a Conn organ, previous house owner and "Madame" Mammy Pleasant's photo of her son built into the fireplace with cobblestones and debris from the 1906 San Francisco earthquake, several statues and paintings made for LaVey, and of course the majestic altar "Baphomet" pentagram: the symbol of the Church of Satan.

Beatrice and I faced the altar while LaVey and Blanche were behind us. LaVey placed Dashwood's chair right behind us and sat down. Then he began with a magnificent oratorium, which I didn't recognize from any older Church of Satan sources. He conveyed that our need of each other creates a free-spirited and also dangerous cell, in which our mutual dependency creates a strong freedom more than anything else. There is a force field inside the cell with which we can build and create. After his ten-minute speech, LaVey declared us man and wife, "In Nomine Satanas." We kissed and hugged, and then LaVey and Blanche joined us in a very special Satanic group hug.

After this beautiful ceremony, we sipped champagne in the subdued light, while LaVey showed us many of the priceless objects in the room. Afterward, we drove in the Jaguar to MacArthur Park to celebrate, and I watched San Francisco pass by as in a dream. After which, as usual by now, we returned to 6114 California Street to talk more, and also watch *Roman Scandals* (Frank Tuttle, 1933) with Eddie Cantor. I remember how LaVey liked to point out how Joseph Goebbels was like the spitting image of the great Eddie Cantor.

The following evening we got together at the exquisite La Bergère on Geary. Beatrice and I were tired but very happy newlyweds; very much living in a perpetual state of, if not disbelief, then at least blissful amazement. And it certainly didn't get any worse when we got back to the house again. LaVey was in a splendid mood and hammered out another classic medley: "Get Thee Behind Me, Satan," "Old Devil Moon," "Somewhere Over the Rainbow," as well as the Russian national anthem!

And more praise all along the way. We kept talking about future projects. The big one being the Swedish translation of *The Satanic Bible*, which I had begun work on and also bought the rights to at that time.

We watched two great Jayne Mansfield films: *The Wayward Bus* (Victor Vicas, 1957) and *Single Room Furnished* (Matteo Ottavio, 1966/1968). Beatrice, herself a voluptuous twenty-year-old blonde, was overjoyed to hear LaVey's many stories about Jayne Mansfield and Marilyn Monroe.

When we left in the morning, we were exhausted and elated at the same time—probably the best way to describe the post-6114 experience. You were infused with a solid mix of intelligence, humor, orgone, and joie de vivre. When you eventually woke up in the afternoon, the borders between dream and waking states were always pleasantly blurred.

In the summer of 1993, I visited San Francisco again; this time alone. It was apparent to me that LaVey wasn't well physically, but he was certainly happy. When I came by, he told me what was already apparent at the time: Blanche was six months pregnant! They were both beaming with pride and joy. I put my hand on Blanche's belly, and LaVey smiled and said, "See, Carl, I can still cut the mustard!" It was fantastic to be part of this genuine happiness, albeit for only an evening.

We had dinner at a great French place called Le Trou, an experience slightly clouded by some loudmouth cokeheads at the table next to us. They were yapping away aggressively, completely disregarding any sense of courtesy, and we were genuinely disturbed. Blanche carefully opened her purse to show me an elegant ladies' gun with a mother-of-pearl grip. Should it be needed, she was more than ready to solve the problem right there and then. I could also viscerally feel LaVey's anger, and him working his magic. Although the morons were only half done with their meals, they suddenly tossed some money on the table and left! Finally, we could enjoy our food and wine in peace!

Back at the Black House we had some more coffee and talked away. I told LaVey about my pen fetishism, which made him very happy. He showed me some of his own—most of them were fountain pens from the 1930s.

And while we were on the subject of cherished objects of fetishism, he also showed me some of his guns and "Al Mar" knives, phenomenally beautiful objects. Given his sincere reverence for these objects, it was like being inside a Sanctum Sanctorum filled with amazing human craftsmanship and ingenuity.

Since I was leaving for Sweden the very next morning, I asked if I could crash on the couch in the Purple Parlor for a few hours. This was perfectly fine, and we said goodbye in the wee hours of the morning. Luckily, Blanche made sure I got up again, or else I would have missed my plane.

As I got into the cab outside this legendary "Hotel California," waving goodbye to the radiant mother-to-be, the immortal words of the Eagles bards resonated inside my mind: "You can check out anytime you like, but you can never leave." I found it to be not only poetically poignant but also existentially astute.

3

ANTON LAVEY, MAGICAL INNOVATOR

This is the circus of Doctor Lao.
We show you things that you don't know.
We tell you of places you'll never go.
CHARLES G. FINNEY, *THE CIRCUS OF DR. LAO*

Assuming that there is already a fundamental knowledge of Satanism in this illustrious crowd, I'm going to allow myself to delve deeper into a few specialized sections of Anton LaVey's contribution to contemporary magical philosophy.*

Let's generalize a bit and say that the first half of the twentieth century was all about synthesizing. East met West, and this was integrated into esoteric systems by intelligent structure-makers. The Golden Dawn was one such group of structure makers; Theosophy under Blavatsky, also. Gurdjieff was another protagonist, and Steiner another; Aleister Crowley perhaps the most well-known one. They all made nutritious stews but basically out of already existing ingredients.

---

*This chapter was originally a lecture I held at the occult bookstore, Nekropolis, in Copenhagen, Denmark, on December 7, 2013.

The second half of the twentieth century was more violent and also more creative in many ways. As the recent structures had become established and their once-so-pioneering key people had become accepted teachers or gurus, a new breed bred on first-generation Thelema, Golden Dawn splinter groups, and assorted pre-1960s swamis from the East concocted their own syntheses and groups—however, taking considerably more contemporary fodder into account than previously.

Science, psychology, irony and humor, art, speculative philosophies, and other previously rare phenomena within occultism suddenly overrode arcane concepts such as invocation, banishing, Kabbalah, tarot, wands, astrology, mystical angelic languages and ancient demonic names, et cetera. Instead, the focus lay in spheres of experimentation, neurology, psychodrama, sexuality, and other nonsectarian core human phenomena. Old structures were dissolved in new ways of looking at things.

The Church of Satan was one of these precursors of radical change. Established in 1966 by Anton LaVey, the Church's first phase until the late 1970s was one of visibility and provocation. LaVey's colorful presence made both him and his Church celebrities. As a well-formulated and intriguing antidote to the mellow and essentially selfless hippies of the era, LaVey was cabled all over the world into news and men's magazines, who found the naked women on his altar just shocking enough to print.

During the second phase, from the late '70s and until his death in 1997, LaVey became much more of a recluse and solitaire. He was established, and *The Satanic Bible* kept on selling and generated an income, which meant he could thereby devote his time and energies to one of the key concepts of the Church of Satan: indulgence instead of abstinence. One of the things he enjoyed and indulged in was writing.

Although his books *The Satanic Bible, The Satanic Rituals,* and *The Satanic Witch* are his most well known, I would say that the later anthologies *The Devil's Notebook* and *Satan Speaks!,* are much more substantial when it comes to his own thinking. The *Bible* and the *Rituals* were basically assemblage volumes, in which pragmatically chosen material was edited together and augmented further by initiated comments. But the two volumes of essays and maxims that followed much later—*The Devil's Notebook* and *Satan Speaks!*—genuinely contain the essence of LaVey's latter-day wit and creativity.

The essays are also a great source of some groundbreaking magical concepts, both on the lesser magic level (willed manipulation of everyday life) and greater magic level (ritualized programming of a willed "Is to Be" situation or development).

Already in *The Satanic Bible* LaVey had shown considerable creativity. Concepts such as psychic vampires and the Balance Factor quickly became household terms in America and the rest of the world. His description of the ritual space as an intellectual decompression chamber also hit home outside the strictly Satanic perimeters, as did the slightly later term *occultnik,* signifying a person who is lost within old structures of occultism without being able to see what's really of use on a practical, material level.

In *The Satanic Bible* we can also find an old-school method within occult writing: creative appropriation of an older source, in this case, LaVey's use of the Enochian keys originally written by John Dee and Edward Kelley via the biographer Meric Casaubon in 1659 and then regurgitated throughout the centuries until Crowley. LaVey exchanged the final intonations traditionally translated as "the highest" with *Saitan,* claiming the previous translations and vibrations had been erroneous: "The barbaric tonal qualities of this language give it a truly magical effect which cannot be described."[1] He also claimed that the nature of the scrying that Kelley as the "gazer" used had been mis-presented as via the grace of angels, when in fact, according to LaVey, it has to do with ocular and psychic angles, which can, metaphorically or not, open wide the Gates of Hell.

The Satanic Witch was a primer in applied, practical feminism. It also brought in concepts such as the LaVey Personality Synthesizer, or the Personality Clock. This is a method to be used in various kinds of matchmaking, human as well as within other areas of choice and resonance, not as a spiritual oracle of some kind, but as a down-to-earth method of applied psychology.

There was also the important concept of ECI, or Erotic Crystallization Inertia. Meaning that our very first defining erotic moments, such as the first orgasm, will be forever linked to the surroundings, emotional atmospheres, et cetera, inside our psyche. That crystallizing moment will be with us forever and affect us all throughout life. As it is an overwhelmingly emotional moment, for good and bad, it can be tapped as a source of energy in magical workings. As with a general and honest definition of one's own sexuality, the conscious working with ECI brings several benefits to the magician.

One telling example most of us can see within our own culture is the fact that both men and women seem to get stuck time- and lookwise in the period when they were most sexually active and attractive. LaVey pointed out some concrete situations where ECI is usually unconsciously used but even more visible. Solitary elderly people, such as widows or widowers, usually become depressed and lacking in motivation. When in the company of people of the same generation, and in an environment that is created to evoke this sexual peak period of life, vitality and general health come back in almost miraculous ways. We'll return to this in the form of another LaVeyan construct: the total environment.

One important aspect of *The Satanic Witch* was the development of what LaVey called "The Law of the Forbidden," meaning that to attract a person or a desired situation, one needs to be genuinely aware of one's own qualities (this is very tied in to the Balance Factor mentioned earlier) and the alluring display of sections but *not* all of it. Showing a little bit of flesh by "mistake" can create a greater jolt and impact than quickly undressing and revealing it all. "Nothing is so fascinating as that which is not meant to be seen." There is even a chapter in *The Satanic Witch* called "The Secrets of Indecent Exposure." However, the dynamic need not be sexual at all. The Law of the Forbidden can be used in many different areas.

Sexual honesty is paramount in the LaVeyan universe. Personal fetishes are also extremely important, whether sexual or emotional. To feel strongly about something that concerns no one else is to generate a force field that can be tapped indefinitely. To feel strongly about something that concerns a multitude of people is to generate leakage and distortion. To savor small items of active preference in a fetishistic way thereby becomes a highly conscious magical act. Emulation is *not* a key to Satanism. Passion, on the other hand, is.

What follows here is an overview of some further key concepts that I hope can inspire the student to delve further into the mysteries of him- or herself via the Satanic grid.

Integration of the ego: Almost all previous magical systems were developed within a dichotomy that was structured around the relationship between higher and lower. No doubt having to do with monotheistic religious imprints in which *this* life is insufficient and that some kind of idealized "pie in the sky" is better.

The heavy influx of Freudian energy during the twentieth century revealed the power of the conscious ego. LaVey integrated the ego as a valid and relevant component in magical thought and thereby made void invisible moralisms that had until then permeated the world view of practically all previous magical conceptualists.

Higher/lower is in itself a concept imbued with value, and that value stems from control systems stressing that the ideal can essentially not be reached within the span of one human lifetime. LaVey, on the other hand, stressed that the uncertainty of karmic relations *possibly* transcending this lifetime is too strong, and that gratification of desires in the here and now is more of a natural given, and certainly more worth striving for.

One also has to take into consideration that will is always expressed through ego, and that even demigod characters projected with selfless, altruistic, and spiritual existence (the Dalai Lama, Gandhi, other Eastern figures, gurus, the pope) all make choices through their egos.

The LaVeyan perspective disrobes a great deal of hypocrisy in our zeitgeist, whether the proponents be political, religious, magical, or just generally altruistic. There is always ego involved in decision making, and if this is not recognized and exposed, obstructing illusions will dominate the analytical faculties of those taking part. This illusion would only be deemed "Satanically sanctioned" if the person in question allows him- or herself to be duped in order to gratify his or her *own* masochistic need of servitude.

The LaVeyan magical system favors the eloquent will of the ego—as well as its underlying libidinal and compensatory forces—as the most relevant ideal to strive for. Whichever clothing this ideal is individually dressed in, it rids itself of the illusions stemming from other people's projections, as well as from *their* individual ego-based wills.

Although LaVey and later LaVeyans have expressed a critical stance in regard to a concept such as spiritual, the concept itself would be better off in a dichotomy called "inner" and "outer" (thereby leveling or at least decimating any inherent value-based interpretations). We all work with processes of thinking, willing, feeling, et cetera, and they could all be seen as being inner or related to the workings of the mind. These processes are then expressed in the outer, filtered through the ego.

If the inner is inspired somehow by what is traditionally stamped as spiritual, or higher (adherence to a certain technical language or certain techniques such as yoga, meditation, or even specific religious thought or iconography), and this is expressed through a conscious ego, the ball game is moved from an externally controlled or imposed field of values to the highly magical and ego-gratifying field of well-being in resonance.

All altruism stems from decisions made by the ego, as does all non- or antialtruism. This integration of a considerably more stripped attitude when it comes to the human psyche and its motivations is probably LaVey's most important contribution to magical thought.

The validation and integration of emotion: Where previous Western magical systems had been based on an intellectual and systematized/

structured approach, Anton LaVey brought in the emotional as a key agent. No greater magical working can, according to LaVey, be successful without an evocation of relevant human emotions. Although this sounds simple enough, it becomes a dilemma when the individual is armed to the teeth with fancy elemental weapons and a perfect *intellectual* understanding of "how" to perform a traditional ritual. But what about "Why"? Why is this ritual performed? Usually, to "cause change to occur in conformity with will," to paraphrase Aleister Crowley. That's fair and fine enough, but if the magician in question only works within a strictly intellectual sphere with a rational approach, he or she might just as well focus on lesser magic (i.e., a Machiavellian manipulation of the surroundings).

Any working dealing with greater aspects needs emotional investment in the ritual moment. LaVey's term for the temple space—the intellectual decompression chamber—pretty much sums it up. It is a challenge for most people to honestly know themselves and to have the courage, even in solitary settings, to display weaknesses and emotions not in line with the desired self-image. But how else can you develop, overcome, or banish these weaknesses?

A sense of humor: Of course, this was not invented by Anton LaVey. But few magicians have stressed it as an important quality and also a tool. "A Satanist without a sense of humor would be unbearable," he says in the documentary *Speak of the Devil*.[2] The use of tricks, jokes, and pranks can be integrated in complex and highly serious magical workings, especially if it entails ridiculing a pretentious person or force or strategically demeaning or belittling oneself to gain a better perspective or position. The clown or the joker is indeed a powerful figure or type.

The Devil's Notebook is suitably dedicated to "the men, whoever they are, who invented the Whoopee Cushion, the Joy Buzzer, and the Sneeze-O-Bubble."

Invariably, those with the most finely honed sense of humor find serious meaning in what everyone else ridicules. The very nature of the joke is its foundation of misfortune. The joke maker can spot the sham in acceptably serious situations. Then, having called attention to the deception, he may stand forth as a Satanic tribune. Not so easy is the reverse. The same rebel who defends the unpopular and the ridiculed, plays to an audience whose only illusion of strength lies in its ability to ridicule. It's interesting to observe how lower man, while realizing the sadness of clowns, seldom pays attention to them when they have serious thoughts to offer.[3]

Incidentally, the Satanically important character of the villain, by his very antithetical stance, also makes fun of the existing order and morals and hence functions as a liberating character—if intelligent and conscious about it. Scapegoating is an important and apparently necessary function in the human psyche. At least for egos that are not healthily gratified. To take on the persona of the vilified or the mocking catalyst requires an inner strength not often found among the "herd," according to LaVey.

Artificial human companions: Inspired by his own misanthropy, nostalgia, and will to be in charge, LaVey early on started creating humanoid dolls—often as memories from his own youth. In the basement of his Black House in San Francisco (the house immortalized by the Eagles in their chart-busting song "Hotel California"), LaVey had a bar called "The Den of Iniquity," complete with several artificial human companions. This environment and its denizens acted as an intellectual decompression chamber as much as the classic black temple space upstairs or the kitchen where he kept his vast collection of synthesizers and other musical instruments. To be able to make small talk with the drunks, the bartender, and the old lady on the floor who was a drunken exponent of LaVey's own sexual fetish— watching women piss their panties—became a sanctuary and a zone free of rational processes and expectations. Anything could happen. And often did.

The emergence of commercially available nonhuman companions (for instance, those made by the company RealDoll) not solely intended for sexual use is a clear current example of a LaVeyan concept manifesting outside of the strictly Satanic environment.

> I have great respect for those who pioneer their own artificial human companion, crude as they might initially be. They will have come a small step closer to playing God and creating man or woman according to their desired image. With a creative outlet as cloaked in age-old taboo as this, innovation may now run rampant—more so than any art form man has yet known. The bizarre twilight world of the ventriloquist, the puppet-master and the doll maker can perhaps be understood through other than the minds of psychologists. The acceptable schizoid element in all of us—the one that selects our mates—has a fresh, new, open portal to pass through. Through surrogates the race will survive.[4]
>
> The prime appeal of the humanoid lies in its approximation of the purchaser's "other half.". . . Artificial companions that are pleasingly heard, smelled, and felt also constitute positive selling points. But that an artificial companion looks right is of primary importance.[5]

The total environment: One of the most important ideas or concepts along with that of artificial human companions is the total environment. Consistent in his exclusion of the herd that provokes deep misanthropy and his inclusion of personal aesthetics and fetishism, LaVey's development of total environments is a key to understanding the subtleties of his magic.

In a world that becomes louder and louder and more and more fragmented, the existence of a sacred space filled with perfection and maximum personal resonance almost becomes a heretical act. It actually is. Not only does it affect you in beneficial ways such as relaxation, excitement, and inspiration, there's also the possibility of using these spaces (and times, if they are time or era specific) for creative magical rituals in many different ways and directions.

In *The Satanic Rituals,* LaVey stated that "Man's ugly habit of elevating himself by defaming others is an unfortunate phenomenon, yet apparently necessary to his emotional well-being."[6]

With the development of total environments and many of his other concepts, there was no longer a need for LaVey to be a frustrated outsider in conflict with the herd. The Satanist's creative isolation in a space/time-warp-possible mind frame is one of silence and subtlety, and one of the greatest tools of the Satanic trade.

This, combined with honest self-knowledge and a proud appreciation of one's own kinks and complications, makes for a good, solid Satanist. There's always a strong focus on real-life material success, too—but only based on the Balance Factor, and what is actually possible for an individual in that position. Self-deceit is not a popular quality in LaVey's cosmos. "The most successful individuals throughout history have been the people who learn a few good tricks and apply them well, rather than those with a whole bag full who don't know which trick to pull out at the right time—or how to use it once they get it out!"[7]

The total environment encompasses many of the central LaVeyan concepts in one confined yet endless space. Personal preferences, esthetics, the intellectual decompression chamber, fetishism, misanthropy, and possibly artificial human companions to share the magic with. . . . It's a sphere of clear-sighted yet romantic protocreativity previously unheard of in "classical" magical lore.

Integration of music: LaVey was a skilled musician who loved music. No wonder then that he had explored magical aspects of tone, vibrations, rhythms, the human voice, and all of these things put together. His own rituals often included his own playing suitable instruments. Sometimes the ritual itself *was* the actual playing of one selected piece of music with heavy emotional gusto. "Music is the most effective tool for evocation, as the entire body rhythm is helplessly taken up by the pattern of life associated with the musical selection. A meaningful idea never dies, nor does the emotional response generated by certain compositions. If enough people are inspired or moved by these compositions, the selections become sonic repository for the accumulated emotions of all those affected by them. Becoming an all-encompassing sensing element to the collective feedback of a particular composition can yield a total evocation."[8]

Again, the integration of emotion is fundamentally important. There is probably no art form more emotional than music. To get into the mood of a specific working, the inclusion of a musical piece chosen for its evocative qualities is essential. If performed live, the emotional amplification will be even greater.

In discussing these things, LaVey also mentions "emotional chording." There seems, according to him, to exist one chord for each emotion. Animals respond to very few—basically pleasure and pain. "Humans have added certain chords to their internal lyre, such as sentiment, which sometimes appears as nostalgia—a combination of pleasure and pain. Humans' internal chording is more complex because humans experience a wider range of stimuli than do other animals (though, alas, the reverse is often true)."[9]

The villain: Satan was defined by LaVey as a symbol with the powerful potential of accusing and revealing hypocrisy and double standards. Satire, irony, and scathing intelligence here become magical qualities, as personified in LaVeyan inspirations such as Mark Twain, Ben Hecht, and H. L. Mencken. Wherever there is dogmatic hypocrisy and attempts at control through intimidation, there will be counterforces. When direct causal balancing is not possible, then a sardonic strike can do just as well.

In all cultures, the antihero, rebel, or villain is usually more popular than the (self) righteous hero running the errands of the corrupt. Even worse than the hero is the person cheering on the righteousness imposed by others. LaVey describes these people as those bearing a good guy badge. Gather two or more of these together, and an intolerant lynch mob is never far away.

The balancing force is the "Lone Ranger"—often a truly good and just person, but with methods and an intelligence in direct opposition to the status quo behavior of the herd. LaVey: "The more grandiose the villain, the more beneficent he is to society"; and "the greater one's natural degree of nonconformity, the greater are one's magical powers."

This in no way automatically implies that nonconformers or outsiders are villainous or vice versa, but there's something in the isolation from the herd or the collective that is absolutely central in the LaVeyan Weltanschauung.

Besides the integrated sense of dark humor, there's also the concept of noir justice in both Satanic and criminal environments. The antihero of hard-boiled crime stories of the 1940s and '50s, and his stern cinematic counterpart in film noir, often represent justice but very seldom the legal system. And the criminal world is truly one of Machiavellian strategies and the protonatural lex talionis* that LaVey was such an avid advocate of.

The third side: Oppositional transcendence is a fairly new construct in Western magical thought. Where Chinese Taoism has always favored the both/and rather than the either/or stance, Western occult philosophy has until the twentieth century been bogged down by religious dualisms and simplified divisions.

Aleister Crowley was instrumental in this transcendental process with his famous definition, "The Magick of Horus requires the passionate union of opposites." It is not only a magical way of solving problems or looking at things but also acknowledges modern scientific thought. Where opposites either clash or unite, there is a great amount of energy set free. For the magician aware of the mechanisms involved, the energy can easily be directed to do his or her bidding.

What's interesting here is what LaVey called the "third side" of any issue at hand. This side he described and defined as Satanic because

---

*The law of retaliation equivalent to an offense.

it challenges dim-witted dualism. Reality is always more multifaceted than a Yes or a No, and especially if one is on a pragmatic prowl for success and pleasure for oneself. Aligning oneself with either the *either* or the *or* is usually to take the safe way out. The third side may be controversial, but that's never a problem for a Satanist. "The third side can be the crackpot stuff of conspiracy theories, or it can be the most logical and simple, yet *deliberately neglected* conclusion."[10]

In *Satan Speaks!,* LaVey gives an example of how this dynamic could work as a pragmatic magical formula mixing two iconic, almost mythic energies of twentieth-century life and culture: National Socialism and Judaism. LaVey himself was Jewish by birth and at times even expressed Zionist leanings, but at the same time he admired fascist aesthetics from both Italy and Nazi Germany.

> It will become easier and more convincing for any Satanist to combine a Jewish lineage with a Nazi aesthetic, and with pride rather than with guilt and misgiving. The die is cast with the vast numbers of children of mixed Jewish/Gentile origins. They need a place to go. They need a tough identity. They won't find it in the Christian church, nor will they find it in the synagogue. They certainly won't find acceptance among identity anti-Christian anti-Semites who use noble, rich, and inspirational Norse mythology as an excuse and vehicle to rant about the "ZOG." The only place a rational amalgam of proud, admitted Zionist Odinist Bolshevik Nazi Imperialist Socialist Fascism will be found—and championed—will be in the Church of Satan.[11]

Criticism of Anton LaVey and his genuinely creative concepts most often stem from blunt prejudice within the critic. When the individual feels safe and comfortable within a system, even systems of otherwise radical and provocative concepts, the critical faculties toward that system become void, and scapegoating toward others begins. While often being brushed off as a con man or a charlatan by these kinds of critics,

Anton LaVey still lingers on as an important player in contemporary magical philosophy. He was decidedly a heretic but perhaps not so much against the Christian church and other monotheistic control systems (these being already increasingly redundant and far too easy to mock), but more so in relation to the magical moralists all too happy to do some unconscious scapegoating and all too happy to flaunt their degree-studded good guy badges.

There are many other concepts that deserve a closer study: LaVey's thoughts on masochism in relation to beneficial slavery, the Law of the Trapezoid, and Lycanthropic Metamorphosis, to mention but a few. I hope this lecture has at least laid a solid base as an overview for future interest and attention.

When I think of all those who would rejoice at my discomfort, I am energized and strengthened to the extent that I might overcome any malaise. It is not my love for mankind that sustains me, but rather mankind's resentment of me. My disdain and contempt for the mediocre masses in general and those who calumniate me in particular angers me to regeneration.[12]

4

CANON FODDER

I am convinced that the only people worthy of consideration in this world are the unusual ones. For the common folk are like leaves of a tree, and live and die unnoticed.

THE SCARECROW OF OZ,
FROM *THE MARVELLOUS LAND OF OZ*,
BY L. FRANK BAUM

Growing up in the 1930s and '40s certainly had its advantages, the biggest one being that there was no TV. Kids read books, magazines, and comics; listened to the radio; went to the movies; and shared these experiences with friends.

Anton LaVey was certainly no exception. As he immersed himself in the adventures of the Lone Ranger, Superman, and Batman and the eventful stories of Jack London and Mark Twain, a sense of philosophy and justice grew inside the young boy.

This was also amplified in his teens, when his love of film noir was being established. The antihero was more often than not the real hero; the antihero brought justice, and often by anachronistic or even illegal means. There was seemingly a world underneath the normal world—a world where real changes take place, initiated by people who despite hard knocks in life know what real justice means. It's not really the people who claim to be good who are good. Against most, if not all, odds, a sense of human pride and force will knock over the corrupt and deceitful—albeit temporarily. That moment of pure accusation and opposition LaVey would later on in life define as *Satanic*.

There were other literary sources beyond such obvious boy favorites as London and Twain, especially as LaVey grew older. Although a musical prodigy first and foremost, the young LaVey showed an equally massive appetite for literature and movies. There were also interesting intersections going on at this time; many successful and influential authors, both from the United States and Europe, were lured into the web of Hollywood by the promises of fame and fortune. Although Hollywood seldom allowed writers full creative freedom, many literary authors definitely left a mark of intelligence and quality on the cinematic output, which was script driven more than anything else.

Ernest Hemingway, Christopher Isherwood, Raymond Chandler, John Steinbeck, Tennessee Williams, Aldous Huxley, William Faulkner, Truman Capote, Gore Vidal, and Dalton Trumbo are only a few examples of intelligent and erudite authors active in Hollywood, before 1950s America's psychotic breakdown in the purge of communists both real and fictional. That this allure was a creative dilemma for many authors is understandable.

One of LaVey's favorite Hollywood people, Ben Hecht, often wrote about how he would have preferred to write novels instead of churning out scripts for popular films, which, on the other hand, made him a whole lot of money.

Ben Hecht was a prolific writer and covered a lot of ground as an author of novels, as a tough Chicago reporter, and as a celebrated scriptwriter. But it is to his early novels *Fantazius Mallare* (1922) and *The Kingdom of Evil* (1924) we must turn to fully understand the attraction for LaVey. Although these novels are essentially pulpy, in the sense that they carry an undefined and deep-reaching horror so frequent in the pulp magazines, they are neither in the Lovecraftean vein of cosmic horrors nor blood-drenched, causal moral tales of rebounding inflictions. Hecht's dark duo offers a disturbing look into a truly deranged (yet undoubtedly artistic) mind that questions everything in life: *Fantazius* is like the bastard love/hate child of Nietzsche, Lautréamont, Bloy, and Dostoyevski. The narrative is like a feverish eruption of unconscious accusations against anything and anyone claiming to be orderly or "sane."

> To possess! What a delusion! And for its sake I threw my genius away. I stripped the world from my eyes that it might not intrude upon the universe within me. A paradise in which I might strut alone. Possess myself. Yes, and here I am, aware at last of folly. For my senses belong to life. And though I buried myself in a madness deeper than night, they would still cling to me. Though I castrated myself, they would remain—five invisible testicles. It is impossible to possess. Folly to attempt. As long as the senses remain life clings like a dead whore to my darkness. Even my madness that I prided myself upon is a babbling witch astride a phallus, her lips bending over it with grewsome hungers.[1]

Pretty far removed from the romantic comedies *It's a Wonderful World, A Star Is Born,* and *Her Husband's Affairs* that Hecht penned in the 1930s and '40s.

If one wanted to highlight one specific era or phase that was extra important for the young "Tony" LaVey, it would have to be the Golden Gate International Exposition in San Francisco of 1939–40. Treasure Island, an artificial island between San Francisco and Oakland, housed a large number of spectacular buildings, attractions, rides, and sideshow oddities, of interest to both young and old and, not forgetting, those somewhere in between. An island basically built of landfill also became filled with wide-eyed lustful dreams.

LaVey has recounted how he snuck into the Sally Rand "girlie shows" to see young maidens pose, get up on horses, and just basically do anything that displayed their bodies. The girls were often adorned only with small pieces of textile covering their pubic region, and the assembled men (and boys) watched the titillating spectacle in delightful awe. Because of his young age, LaVey was thrown out, but he had definitely had his prurient appetite "whetted for life."

Exhibited at the Exposition were also various kinds of popular artworks, including colorful vistas of circus life, signed Robert Barbour Johnson (1907–1987, a.k.a. "Rubber Bubber"). A former journalist and circus worker who had handled big cats such as lions and tigers, Johnson dabbled in painting circus scenes from memory. But he was mainly known for his chilling and macabre short stories for such pulp magazines as *Weird Tales*—magazines that the young LaVey devoured. Later on, the two men became friends; it seemed almost inevitable. Through similar friends, and friends of friends, who passed by his Black House and its interesting evenings, LaVey also got to know *Weird Tales* contributor Clark Ashton Smith (1893–1961), Lovecraft's friend and Arkham House publisher August Derleth (1909–1971), and collector and publisher of the highly influential magazine *Famous Monsters of Filmland* Forrest Ackerman (1916–2008), as well as many others.

The pulp literature was at this time (1930s–1950s) a popular manifestation of a genre (or several)—the "fantastic"—that had been present in Western culture for a long time, often including diabolical or occult themes or characters.

LaVey at several times touched on his love of literally fantastic literature during the Magic Circle lecture evenings and often read favorite passages out loud to the assembled. Authors such as Edgar Allan Poe, Washington Irving, Charles Dickens, Ambrose Bierce, Robert Chambers, Edward Lucas White, William Hope Hodgson, Guy Preston, and of course Howard Phillips Lovecraft were mentioned, for instance at a lecture at the Black House about supernatural fiction on April 1, 1966:

> Bierce was a gentleman of many mysterious qualities who vanished in
> the wilds of Mexico; never to be heard from again. Ambrose Bierce

set a style that was followed by Robert W. Chambers, and his masterful work: *The King in Yellow*. Chambers in turn inspired a contemporary writer of our modern time, Howard Phillips Lovecraft, who has picked up the pieces and all of these little-known aspects of terror in the printed word, and added his own cataclysmic additions to these. Lovecraft lived as he died: a strange, reclusive man who had no aim in life other than to wander the strange, deserted streets of New England in an attempt to find the lore, the legend, and any kind of superstitions that would enhance his subsequent writings.

Lovecraft himself had written admiringly to Robert Barbour Johnson in the 1930s, commending him on his stories. To catch older gentlemen like Johnson, who had been immersed in all the things LaVey had fantasized about—and then some—became an intuitive magical transference that helped shape his own destiny. But it also went far beyond purely personal admiration.

Many concepts drawn from pulp stories like those LaVey lectured about also ended up in the actual rituals of the Church of Satan—as did concepts from German expressionist cinema. A lot of the practical uses stemming from ideas or emotions formulated by these masters of the uncanny were taken on as aesthetic cues—*not* necessarily philosophical or intellectual ones. If you can change the atmosphere of a more or less confined space, you can change whatever or whoever exists within that atmosphere. In this sense, Lovecraft was a master, according to LaVey: "While Freud and Einstein wrestled with their respective disciplines in the isolation of academic specialization, Lovecraft was describing the astonishing influence of physical and geometric law on the psyche. While he might have hesitated to style himself master of scientific speculation, he is no less deserving of that title than are Asimov and Clarke."[2]

It is through style and aesthetics one can efficiently open up the human psyche—for good or bad. LaVey had already seen this clearly in the circus and sideshow work, but also in the way people projected awe and hope on those claiming to know or perhaps even master the "occult"—whatever this actually meant.

Another very tangible source of inspiration in San Francisco for LaVey was the British-Austrian inventor and artist Cecil Nixon (1874–1962). This remarkable and larger than life character lived in a house on Broadway and Van Ness called The Castle of Indolence by Nixon himself and The House of a Thousand Mysteries by a San Francisco endlessly fascinated by this former dentist's mechanical achievements.

Although of a kind of Apollonian bent—in the Nietzschean sense—where LaVey was decidedly much more Dionysian and sensual, Cecil Nixon made a powerful first impression on the curious twenty-three-year-old organist in 1953 that lasted a full remaining lifetime and even seeped into the design of his own Satanic "Castle of Indolence" on California Street.

Nixon's main claim to fame was the construction of a mechanical doll called Isis, who could play three thousand different tunes on a zither. Isis was a stage magic superstar completed in 1919, and she (and Nixon) entertained many a guest at his legendary soirées at home, including Harry Houdini, Lon Chaney Sr., and Arthur Conan Doyle. He had also constructed a large pipe organ in his basement, but as he didn't play himself, he engineered it to play the standard perforated music rolls that were common around the turn of the century. But in case there would someday be a suitable organist for the soirées, he also added a keyboard function.

When Anton LaVey got to know this gentleman in the 1950s and displayed his musical skills, it was immediately decided who would be a main organist at Nixon's castle. A favorite piece was always Chopin's Funeral March, which LaVey performed reverently: "I never burlesqued these things. I would put myself back into the past and imagine how tender and meaningful these songs could be before they became cliché."[3]

In this new capacity, LaVey was introduced to, for him, unknown segments of San Francisco: aging society ladies with many a bizarre quirk, as well as younger talents who appreciated the odd and anachronistic. It didn't take long before LaVey was regarded as a son of sorts by Nixon. The mechanical genius also became a frequent guest at LaVey's Black House and especially enjoyed LaVey's first wife Carole's home cooking. LaVey remembered his mentor warmly: "He was right out of fiction, out of a Merritt novel. He is one of the original Satanists. He didn't think of himself as a Satanist, but he would always bring that up—Lucifer, Mephistopheles, the Dark Prince. To him that was magnificent."[4]

Just as LaVey's house had many nooks and secret passages, due to its history as a brothel and, later on, speakeasy during Prohibition, Nixon's bizarre castle was mainly constructed by himself in endless mechanical developments. The doorbell played "Taps," recorded bird sounds were emitted every twenty minutes, the large hand-carved panels were in turn adorned with giant paintings, and there were even several indoor fountains. A door with an imposing satyr's head on it opened up if one said, "Open, Sesame!" loudly enough. The entire furnace and heating system had been removed so the sounds of the basement organ could travel through the vents of the house more freely. Et cetera!

Whatever had happened at the castle during the evening—a musical performance, recitals of poetry, hypnotism sessions, or magic performances—refreshments were punctually served at midnight in the form of ham and chicken sandwiches, candy, chocolate cake, and coffee. The people Nixon approved of were allowed to linger on and admire the house.

There was another big project after Isis that was never fully finished: the lovely Galatea, who was to become a relative of sorts of Isis's. She would be blonde and play the violin rather than be an Egyptian goddess playing the zither, but with an even more advanced capacity and interaction. Although begun already in 1922, Galatea unfortunately never fully manifested.

The story of the lovely yet inanimate Galatea who comes alive through Pygmalion's magic displays most of all (at least in the

George Bernard Shaw version of the myth) a defiance against the causal rules of life and nature that the religious have called "God" in various languages. What if humans could create new life themselves, wholly on their own terms—and beyond mere biology?

It's a thought as fascinating and appealing as it is dangerous. Dangerous in the sense that it requires a pretty stable psyche to fully realize how much we can actually create on our own in order to fully satisfy our needs—whether these be sexual, sensual, or intellectual. The creation of new life beyond the causal to satisfy the needs of the creator is then by definition truly diabolical. It removes the power of the apparent authority of the primordial monotheistic daddy and puts it in the hands of anyone advanced enough to create life on their own terms.

What, then, constitutes this life force? Comparing Nixon's musically eloquent Isis and, in extension, his Galatea, with LaVey's haunting (and haunted) customers at the Den of Iniquity,* we see that the key is a magical evocation that only passes through the physical on its way to the real goal: the emotional sphere.

People who had the good fortune to hear Isis play quickly forgot the question of "How?" and instead were drawn into an eerie form of brilliant beauty that made them *feel* beyond the music itself. People who had the good fortune to see the seedy clientele of LaVey's Den quickly realized that this was a complete evocation of a space, a time, and also people that LaVey had experienced, and who were there for a reason. The investment in this total environment—whether that be of money, or of hours of work, or of emotional or sexual energy—is one of the main keys to why the environment will eventually come "alive."

Nixon had realized this early on, and LaVey took the concept one step further, imbuing it also with the relevant and revealing theories of Freud, Reich, and many others. Not as any kind of justification for or to other people, but mainly to pragmatically apply whatever was there

---

*A bar in LaVey's Black House, complete with guests that LaVey had built himself of mannequin parts.

in the zeitgeist to make the creation more understandable to himself.

In the very same zeitgeist there was also a book definitely known to LaVey: *Witchcraft: Its Power in the World Today,* by American author William Seabrook. Seabrook is one of the dedicatees in *The Satanic Rituals,* and it's easy to see why: he was an adventurer, a compelling hard-boiled writer, and someone who appreciated a good mystery. This particular book of his has an entire segment called "The Witch and Her Doll" and displays both personal knowledge and literary panache:

> Dolls of every sort and size have always intrigued humanity—rag dolls, plaster saints, and brazen idols, images in bronze, wood, and marble; kewpies, Teddy bears, Madonnas, and St. Josephs; Jupiter and Venus, Mammon, Memnon, Vishnu, Baal, and Buddha; fashion-decked dummies in windows and blood-spattered Juggernauts on wheels; sacred, Satanic, or silly, from Donatello's wooden Christ on the Cross to Bergen's wooden ventriloquist dummy on its owner's knee. I have been a "collector" and connoisseur of a peculiar type of doll for many years—the kind that are made in secret, then pierced with needles; or wound round with scarlet death thread; or made of wax to melt before a fire.[5]

As the vitality of the old eccentric Nixon dwindled, he entrusted LaVey with type- and handwritten instructions for how to handle Isis properly. Burton Wolfe, LaVey's first biographer, wrote that "Anton locked Dr. Nixon's secret instructions in a vault and refused to let anyone read them."[6] These documents, and the very secrets in themselves, were regarded by LaVey as genuinely occult items, as talismans of magic. In part because of the absolute secrecy and trust, and the power this generated, and in part because Isis herself was such an incredible, intricate creation that, later on, actually did puzzle the new owners—including casino owner Bill Harrah in Las Vegas. There was simply no manual for Isis—it was all hardwired in Nixon's one-of-a-kind mind and, possibly, in those secret papers LaVey must have regarded as his own "dead sea scrolls." To fully be able to work the magic, you need to know what to do, and when.

LaVey described Cecil Nixon as an original Satanist, and it was certainly true even beyond the basic definitions concerning outsider eccentricities and anachronisms. Nixon looked down on the herd in a genuinely Nietzschean sense and had a stern, elitist outlook. He loved and lived life to the fullest and was not willing to compromise one bit: "Death is monstrous, an insult. I shake my fist at the deity."[7]

Nixon was also present at some of the Magic Circle's early meetings, which would indicate an interest in decidedly occult subjects. That Nixon was not only a role model for LaVey but also a source of genuinely esoteric information is beyond any doubt. Among other things, Nixon left his young friend books on stage magic, including volumes by Jasper Maskelyne.

Nixon's many creations were always very well publicized, as was his house. This is another parallel between the two men that we shouldn't forget. When Nixon died in 1962, LaVey was active with his Magic Circle and Witches' Workshops but there was no Church of Satan as of yet. He did get attention for all his strange endeavors, and also sought it out, but it was mainly on a local level. The Black House was usually part of the "deal," as were his exotic pets: the black leopard Zoltan and the Nubian lion Togare. In many ways, LaVey and his family were portrayed as a local variant of Charles Addams's popular fantasy family.

This endearing media focus changed quite radically when LaVey, on the recommendation of his longtime friend, police inspector Jack Webb, concocted the Church of Satan as an organization and focused the lectures and meetings on more literal Satanic material. Suddenly, LaVey went from local to national, and then even international, interest.

The fact that this was a conscious "construction" on LaVey's part, adapted to a media-driven culture, seems to have frustrated some of his critics deeply over the decades. But they usually forget the times in which the concept as such was constructed. I'm not merely referring to the commonsense aspects of simply being able to be more visible, and thereby able to make money from your creative mind and work, but mainly to the zeitgeist aspects of books (and ideas) such as Marshall McLuhan's *Understanding Media* (1964) and *The Medium Is the Massage* (1967) and Orrin Klapp's *Symbolic Leaders: Public Dramas and Public Men* (1964).

McLuhan famously stated that the "medium is the message" and that a culture permeated by mass media, for instance, will be shaped by that particular machinery. LaVey clearly understood this and put it to use for his own benefit; acknowledging that if a Church of Satan is needed to get the attention via mass-market magazines, newspapers, TV news, et cetera, then, fine, he could certainly create one. Through that presence or "egregorian" potential, ideas could be disseminated much more efficiently (and profitably) than during a weekly meeting for some twenty people, each paying him $2.50.

American sociologist Orrin Klapp (1915–1997) is one of the esteemed dedicatees of *The Satanic Bible,* and it's easy to see why. Klapp eloquently elaborated on and structured the American mass-media psyche in relation to its heroes, villains, and fools—and how important these were/are for the American public when it comes to understanding their own overall reality and identity. In his *Symbolic Leaders,* Klapp wrote: "The symbolic leader is an emergent phenomenon, and that is why we so often do not know in advance—nor does he—what he will become. It is typical of a dialectic—an argument or other prolonged give-and-take in which interaction is creative—that neither party knows the outcome; it is a discovery for both."[8]

This advanced yet popular argument is not only an expression of the zeitgeist that was permeated by celebrity culture, and aggressive attempts at manufacturing "stars" of all kinds. It also vibrates with LaVeyan resonance in his formulating the Church, *The Satanic Bible,* but also, first and foremost, his own persona. What seems to be an overt initial alliance with the villain has over time come to include the other main roles as well—and, of course, many kinds of mixed nuances and fragrances.

For the general American society of the 1960s, LaVey played the villain, willingly. By doing this, and also taking the flack from peers (other more or less similar occultists, magicians, and countercultural groups) by having the fool projected on him ever since the 1960s, he has also grown into the steady stature of hero—as he has undoubtedly, by personal presence as well as by proxy dissemination, affected culture for several generations.

The interesting thing with Klapp is that he wasn't only a man with ideas that insightfully resonated with the psyche of the times. His packaging of complex ideas and interrelations in society as an exciting bag of tricks that was accessible and palatable to anyone who bothered to read it was, according to me, of equal importance to LaVey. There are distinct echoes of Klapp even in LaVey's approaches in presentation; LaVey's philosophy of magical accessibility and tangible effect was eloquently clothed in a clear and quite often satirical signal.

There is one author who deserves a special honorable mention in LaVey's canon. The successful and suave British author and dramatist W. Somerset Maugham seemed to be one of those natural Satanists who did everything right in life. His novels laud strong women and often focus on pleasure and egotism as benevolent driving forces. His disdain for Christianity and other organized religions was as fierce as it seemed to be vis-à-vis reactive rebels such as Aleister Crowley. In 1908 Maugham even wrote a novel called *The Magician,* in which a pretty obvious Crowley definitely isn't painted in a pretty light.

If organized religion, and its apparent shadow-side phenomena like Crowleyan magic, didn't quite cut it for Maugham, then an unabashed self-love and an indulgence in the pleasures of life certainly did. Particularly *The Summing Up* (1938)[9] and *A Writer's Notebook* (1949)[10]— books that are not works of fiction but of memories and thoughts—are absolutely jam-packed with what could be called LaVeyisms:

What mean and cruel things men can do for the love of God.
(*A Writer's Notebook,* 68)

That we do not often consciously make pleasure our aim is no argument against the idea that the attainment of pleasure is the object to which all actions tend. (*A Writer's Notebook*, 74)

I have loved individuals; I have never much cared for men in the mass. (*The Summing Up*, 33)

I liked life and wanted to enjoy it. I wanted to get all I possibly could out of it. I was not satisfied with the appreciation of a small band of intellectuals. (*The Summing Up*, 81)

Men think him cynical because he does not attach importance to the virtues and is not revolted by the vices that move them. He is not cynical. But what they call virtue and what they call vice are not the sort of things that he takes any particular interest in. They are indifferent elements in the scheme of things out of which he constructs his own freedom. Of course common men are quite right to be indignant with him. But that isn't going to do him any good. He is incorrigible. (*The Summing Up*, 135)

In terms of other writing inspirations, we shouldn't forget Henry Louis Mencken, the world-infamous, Baltimore-based journalist and editor. Although Mencken stuck with the facts and never dabbled with fiction, his sense of style and wit made positive impressions on LaVey. Mencken had strong views and never backed down; he thoroughly enjoyed punching stupidity smack dab in the face and making fun of everything that was just downright idiotic. But he wasn't merely someone who *reacted* to American stupidity, albeit eloquently. Through his work with the magazines the *Smart Set* and the *American Mercury*, he also actively promoted intelligent American culture, and beyond. Hence, Mencken was more of an acerbic realist than a cynic, or even nihilist, and I'm sure LaVey found a resonance in this attitude. As Blanche Barton points out in her interview for this project: "LaVey was a man of deep conviction, and for all of his misanthropy I would have to say he was an idealist, or else he never would have done what he did."

Particularly in LaVey's collections of essays, *The Devil's Notebook* and *Satan Speaks!*, there are traces of Bierce, Maugham, and Mencken that spice up his many radical ideas in a great stylistic way. Had these not been expressed with such a suave tongue in Satan's cheek, most of them would probably not have been acknowledged as the real gems they are. The aesthetic form must be in solid union with the diabolical content it carries. And preferably at a slightly askew angle.

5

BEWITCHED, BOTHERED, AND BEWILDERED

If you know how to imitate the woman a man carries within himself, you may have anything you wish that another man can supply.

ANTON LaVEY, PROLOGUE TO *THE SATANIC WITCH*

Would LaVey have found our contemporary times interesting? Absolutely.

In a 1989 Church of Satan–produced infomercial called "Hail Satan!" LaVey stated that, "The future of Satanism is assured. There is nothing I can say or do that's going to retard it or advance it. The die has been cast, the show's on the road, and everyone is just sort of waiting to see what's going to happen."*

Anton LaVey had by this time already seen enough to know that his concepts were being cleverly disseminated and growing stronger. Individualism was on the rise, and occurrences like the Satanic Panic merely showed an inert environment's death rattles, *in absurdum*.

But what he probably couldn't fully foresee was that in many ways anything that's good and strengthening can also backlash into opposing

---

*Transcribed portions of this infomercial are included in Appendix I of this book.

forces—even stronger than those one originally rebelled against.

At times, LaVey did mention that he felt as if he had opened a Pandora's box filled with empowering opportunities, but that these had simply revealed how most humans actually function. Given some form of empowerment, humans will do their best to destroy for others. Very few people are content to just grow stronger and be happy as individuals; most also need the amplified acknowledgment of others that they either suck up to or kick down.

Just as Satanism in itself was a conscious provocation for the inert America of the 1960s, its expansion through *The Compleat Witch, or What to Do When Virtue Fails* (1970, reissued in 1989 as *The Satanic Witch*) became a contemporary 1970s mirror that keeps on reflecting philosophical fodder to this day. And before there was a book called *The Satanic Witch,* or even a Church of Satan, LaVey had for many years run what he called the Witches' Workshop.

Based on questions and suggestions from women (young and old) who sought him out, he provided them with tools to work their own magic. Whether based on previously occult techniques such as spells and love potions or on contemporary psychological insights into simply how to deal with other people, LaVey provided his witches-to-be with hands-on techniques and information designed with only one purpose in mind: their success.

These hundreds of cases gave him firsthand data on what women in general seemed to be preoccupied with and, more importantly, how to fix their problems or predicaments in real life. This mass of data percolated inside him and eventually became the bulk of *The Satanic Witch.*

So although there are certainly a lot of LaVey's own preferences, systems, and concepts in the book, it's still based on what the witches had taught *him;* not necessarily, nor exclusively, the other way around.

In the late 1960s and early 1970s, LaVey also had a regular column called "Letters from the Devil" in magazines such as *National Insider* and the *Exploiter.* The focus was often on the sexual aspects of Satanism, and the column can definitely be regarded as a sketchbook for

The Compleat Witch. His erudite mix of matter-of-factness and satirical wit was well stirred in these trenches and basically formed his signature style in all of the writings and books that followed.

> The Satanist recognizes ALL aspects of sexuality, whether it be heterosexual, bisexual, homosexual, sadistic, masochistic, voyeuristic, ad infinitum, so long as they are practiced with due observance of legal boundaries and the well-being of the persons involved, who, of course, must be consenting adults. . . . Bisexuality is as prevalent in the realm of our four-legged friends as it is among the species *homo sapiens;* therefore, let none be guilty of harboring the insidious teaching of Christian sexual "abnormality." To the Satanist, nearly all sex is "normal"—provided we do not inflict ourselves upon those who do not desire our attention.[1]

LaVey's mention of the fluidity of human sexuality, and of the sliding scale of masculine/feminine traits within each human being, definitely placed him ahead of his times. That such an emphasis was placed on both identity and sexuality being performative also made him a pioneer. Some twenty years later, academics such as Judith Butler presented similar theories in such books as *Gender Trouble* (1990). However, LaVey's original encouragement of individual empowerment through experimentation and manipulation of preconceived (or imposed) notions in strange ways seems to have been co-opted and commodified throughout the decades, merging with a new form of collective moralism that in many ways goes against the original ideas. As previously noted, Anton LaVey left behind many exciting and groundbreaking concepts: ECI, the total environment, artificial human companions, the cult of victimization, and the good guy badge, to mention but a few.

LaVey's experiences at the Golden Gate Exposition in 1939 to 1940 brought on a lot of things. Not only was there revelry in a sideshow kind of fun way, there was also a revelation in terms of his own ECI—his Erotic Crystallization Inertia. Seeing the seminude girls from the Sally Rand Nude Ranch made an impression that lasted a lifetime. The fact that he was not actually allowed to be there (because of his humble age) simply added to the thrill.

There was also further voyeuristic stimulation from visits to Coney Island in New York in 1945. The Pavilion of Fun section of the great amusement park featured something called "Steeplechase Park's Insanitarium and Blowhole Theater." Women of all ages were lured in by clowns, who sometimes even spanked them to get in the right position. The "right position" being just over air vents where blasts of compressed air from below made all skirts and dresses fly high, to the jubilant cheers of everyone present. Regulars of course knew what was going to happen and often stayed put for hours to get their voyeuristic kicks. The seats were attractive, and the young LaVey offered to keep seats for people for a quarter of a dollar when someone needed to visit the restroom or get some fresh air. Business was literally a blast!

This environment—a sexually titillating one for both himself and others—within the loose confines of a sleazy carnival (literally, a "celebration of the flesh") was an obvious ECI for LaVey.

As the curious boy came of age in more concrete and hormonal ways, there was a certain type that appealed to him; initially personified by the actress Iris Adrian:

My idealized woman, my idea of the perfect Pygmalion's Galatea, is, and was when I was a kid, the sort of overblown, slightly chubby chorus girl; the one that was always in the back, not in the front line; the one that was sort of unnoticed. I had real fixation for Iris Adrian, who was a character actress. Later on, I was to meet her, too. I told her that I was just completely smitten with her as a young boy. She couldn't understand that anybody could accept her as the ultimate sex symbol. Subsequently, I think my taste has run toward fleshy blondes, rather sleazy, overused, rather disheveled looking women who look like they're not quite what they should be.[2]

Iris Adrian represented the physical female type that he sought out for both short- and long-term relationships for the rest of his life, whether in flings with Marilyn Monroe and Jayne Mansfield, or in devotions to Carole Lansing (mother of Karla LaVey), Diane Hegarty (mother of Zeena Schreck), and Blanche Barton (mother of Xerxes LaVey).

LaVey's work at bars, lounges, clubs, and events as a diabolically skilled and sensitive organist exposed him to hundreds of young women of this type, who all "strut their stuff," and definitely enhanced the orgone charge of the spaces in question. For LaVey to be an active part of this nightly ritual must have been empowering beyond belief—both in terms of personal pleasures and of a validation of his budding theories.

No wonder then that he later on in life wanted to hang on to these moments, areas, and eras. With the concept of the total environment he encouraged anyone brave enough to construct their own perfect space-time, in which the ECI would be continually regenerated as much as possible. His own Den of Iniquity at 6114 California Street was just one of many such space-times and time-spaces. One could indeed argue that the entire Black House was a total environment.

The artificial human companions within this space brought him back to an era he had experienced and played music in: a sleazy bar, complete with an aloof (cynical?) bartender, and guests who "know the score" (some more than others). On the floor was a lady, slightly beyond her prime, who in her inebriation has wet herself so that everyone can see it. LaVey never hid from the fact that this was one of his own sexual fetishes. On the contrary, he indulged in the fantasy and left behind some wonderfully funny yet empathic drawings of women in a similar "shameful" predicament of inebriated incontinence.

Whatever things LaVey wrote about were meant as pointers and encouragements for other Satanists to deal with their own carnal kinks and possible perversions. Not to emulate or imitate, but to truly be creative and concoct similar paradises based on their own ECI experiences. We see here one distinct personal trait: the young LaVey matured into the old, filled with not only pleasure and experience but also of the conscious awareness of it. All of this he decided to share, even though not doing so wouldn't in any way have been clashing with his philosophy. He simply must have derived further pleasure from being the disseminator of all these ideas, and in being acknowledged as such.

There was something almost unexpectedly altruistic in many of LaVey's ideas. Although misanthropic and doubtful about the benevolence and usefulness of *any* collective, there were indeed also aspects that revealed concern instead of merely consternation: "Sex surrogates will be a giant step toward the lessening of man's destructive aggression, and channeling it into pure sexual expression. We would all be much better off if we concentrated on this step, on this present ball of dirt, instead of on how to step onto the moon."[3]

Containing ECI or other particular emotional clusters inside protected, hermetic total environments becomes a generator of the desired (in energy and, in extension, hopefully also of result) in a conscious insulation of basically unconscious impulses. In order to share these experiences, and this level of honesty, one either needs a partner or magical assistant one can truly trust with the secrets, or . . . perhaps invent one's own?

The concept of artificial human companions within the total environment is a logical extension of the space-time itself. Not necessarily constrained to a psychosexual ECI impulse, specifically, but as a stimulating agency for one's own formulation of whatever desire there may be right there and then. There can be no stronger bond than between yourself and the companion you have invested your trust in. These are all ingredients of a full evocation of yourself in a confinement undisturbed by others. That doesn't mean that you can't share it with others, but again, there needs to be more or less total trust. If it squeaks, it leaks.

The use of mannequins was in many strange ways part of the zeitgeist. Various surrealists had used store mannequins—from Marcel Duchamp's "punny" window display for André Breton's *Le Surréalisme et la Peinture* (1945), over Fernand Léger's sequence in Hans Richter's magical film *Dreams That Money Can Buy* (1947; the sequence is called "The Girl with the Prefabricated Heart" and contains mannequins acting out the lyrics of the haunting song), to the nightmare visions of Hans Bellmer's experiments and documentations of disjointed (and reassembled) mannequin and doll parts.

We also should not forget the cultural impact/trauma of the famous Black Dahlia case, which to this day remains unsolved. The young starlet Elizabeth Short was found murdered and mutilated in Los Angeles in 1947. The gruesomeness of the murder shocked America, and published photos of the crime scene were not as censored as one would have thought appropriate of those times. The dehumanization of Elizabeth Short—her body was cut in half, a gash had been added to her vagina, et cetera—evoked a lifeless mannequin whose loose parts could easily be disassembled in the dark of night (but not be put back together again). And this to an entire nation!

One year before this spectacular murder case, in 1946, Marcel Duchamp started conceptualizing his secret masterpiece, *Etant Donnés*. It's an installation that wasn't finished until 1966 and was eventually installed at the Philadelphia Museum of Art in 1969 (one year after Duchamp's death). It displays an uncanny scene, which you can only peep into via a tiny hole in a big wooden, barnlike door. What you see is the body of a woman, seemingly headless, lying in grass with her legs wide apart, and with a hairless gash more than a normal, labia-adorned vagina. There are other elements to it, too, but these pertain more to the magician Duchamp's total environment and will forever be a mystery.

But what's interesting from our point of view is that the "art installation" carries a confined space in which an obvious ECI processing was going on; in doing so, it definitely invoked and evoked the Black Dahlia. Duchamp's work was secretive, but once launched it was regarded as the master's brilliant swan song—and so it remains to this day.

Georges Bataille, the surrealist who wrote many seminal, insightful, and provocative texts about sexual psychology and pathology, had his own group of artists (and a magazine) called *Acéphale,* which means "headless."

The human (or mannequin) body as a malleable tool for enhanced interaction and symbolism was definitely around, and of course Anton LaVey was no less exposed to these things than other Americans at the time.

I would also argue that LaVey's presence in burlesque strip shows added to his ECI, and to his interest in artificial human companions. The gradual display of parts of the female anatomy in a sensual-seductive environment (the male gaze, the bump-and-grind music, atmospheric lights, etc.), all leading up (or almost) to "the source of life" itself, made the separate parts as influential as the whole woman—sometimes perhaps even more so if one had a preference for a particular part.

To create his own companions in a form that sufficiently suspended disbelief wasn't easy for LaVey. In a conversation with his old friend (and first biographer) Burton Wolfe, he revealed his insights: "Vinyl. Fiberglass. Dacron fill. Polyurethane foam. I've already been able to combine materials like these in a way that you can touch the ass of my people and your finger sinks in. It's a lot better than these inflated dolls you buy; they have about as much sex appeal as a Goodyear blimp. Awful stuff. What I've done is of much higher quality, but still a long way from being lifelike enough."[4]

In an interview with Dick Russell for the magazine *Argosy* in 1975, LaVey elaborated: "Yes, I make people. They're partially automated. I move them with solenoids. I suppose most of them are actually disgusting human beings. Drunk floozies, sailors trying to pick up women, and one of them even passed out under the bar! But *I* created them. So they become not reprehensible, but people you would meet at any neighborhood bar. Friends that you sit and have a drink with."[5]

For a period of time, Anton LaVey worked as a police photographer in San Francisco. Although it's easy to romanticize the work of Arthur

"Weegee" Fellig and his often-poetic documentation of crimes in New York from your own comfortable couch, LaVey was confronted, as was Weegee, with the very worst of the worst of human behavior. His experiences of murders, suicides, car accidents, drunken assaults, domestic fights, et cetera, helped shape the philosophy of Satanism, in the sense that the nightly excursions in the company of tough cops showed LaVey just how feral human beings actually are.

You can argue back and forth about what's good or bad, or you can accept that human beings are essentially brutal and cruel animals who would stab anyone in the back to get ahead—symbolically or literally. Seeing a multitude of damaged human bodies that had only recently been filled with esprit, joie de vivre, hope, and love creates a discrepancy in the human mind that will either lead to religious denial or absolute clarity (which can be hard to bear for most people, many of whom will therefore turn cynical). Isn't this in essence what most film noirs are about, too? The unwanted, harsh realization of how things and people *really* are?

One could argue that LaVey's Den of Iniquity is a containment of the things and people he really liked in the seedy underworld of San Francisco; knowing by firsthand experience that once these creatures left the relative safety of the Den, anything could happen to them—and probably would. LaVey's creation could be seen not only as an evocation of his own pleasure, but also as a misanthropic purge of his experiences on the outside.

What changed on that proverbial, pervasive outside, specifically during the 1970s, was a strange American cultural phenomenon in which the active hero and self-made man/woman ideal was replaced by the acknowledgment that actually being a victim (of basically anything), a disgruntled employee, a wronged citizen, or a representative of a bullied minority could be much more profitable than trying to break out of the mold and prejudice and overcome any resistance—thereby gaining the respect of those around them. On the contrary: all you needed was an aggressive lawyer to do the work for you. The more decrepit, suffering, and sad your life story was, the bigger the potential mega bucks—not forgetting nor neglecting possible spinoff deals of books, movies, made-for-TV-movies, TV talk shows, et cetera.

This fetishizing and implementation of inability and ineptitude within a context of handing over one's own responsibility to someone else (a spokesperson, a collective, an attorney) has increased exponentially over the decades and is today a phenomenon that affects our culture in severe and detrimental ways.

Where Anton LaVey preached that "Satan represents responsibility to the responsible, instead of concern for psychic vampires!"[6] contemporary Western culture seems to move in a diametrically opposed direction. LaVey, being a self-professed Freudian, would no doubt argue that Satanism represents the healthy libido in culture, whereas the contemporary cult of victimization represents society's death drive. The denial of individual strength and pleasure in favor of a collective cry for sympathy (quite often with an agenda of its own), carries implications that we can daily see reflected in increasingly chaotic politics, "cancel culture," "trigger warnings," and other similarly dystopian phenomena.

This strange phenomenon is personified by those carrying yet another LaVeyan concept: the good guy badge. Whoever wears it proudly will hide his or her own misdemeanors or weaknesses behind viciously scapegoating *anyone* who has a divergent point of view and the guts to speak out and up. It's a malady of career-opportunity "spokespersonism" in which someone takes on the role as defender (of the weak, the faith, the disgruntled, or just the plain old whatever) and thereby makes a name for him- or herself—but rarely doing anything for the cause itself.

The good guy badge is the result of centuries of implicit moralistic decay stemming from monotheistic sources, clothed in the optimism of enforced communal cheering but eventually displaying the usual elements of greed and corruption. Lost causes are unfortunately a dime a dozen, and that's never because of any original impetuses or real injustices—it's always because someone with a good guy badge profits at the cost (and increased suffering) of the originally disgruntled.

People today seem uninterested in a personal application of an idea that hasn't been approved by their dominant tribe. That's why renegade ideas like LaVey's are always the most powerful and feared; they represent a threat to those who have claimed the mighty prerogative to interpret.

Taking all of these concepts into consideration, we see in LaVey's *The Satanic Witch* an attempt to empower *individual* women specifically, in ways that are untainted by *any* collective or cultural distortions. But it's clear to see that the wisdom of his book can be applied to anyone of any gender, and of any sexual proclivity or kink. Provided, of course, that this person is willing to be responsible for his or her own life and actions.

Throughout his various disseminations, LaVey made frequent references to Basil Zaharoff, the arms dealer and gray eminence of international politics during the first half of the twentieth century, and it is in many ways because he applied a manipulative realpolitik behind the scenes—that is, in the occulted spheres of influence. Everyone has a soft spot or weakness, and quite often these are of a sexual nature. Knowing those secrets immediately brings an upper hand for the enemies.

When contemporary emperors seem to have no clothes on in their political or public life, it's very likely because they've literally had none on in some compromising situation or other that has been documented and then displayed back to them in private. Blackmail is a timeless and efficient technique, provided that the culture in question is: a) inherently corrupt, and b) encourages sexual hang-ups via stifling monotheistic morals. "Nothing is so fascinating as that which is not meant to be seen."[7]

The above LaVey quote from *The Satanic Witch* is filled with many meanings. Initially it brings to mind what every girl learns as she grows up—a quintessential female wisdom—but it could of course be applied to a greater societal prurience, too, in which celebrities and politicians in the public arena can manipulate their own visibility by leaking what the voyeurs want to see. Or they can *be* manipulated by a negative exposure of what should *not* be seen. The one who controls the soft spots of power controls the world. And of course, this is valid for the individual sphere, too.

The Satanic Witch is a grimoire of previously unheard-of potency, simply because it is stripped of any symbolic noise, or any arcane trappings. It isn't filled with weird symbols or incomprehensible harangues in languages no one will ever know. LaVey quite literally "spelled" it out—in *The Satanic Witch* as well as in his other magical writings.

When the *demonic* is mentioned in *The Satanic Witch,* it doesn't refer to some old ghosts of medieval Christian fantasies, but simply to the exact opposite of your position on what he called the LaVey Personality Synthesizer—basically a schematic overview of general character traits projected onto a clock structure so that qualities at twelve o'clock are regarded as most attractive to the six o'clock. The exact opposite is what will be most attractive to you, and probably unconsciously so (hence the term *demonic*).

When LaVey repeated the old adage that "men should be men, and women, women," it's not an example of retrograde, reactionary feelings of a man born in 1930. It is rather a revolutionary jab at the inert and basically asexual "uni-sexism" of the 1970s. LaVey's approach was to accentuate and amplify *any* differences between the sexes (or roles/ identities), in order to strengthen the force field of Wilhelm Reich's orgone energy.

Pick any era, style, or look you want (preferably as far from contemporary fashion as possible), but make sure it flaunts who and what you are, that it *doesn't* hide you in a soul- and sexless herd steeped in imaginary equality.

If you can't find your demonic person in the flesh, then you can certainly integrate the demonic in the privacy of your own intellectual decompression chamber, in your total environment. A calling forth of your demonic self, according to LaVey, will promote not only temporary pleasure and satisfaction, but also lead to a much greater degree of self-knowledge—regardless of whether this is explored by yourself or in the company of someone else. "The transsexuals and transvestites, bless them, come closer than anyone else to a complete recognition of the Demonic element within them. These people who, because they truly admire and recognize the sensual qualities of the opposite sex, would do nothing to discourage whatever trappings add to the *difference*. That is why transvestites and transsexuals often are said to 'make better women than women.' They employ all the devices of overcompensation and frequently come out actually looking more convincing."[8]

Self-knowledge and honesty are key elements in LaVeyan Satanism. This then is also of the utmost importance in explorations of the self. Sexual adherence can be a powerful thing to both flaunt and keep secret, depending on who you are. It only really becomes a problem if you flaunt it to people who have no interest in your proclivities, or if you keep it a secret against your will because your surroundings are threatening.

In this sense of protection and privacy when it comes to initial exploration, LaVey advocated masturbation as the best tool; and one to fully make use of in magical ritual:

Masturbate. Fantasize as you do. First-rate fantasy is infinitely superior to a fourth-rate fling. Don't try to force or look too hard. It's better to use your imagination fully than your prick foolishly. It costs less, too. Now, understand, I'm talking about substitution, not sublimation. I don't believe in sublimating your sex drive, channeling it into other activities, even creative ones like art. That's strictly for the guilt-ridden. Go ahead and masturbate and get rid of the tension. Make yourself feel better. Masturbation is the most selfish of all acts, with no need to concern yourself with anyone else's pleasure.[9]

Feminists have at times been critical of LaVey's insights, as these stress lesser magic manipulation via the use of sex or sexual allure. To these critics, LaVey merely objectifies women when telling them how to make use of sex and sexuality as a tool to get what they want. But the critics seemingly have never been able to leave their collectivist perspective, in which billions of women are somehow lumped together as one. Instead, I would argue that LaVey strongly subjectifies women (and men as well) and leaves it to them as individuals to fend for themselves.

If the lesser magic required in life involves the use of sex or sexuality, then that is something to joyfully master—*not* be mastered by. By sharing his experiences and synthesized observations, LaVey wanted the Satanic witch to be free and successful—regardless of what she does or doesn't do. The realistic perspective always clashes, sooner or later, with imposed moralism. The Satanic witch is simply a realist who makes life work for her—while enjoying it.

In a 1980s wave of cheap debunking of LaVey, many of the things he claimed were questioned. Had he actually worked in this or that circus, had he ever met (and had sex with) Marilyn Monroe, had he ever played with this or that orchestra . . . ? The obvious goal was to literally paint the man black—ironically, from the perspective of some kind of illusory balanced history writing. This endeavor eventually backfired into actually strengthening his position, and we can learn a lot about LaVey by looking at why it did so.

Already in the 1950s, Anton LaVey was a larger-than-life character who knew how to attract attention and keep it, "for fun and profit." He nurtured his own nature and concocted an identity as a colorful organist, a talented musician, and someone with obvious experience from circuses and sideshows (as documented in photographs). And then the big cats. . . . You don't keep leopards and lions as pets unless you know how to deal with them. He learned that at the circus, just as his mentor Rubber Bubber Johnson had. What LaVey did was to consciously and consistently augment an already fascinating life and lifestyle. You are who you are, but also to a great extent what others project onto you. Add some stardust to the already twinkling star, and people will joyfully accept it—and keep on projecting.

Most famous and infamous magicians of history have done exactly the same thing; it's part of their identity and their mythology. To mention but a few: St. Germain, Cagliostro, Rasputin, Blavatsky, Gurdjieff, Crowley, Gardner, and Spare all told "a truth and a half," and this is *exactly* what wrote them into history—*not* their capacity to evoke this or that spirit. And that also goes for many other magicians (not of the hocus pocus kind) in and on LaVey's mind: Nixon, Lovecraft, Zaharoff, and Capone, for instance, in themselves larger-than-life characters that people have then sprinkled their own mythological stardust on. The dedicatee lists in LaVey's books tell, as we have seen here and there in this book, a very rich and inspiring story. This story doesn't really need critical nitpicking to be effective, as it's not mainly working in the arena of materialist, academic analysis but rather in the sphere of contemporary mythology.

However, what I actually found most refreshing when visiting LaVey at the Black House was not that the stories he told were great and amazing—beyond belief, even; it was that they were actually verifiably true. It really takes someone with a great story to make a great storyteller.

In conclusion, and in essence, the critics' attempts at debunking Anton LaVey have failed because they all seemed to forget what P. T. Barnum, Mae West, Jayne Mansfield, LaVey himself, and a large host of other magicians have stated so clearly, time and time again: "There is no such thing as bad publicity." Any little mention in any little arena will greatly help the myth to live on.

Orrin Klapp couldn't have agreed more:

A good story is by no means always moralistic. It has specific earmarks: spiciness, novelty, vividness, simplicity, thematic significance, and "human interest." One of the first spots of "coloring" a man, then, is to search his life for the stories that fit him, point up his good qualities (and even a few "bad" ones), and create an unforgettable tale. There is literally no end to a good story, because people not only keep repeating it but cannot forget it. The general direction is clear: if you are going to give a man color, find something lively, avoid the clichés of goodness, and take a little chance.[10]

What Anton LaVey presented to the world was (and is) colorful enough to draw a lot of attention. When scrutinized by critics for being too fanciful, or possibly even deceitful, the results seem to, more often than not, (re)turn to and in his favor. To quote Klapp again: "Everybody loves a hero, a villain or a clown." If Anton LaVey suffered from any pathological affliction (seen in this ex post facto regard), it would only be a slight bout of *maior quam vita*-ism—a condition his enemies will always be thoroughly immune to.

6

MAYBE WE SHOULD WATCH A MOVIE NOW?

It is for amusement that I exist. It is for that alone that I remain upon a world in which, when all is said and done, amusement in some form or guise is the one great aim of all, the only thing that makes life upon it tolerable. My aim is, therefore, you perceive, a simple one. But what is it that amuses me?

ABE MERRITT, *SEVEN FOOTPRINTS TO SATAN*

Anton LaVey was one of the finest film buffs I have ever met. It was reflected not only in the choice of films we watched on video while I was at the Black House, but also in his constant references to both on- and offbeat Hollywood masterpieces—and beyond. To really hammer in the magical significance of certain movies, there is the official movie list in Blanche Barton's *The Church of Satan* book.[1] A lot of groups and people love to show off fancy esoteric reading lists, but how many magical orders actually have their own list of recommended films?*

---

*The list is also available on the Church of Satan's website, churchofsatan.com, and in the vastly expanded version of Barton's book, called *We Are Satanists* (La Quinta: Aperient Press, 2021)

As it's sometimes justified to call LaVeyan Satanism a "perpetual ECI nostalgia crusade," that outlook would of course also include movies from one's most ECI impacted/dominated years. The official CoS film list is part LaVey's own ECI crusade and part later films that amplify his perspective—basically, a celluloid codification/reinforcement both in emotional tonality and intellectual, philosophical fodder.

In our particular context, it's interesting to consider how LaVey himself, as well as the Black House, has been portrayed on film. Already in 1969, there was Ray Laurent's *Satanis: The Devil's Mass,* an underground documentary about LaVey and his Church. The film contains ritual footage, interviews with Church members and the LaVey family (Anton; his partner at the time, Diane; and his daughter from a previous relationship, Karla).

Satanis is an ambitious film of meager means. What it lacks in snazzy production values, it makes up for in glorious 16mm integrity. It is neither pro nor contra the Church of Satan but certainly allows LaVey and his epicurean congregation to speak freely about what they believe in. As comical counterpoints, we hear how LaVey's neighbors are disturbed by the nightly sounds of Togare, LaVey's Nubian lion, his "ill-kept" backyard, and the fact that he doesn't seem to have a "normal" job. As one of LaVey's neighbor ladies interviewed in the film expresses it: "He could work as anybody else. You know, we are working people who make our living in a decent way, you know, but probably it was too much for him."

There are also scenes of ritual from inside the black chamber; for instance, a "compassion" ritual for members of the congregation, which seems to also include a destruction ritual (at one point, needles are stuck in an effigy). Just as with the men's magazines, LaVey was more than willing to show off and stage rituals, so that the photographers got everything they wanted in terms of naked ladies and spooky men. But the scenes in *Satanis* definitely carry more weight. The people involved are real members—including a young Isaac Bonewits (neo-pagan author of such books as *Rites of Worship* and *Real Magic*), who asks Satan that "the powers of darkness should be bestowed upon a certain faction of my anatomy, that will enable it to perform its duties better to my satisfaction and its own."

Bonewits later disowned this erect request, the experience as such, and his time in the Church of Satan, claiming that "since I was still an enthusiastic ritualist, I was drafted to play various silly parts in these [fake rituals]. I climbed into a coffin with a naked woman while wearing a bishop's costume, stabbed a puppet with a knife, asked the high priest (Anton, in his Red Devil costume) for Satanic blessings, etc. I can't remember any of the dialog at this point, but I do recall Anton telling us that what we said didn't matter much, since everything was going to be translated into European languages for the 'documentaries' the men were making."[2]

Even though *Satanis* is a better documentary than how fate has deemed fit to treat it, it surely must have acted as a great, covert commercial for the Church of Satan at the time. It was released at about the same time that *The Satanic Bible* was published and was picking up speed, and interest in the dark and erotic goings-on in San Francisco was great. The colorful group that was depicted consisted of real adult libertines—people actively developing the arcane and dusty systems of magic that had been dominant until then. And eloquently so.

I suspect most people who hadn't already heard of LaVey by then on TV or radio, or in magazines, must have expected far-out hippie kids flashing inverted pentagrams to provoke American moms and dads. That this wasn't the case at all—quite the contrary!—must have been extra shocking to the average American.

It occurred to me for many, many years that there was a large gray area between psychiatry and religion that was untapped. No religions have ever been based on man's carnal needs or his fleshly pursuits. Religions are based on abstinence rather than indulgence. And while religions therefore have to be based on fear, well, we don't feel that fear is necessary to base a religion on. The fact that religions for thousands of years have been telling people what they should do and what they shouldn't do according to the basic whims of a person who might be running the show, it's very understandable; we're realists. But we also feel that first one has to be good to oneself before one can be good to other people. We feel the greatest sin of all is self-deceit. This is a very selfish religion. We believe in greed, and we believe in selfishness; we believe in all of the lustful thoughts that motivate man because this is man's natural feeling. This is based on what man naturally would do.[3]

The Italian mondo film *Angeli bianchi; angeli neri,* released in the United States as *Witchcraft 70,* contains a seven-minute segment with LaVey, beautifully shot at the Black House. The narrative is structured around a young couple coming to the Black House to be married. LaVey obliges, and the congregation amplifies their desire, while the young smile and "flash the horns." But LaVey also gets the chance to spread the gospel of Satan, squeezed in between hysteric narration and likewise organ pop music (it is, after all, an Italian mondo film!):

> The Church of Satan was formed April 30, 1966, which is now considered the year one of the Satanic age. The primary creed of the Church of Satan is to indulge in whatever one can in life and to not abstain, as we feel that indulgence is the prime motivation of human beings of all animals. The Church of Satan is the first organized religion of its kind in the history of the world. We believe in life everlasting, world without end; we have nothing to do with prophets of doom, or the masochist, or the people in the world that thrive on misery. We prepare ourselves for each succeeding day of life, and we live it to the fullest.[4]

During this initial heyday, LaVey was also filmed by Kenneth Anger, who was riding high after the success of his experimental film *Scorpio Rising* (1963). Fueled by not only critical acclaim but also some degree of revenue from this film, Anger had relocated to San Francisco. His idea was to begin work on what would become his magnum opus: *Lucifer Rising*. This would be a film displaying the awakening of Lucifer, filtered through Aleister Crowley's religious appropriation of the Egyptian god Horus, in his own construction of the "Aeon of Horus." The environment of San Francisco would be a perfect place for this, according to Anger. The hippies and radically different lifestyles appealed to Anger as colorful examples of a loving yet violent over-throwing of the old and rigid.

At the same time as Anger worked on his film, he also befriended Anton LaVey and started attending the Magic Circle. He also lent Crowley books and artworks to the Church of Satan. Crowley's por-trait of his "scarlet woman" Leah Hirsig (1883–1975) can be seen on display in many early photographs from the ritual chamber. Anger also took part in official capacities as a Church of Satan priest, for instance at the funeral of a member of the U.S. Navy, machinist Edward Olsen.

The production of *Lucifer Rising* had begun well, and Anger filmed away for what he knew would be a masterpiece of magical filmmak-ing. He did, however, experience increasing problems with his main cast member: musician Bobby Beausoleil. As the handsome guitarist of the band Love, Beausoleil was a perfect Lucifer for Anger's film. They also shared living quarters at a majestic Victorian house on 1198 Fulton Street that had at one point been a center for czarist émigrés (hence the nickname, The Russian Embassy), but the relationship was not a stable one. Beausoleil, still a minor at the time, kept substantial amounts of marijuana in the house, and when Anger found out, there was a heated argument.[5] In rage after the confrontation, Beausoleil allegedly stole most of the *Lucifer Rising* footage already shot and drove off into the dark night of his own destiny: becoming a part of the Manson "family," murdering fellow musician and music teacher Gary Hinman in a drug deal gone sour, and presently still serving a life sentence in prison.

What would have become Kenneth Anger's cinematic testament, and an aestheticized ushering in of Aleister Crowley's cosmic era of "force and fire," was now suddenly gone with the wind. With support from friends, including members of the Rolling Stones, Anger gradually regained momentum and decided to use whatever scraps he had left—even using material from his cutting room bin—to at least finish something. The result was the impressive *Invocation of My Demon Brother,* which was completed in 1969. The film also contains footage from a Rolling Stones' concert in Hyde Park, London, in the summer of 1969. Mick Jagger agreed to improvise the soundtrack on one of the first Moog synthesizers, and the result is uncanny and powerful. In the midst of this gem of a film, we can see Anton LaVey coming through a door, carrying a human skull. This brief footage itself, as well as the emotional and aesthetic context of Anger's film, creates a powerful moment that in many ways contrasts the obviously staged displays of, for instance, *Witchcraft 70.* Where the PR films were cinematic displays of attraction spells, Anger's footage is more low-key but also, in a sense, more genuine.

Anton LaVey's early love of movies remained an active passion throughout his life, and many people that he met had ties not only to the entertainment industry in general, but to Hollywood in particular. Jayne Mansfield would be the perfect example of this, as someone who was intrigued, sought out contact, and created a "third mind PR Golem" of sorts that lives on to this day. (For more information about their relationship, see Appendix III, "There Is No Such Thing as Bad Publicity")

One interesting filmmaker of note was British set designer and director Robert Fuest (1927–2012). His most famous films, *The Abominable Dr. Phibes* (1971) and *Dr. Phibes Rises Again* (1972), are beautiful gems of poetic schlock cinema—a mix of horror, suggestive plot holes, a set design drenched in LSD, truly magnificent performances by Vincent Price, and substantial inspiration not only from Anton LaVey but also from LaVey's friend and mentor Cecil Nixon.

The character that Price so eerily portrays is called Anton Phibes. He has created a total environment, complete with a mechanical artificial human companion band ("The Clockwork Wizards") and lavish art deco interior design. His main occupation in this splendid isolation is as an organist.

The Phibes films are amazing in many ways, striking you as psychedelic oddities that could only have been made at that specific time— in the chemical analysis of cultural history (not unlike the British TV series *The Prisoner* or the American International Pictures "acidsploitation" gems such as *The Trip* and *Psych-Out*). It is not surprising that earlier in his career, Fuest had directed several episodes of the British TV series *The Avengers*. But there is an eerie quality that permeates both these Phibes films. In one way, they are formally stiff—befitting the proverbial British upper lip—but that formality adds to the uncanny displacement or even dissociation of the viewer.

And then there is the actual story, and its moral implications. In the overall narrative, Anton Phibes's beloved wife had died during surgery (possibly echoing the demise of Cecil Nixon's paramour Elsa Nye Meriweather [1890–1943]; she had spent nine days in severe pain at a hospital in Oakland before dying). Phibes, being a famed medical doctor himself, sets out on an intricate journey of brutal revenge. It's lex talionis squared; not only of biblical proportions but of content—each victim suffers one of the curses mentioned in the Old Testament.

The two Dr. Phibes films are cinematic anomalies in the best possible way, and actually merge Anton LaVey and Cecil Nixon into a single character—and what an honor it must have been to have that union further "ensouled" by Vincent Price. . . . Perhaps that is also why LaVey agreed to work together with Fuest some years later.

In 1975 Anton LaVey played a small but certainly important part in Fuest's *The Devil's Rain*. This mind bender also stars a confused William Shatner, a precareer John Travolta, a postcareer Ida Lupino, and a downright glorious Ernest Borgnine as the high priest of a Devil-worshipping cult. The story (of sorts) is that this cult holds forth in an abandoned desert village while its devilish leader tries to access an important book from the seventeenth century that's been kept in enemy hands since the witch trials of New England. The dorky protagonist (played by Tom Skerritt of slightly later *Alien* fame) tries to fight this, and it all ends with a veritable orgy of melting devil-zombies as the sanctum sanctorum is smashed (a small TV set inside a papier maché ram's head, in which you can see souls trying to break free from the clutches of the Devil—or is it from the Pilgrim moralists?).

Although this film today feels more like a *Cremaster* sketch film by artist Matthew Barney, or a film by equally weird artist Mike Kelley, LaVey's brief presence at the high altar while Borgnine recites ceremonial lines (very likely provided by LaVey, as he was also hired as technical advisor for the film) makes up for any cinematic shortcomings. Although Fuest surely had genuine filmmaking visions, his original admiration for Cecil Nixon and LaVey here turned into drawn-out multicolored mush.

In the early 1990s, Anton LaVey jointly inspired Feral House publisher Adam Parfrey and filmmaker Nick Bougas to team up for the documentary *Speak of the Devil* (1993). This film shows LaVey in the same way as I got to know him: safely situated in the Black House, holding court in the Purple Parlor or by the synthesizers in the kitchen.

In many ways, *Speak of the Devil* is very much an in-house production, and should be regarded as a successful manifestation of a process that began with the abandoned *Hail Satan!* film/infomercial in 1989 (see Appendix I for more information about this film).

LaVey talks to Adam Parfrey about his life, favorite subjects, and philosophy, and it's cleverly edited and illustrated by Bougas with old movie clips. The result is a peek straight into the official mind of Anton LaVey; it was released on VHS by Wavelength Video.

In an email from 2018, Parfrey briefly told me about the production of the film: "I bought a Hi-8 camera to film it, did a lot of the camera work and interviewing with Anton and others. Even purchased the videotapes. Of course Nick had a lot to do with it too, but certainly not all of it. He was the primary editor of the tapes, as this was also his job for that company he worked for, although comments we made seem to affect the final edit. Since I was a friend of both Anton and Nick at that time, I saw it as a group effort."

In 1989 and 1992 LaVey provided the voice-over narration for both volumes of Bougas's morbid video compilations *Death Scenes* (also released by Wavelength Video).

Some twenty-five years later, it was time for another cinematic burst. Spanish director Aram Garriga released his film *An American Satan* in 2020. It's a straightforward documentary with lots of interviews about the Church of Satan and Anton LaVey. Scenes from CoS rituals and performances at the Slipper Room in New York constitute the filmic framework for a multitude of voices, including Church "dropouts" such as artists Boyd Rice, Steven Johnson Leyba, and Diabolos Rex, as well as some footage with Zeena Schreck's son, Stanton.

My own film, *Anton LaVey: Into the Devil's Den,* was first screened at independent cinema Husets Biograf in Copenhagen, Denmark, on November 21, 2019. The proprietor of the cinema, American film historian Jack Stevenson, is also in the film (and in this book), as he screened weird horror films several times for LaVey at the Black House in the early 1990s. Stevenson has also written a great piece about the history of Tod Browning's Satanic masterpiece, *Freaks* (1932),[6] as well as other wonderful essays and books about cinema.

LaVey told me personally, as well as many others, that he had been instrumental in the revival of *Freaks,* and I often wondered how, exactly. Stevenson, inspired by LaVey's display of his own collection of Freaksiana (lobby cards, press material, and many other things), explained that after the film had originally "died" in the mid-1930s, it was first revived by exploitation master Dwain Esper, who let the film travel for a long time but mainly as a sideshow kind of oddity in itself—often splicing in other random "freaks" and also sexual material into the film. Anything to cause a scandal and make a buck from the local yokels in rural America!

Although there was a faint buzz lingering among sideshow aficionados, the film as a phenomenon was soon basically unheard of, as even Esper's crass exploitation eventually dwindled.

Together with his wife Willie, real estate developer Donald Werby moved through different San Francisco social circles and developed friendships with, and supported, whomever and whatever they liked. For instance, the Werbys were often at Cecil Nixon's Castle of Indolence and even bought the famous Open Sesame door at the auction after Nixon's demise. That the couple would eventually befriend LaVey and his Church was not unexpected at all.

Mrs. Werby was not only a socialite but also a big fan of movies. As she was putting together a film program of "A History of the Macabre" for the Camera Obscura Film Society in 1956, local film fans Val and Claire Golding suggested she contact the one-of-a-kind organist Anton LaVey. When she asked her new friend what should be in the program, he immediately recommended *Freaks*. LaVey showed her all of his PR material and told stories of the people who had been in the film—many of whom LaVey had met himself. This set Mrs. Werby off on a hunt for a print of the film that was in good shape and untainted by Dwain Esper's rapacious interference.

Mrs. Werby contacted the attorneys at MGM (the studio that had produced the film), but even they couldn't get her a definitive answer about who owned what and where there could be a decent print. After some real detective work, Mrs. Werby found Esper and bought the rights—something that made the impoverished Esper very happy. A print was eventually found in the basement of the El Rey Burlesque Theatre in Oakland, and from this print a new negative was struck—a Holy Grail for all *Freaks* fans. (Incidentally, Anton LaVey had played the organ at the El Rey several times in the 1950s. This theater is also where "bosomaniac" Russ Meyer worked as a projectionist before emerging as a brilliant filmmaker in his own right.)

Mrs. Werby screened the film at her festival and also lent prints to other film societies, museums, and universities. She eventually sold the rights to an initial competitor, film distributor Raymond Rohauer, at a profit. Rohauer, who specialized in showing old Hollywood films, screened *Freaks* as much as he could, but eventually the actual rights reverted back to MGM. By this time, the film's reputation was solidly reestablished, and it has since been disseminated and shown on all kinds of formats.

The influence of the film during the early 1960s was substantial. Its attitude of using "real" and decidedly "special" people instead of actors (which had been a central critique in the 1930s) greatly inspired such American filmmakers as Andy Warhol, Paul Morrissey, and their immediate spawn, John Waters.

Already in 1961, when the New Yorker Film Society booked a week-long run of the film, photographer Diane Arbus went to see it. As she was in a phase of trying to define herself, her often macabre interests, and her expressions of these, the celebrated art critic Emile de Antonio brought her to see Browning's magnificent odyssey of oddities. She then returned every night to watch the film again. In a letter to her daughter Doon, from August 1961, Arbus writes: "I have a new assignment and several more pending ones for a new magazine called *Show*. The one I am working on first is about HORROR in films, theater, TV, wax-works, spookhouses, any kind of entertainment and although at first I was somewhat cool to the idea maybe that was because I didn't think of it myself because it has begun to . . . GRAB ME."[7]

The film obviously made a huge impact on a creative mind already obsessed by the darkly prurient side of life. Already in 1959, de Antonio had brought Arbus to many places in New York that would provide fodder for her work for a long time—including Hubert's Museum at Broadway and 42nd Street. Although one could argue that the American 1960s fascination with freaks was generally more of a zeitgeist phenomenon than carefully constructed by a handful of loving aficionados, we can never escape the fact that the chain of LaVey-Werby-Rohauer provided this zeitgeist with its most precious and powerful building block. It is also interesting to note how culture and influence move forward in circles. LaVey was certainly aware of the important work Arbus had created in the 1960s, as she is one of the dedicatees of *The Satanic Rituals* (1972).

When Jack Stevenson moved to San Francisco in 1990, he had just published the third issue of his massive fanzine endeavor, *Pandemonium*. This issue contains rare material with Johnny Eck, the actor and performer who was one of the many stars of Browning's *Freaks*. Included, for instance, are Eck's fragments from, or attempts at, an autobiography:

> Time heals all wounds, and many nights I would cry, lying awake in the dark, thinking of how really wonderful and exciting to be working in front of the cameras on all the different giant sound stages. I got to know each member of the film crew; I was accepted not as a Monster Freak—but as one of them—not twenty inches tall, but a miniature super-man! Best of all, I was special to director Tod Browning, and his assistant director Earl Taagart. I would ride many times along the side of these great men on a big camera dollie while they were shooting scenes. Now it was all over.[8]

Johnny Eck fell on harder and harder times and died in Baltimore in 1991. Though he originally worked for big circuses such as Barnum and Bailey and the Ringling Brothers, each decade seemed to bring an increased marginalization on and in the sideshow circuit for the original "incredible half man" Eck. Anton LaVey had met him when working in a "Ten in One" section of a sideshow, where an assortment of human oddities performed. "Johnny was extremely intelligent, always good-natured and one of the best people to be with I've ever known. There are very few normal people I have such high regard for."[9] LaVey described these so-called freaks as the "royalty of the carny world," because they didn't even have to come up with an act—they were simply themselves.

In an unpublished interview with Adam Parfrey from 1992, LaVey was incensed that after Eck had been robbed and beaten up in his Baltimore home in 1987, people vaguely discussed setting up some kind of financial support system. LaVey argued that, instead, fans should have volunteered early on to stand guard and beat up any intruders with a baseball bat—which is what Eck's own fantasy was, had he been able to.

LaVey's sentiments of Satanic solidarity echo those of the original *Freaks* movie: If you in any way hurt or ridicule one of "us" simply because we're different, you will suffer for it. It's a code not only of honor but one of deeply rooted human survival instincts, in which the ostracized and afflicted fight back, with "compound interest liberally added thereunto."

There are two other films that are noteworthy in our context (as film historian Jim Morton specifically mentions in his recollections): the Mexican *Yanco* (Servando González, 1961) and the Swedish *Vaxdockan* (Arne Mattsson, 1962, released in the United States as *The Doll*).

Yanco is a very peculiar and poetic tale about a boy, Juanito, whose sensitivity to noise makes him an outcast escapist. Life in his little village is filled with various forms of noise; some general and some specifically directed at him by bullies. What the boy loves is music, so he takes any opportunity to paddle his canoe to a secluded spot outside the village, where he keeps his self-constructed violin hidden. He brings out the instrument and plays so beautifully that the birds and other animals join him in harmony and also praise the boy for his equilibrist spirit.

Juanito one day hears sweet music close to the village market. It's performed by Yanco, an elderly musician who also sells candy to the village's children. They become friends, and Juanito learns to play the real violin from this master. But when Juanito's mother grows ill and he has to tend to her, old Yanco dies in solitude. Only after the fact does Juanito find the magical violin for sale in the local store. As his mother is too poor to buy it for him, he steals it every night to play the music he loves out in the open. Come morning, Juanito places the violin back in the shop.

The nightly concerts scare the simpleminded people of the village. The fact that the violin keeps disappearing from the store, only to mysteriously return, becomes part of a mystery that of course has to be somehow diabolical. Just as in Frankenstein and other similar myths, the rabble must destroy what scares them. As the villagers are approaching the source of the music with torches, Juanito loses his foothold as the piece of ground he stands on is severed and floats out into the main river and down a maelstrom—as does Yanco's violin.

It is a sad and poetic tale of sensitivity, the magic of music, and the eventual violence of intolerance and ostracism. Although Juanito's outsidership is innocent and basically a reconnecting to nature's higher kind of poetry, the villagers interpret the liberation and insight the music brings him as diabolical. Where old Yanco himself enjoys cultural integration by being a friendly candy salesman and a musician for the ladies of the village while they do their laundry, Juanito's inherent weirdness makes him, by LaVey's standards, a de facto Satanist. Juanito can't help but embrace that which makes him special, and thereby a talented outcast artist. His mastery of the beautiful language of a music that transcends the mere utilitarian human realm presents a threat to those who simply don't have the capacity to understand him.

A similar theme is played out in *Vaxdockan,* and with the added bonus of artificial human companions. Swedish director Arne Mattsson was a successful director of commercial films, like those about the private investigator Hillman. That he would direct a weird film about essentially a dark-side Pygmalion-Galathea drama was probably as strange and unlikely as the film itself. Written by famous Swedish author Lars Forssell, the film tells the story of a night watchman called Lundgren. His life seems completely devoid of meaning, and it depresses him. One night he steals a mannequin from the department store where he works. He takes her home in secret, invests her with his sincerity and love, and . . . watches her comes alive. After initial moments of loving communication, she starts demanding things from him. At the same time, his neighbors begin to wonder what's going on. They can't imagine this oddball having a lady friend in his tiny room, but at the same time they can distinctly hear his voice in there, talking to someone.

The empowerment and ecstasy that affect both the doll and Lundgren also trigger the ensuing madness, completely encouraged by the Galathea character. Lundgren goes on a rampage after having been discovered by the neighbors, smashes his love object to pieces, shoots at one of the snooping neighbors, and drifts back into depression.

For someone already nurturing agalmatophiliac (doll-loving) inclinations, *Vaxdockan* must have been a revelation to Anton LaVey. Not only is it thematically relevant and poignant; it is also a beautifully shot film, with a blatant noir vibe that accentuates its truly eerie and disturbing qualities. Masterful performances by Per Oscarsson as Lundgren and Gio Petré as the doll also forcefully remove the film from what otherwise could have led to a complete disappearance from film history. Instead, it's a film that in a very dark way remains painful and strong; not unlike a cross-pollination between Ingmar Bergman's 1960s eloquence and the warped agalmatophiliac mind of Hans Bellmer.

The focus in both films being pathological outsidership—and how to deal with it—it's interesting to see that neither of them ends on a happy note. But that certainly doesn't take away the stories' absolutely magical moments of liberation and ultimate happiness. It is when the Satanic magician wholeheartedly indulges in his or her intuition that not only excellence comes forth, but that freedom and happiness are allowed to reign—albeit for a fleeting time. We should keep in mind here that what rocks the boat is not Juanito's and Lundgren's sensibilities, sensitivities, or mind frames; it is simply the "normal" people that can't handle the visible and audible discrepancy from their own neurotic and hypocritical worldviews. What they cannot understand, they destroy.

There is a vast number of films that can be enjoyed if one wants to get a better understanding of the LaVeyan mind. The recommended films list on the CoS website and in Blanche Barton's *We Are Satanists* tome is a veritable and palatable menu of what could be (and was) served in the Purple Parlor. To watch a movie was as natural there as having a drink or a plain conversation. The integration of a framework of cinematic fiction was not meant to distance oneself and get out of a social context, but rather to actually heighten (and deepen) the awareness of the atmosphere in the room.

The films themselves were very much curated portals into conversations that integrated larger mysteries than mere morsels of film history. The people who had written the films, those who had directed them, starred in them. . . . There was always a hidden story too good to be true, quite often "beyond belief," and always with a Satanic twist or wisdom to reveal the sugarcoated fantasies spun by the movie studios' PR departments.

No matter how clean-cut the actors and other movie people tried to appear, there was always some connection to the infamous gas station of Scotty Bowers, Hollywood's pansexual procurer par excellence, or other facilitators of letting off the steam of celebrity stress. The more metabolic or sexual secrets there were, the more power those who were actually in the know wielded. Prurience and dirt were hard currency in a hypocritical microcosm such as Hollywood, as it is in the macrocosm of humanity as such.

Anton LaVey loved these kinds of secrets and what they brought to those involved in terms of pleasure as well as pain. The film noir mythos and morality, with its heyday in the mid- to late 1940s, in many ways reflected larger society and its values more accurately than any constructed apple pie (sur)realities of suburban America. The good guys were often not so good at all, and the rugged antiheroes—although harnessing hearts of gold and an infallible sense of justice–were eventually mowed down, taking their secrets with them to an abode six feet under (unless of course they had spilled the beans to some swell dame who would now access the loot in cahoots with some other two-bit sucker). The film noir world is one displaying the possibility of a momentary reversal of the established hypocritical morals and is thereby inherently Satanic.

This angle of looking deeper into film history, and specifically its shady and sleazy sides, has become the trademark of LaVey's close friend, filmmaker Kenneth Anger. In the 1950s, Anger started writing about

the saucy scandals and drug-fueled debacles of Tinseltown. The satirical noir sensibility that Anger had already mastered in his twenties and
then developed in his best-selling *Hollywood Babylon* books was surely
a fast lane into the heart and mind of Anton LaVey. When Kenneth
Anger moved to San Francisco in the mid-1960s, a friendship between
these two enthusiastic film buffs seemed devilishly destined. The fact
that they both also shared an active interest in magic and occultism
certainly didn't make things worse. But why don't we let Anger himself
tell the story. . . .

PART II

THE INTERVIEWS

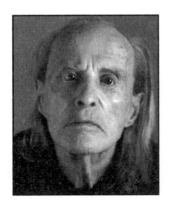

7

KENNETH ANGER

Kenneth Anger, Los Angeles, 2018.
Photo courtesy Trapart Film.

"You don't easily knock out a duplicate of a one of a kind."

I first met American filmmaker Kenneth Anger in 1989, on the same trip as my first meeting with Anton LaVey and Blanche Barton. Although I had some nepotistic door openers via acquaintances, and the fact that I had just written a thesis at Stockholm University about "Aleister Crowley's influence in Kenneth Anger's films," I do believe it was LaVey's phone call to Anger, saying I was OK, that got me into Anger's half of Samson De Brier's enchanted house on Barton Street in Hollywood. We have kept in touch on and off since then, and I have also made a film about him, called *Cinemagician: Conversations with Kenneth Anger* (2019).

How did you first hear about Anton LaVey?

When I moved to San Francisco he was considered one of the most colorful characters who lived there. I soon met him and we became fast friends. I never had any conflict with him, and we were close friends until his death. I made a point of meeting him, and it was not that difficult for me to do so. He invited me over to his house, which was known at the time as the Black House—which unfortunately has been torn down; it no longer exists—at 6114 California Street. He had his pet lion in the basement, and eventually the roars of the lion at night disturbed his neighbors, and he was forced to donate the lion to the San Francisco Zoo.

How did those meetings impact your life?

In a positive way. They reinforced all my ideas about individual liberty and the free expression of ideas, and it was a positive development. They insured that far-out ideas can thrive and be expressed quite freely and still not be oppressed by other people.

Did you bring ideas and concepts to the Magic Circle that he wasn't aware of?

I don't think so. Our ideas enhanced each other because they were exactly parallel; there was no conflict.

You have both focused on the total environment as a magical space. Did you work on this and other ideas or concepts together?

We certainly discussed them in a friendly way, and I guess you can say that we influenced each other. I'm happy to have been part of that influence. If I influenced him, I'm happy about that, and he certainly influenced me.

In what ways?

Well, in the ways of creativity.

What are some specific ideas or concepts that you worked on together?

The idea that groups of people can reinforce the strength of these ideas, if they form a ceremony or a ritual around them. We had our rituals connected with the Church of Satan, which evolved and were part of his life until his death.

Did your impressions of LaVey change over the decades?

Well, they were always positive. In other words, I never had to recant my feeling about him and say, "Well, he turned out to be a monster," because that wasn't so. He was a very thoughtful and creative person, and he was one of the great friendships of my life.

What would you say has been LaVey's greatest contribution to your life?

He showed me that people can work together to create something, and that it is a positive thing to have other people involved. Because before that, I was more or less a loner, and my ideas were my own. I never knew Aleister Crowley, because he died in 1947 in England. I never was able to meet that man, but he was also a very great influence on me through his books, and by talking with people that knew him.

Did you ever discuss Crowley with LaVey?

Oh yes, I discussed Crowley with LaVey, among other people. If anything, he was perhaps a little bit humanly jealous of Crowley, but I think he recognized that Crowley was a true master.

What would you say was the key to LaVey's controversy: merely the word Satan, *or something else?*

Well, the something else was that there were other belief systems that certainly did not correspond to what were popular belief systems at that time; he expressed this as a very active voice in the contrary position.

What were some of the ideas about magic that he would talk about or that you would talk about together?

Basically, that magic is like an underground river that connects everything, and that it has to be recognized as flowing there—that it is there.

Is this something that LaVey openly discussed?

Well, he openly discussed it with me, and his life was a pretty good example of it.

Were there certain theatrics that he had at his meetings or rituals; things that he used for effect?

He was a theatrical person, so everything he did had that aspect. He would make his appearances at these meetings through the fireplace. There was a fireplace in the room, and actually it dated back to the Prohibition days. In the basement was a complete bar, and the access to the bar was through a ladder that went down through the fireplace and ended up in the bar. It was a secret place during those ridiculous years of the Prohibition.

Did he have other sorts of props?

He did have a Tesla coil, and he would turn it on occasionally for theatrical effect, and of course it makes a loud zapping noise and a bright lightning-like flash of light, and he loved that machine. He had some red gels that he used, not all the time, but sometimes. Basically everything was simple, in the sense that all of this was happening in the living room of his home, not on a stage or in some elaborate space. He always used his ability at the Hammond organ as part of what he was doing. He would play the organ, and this would be the background for certain of the ceremonies. In other words, he was always on stage. I never saw Anton, even in his private moments, where you could say, "Well, now he's not performing." He was always performing as if he were on stage, which can be a little, maybe, tiresome for some people. I found it fascinating.

What was the altar like?

The altar was a naked woman, which is traditional in black magic: that you have a naked woman who lies actually before the altar. She just serves as a kind of prop of the ceremony; she doesn't actually do anything except lie there in the naked state, which is the picturesque way of being Satanic, I suppose you could say.

What do you miss most about Anton LaVey?

I miss having a friend who was very well read—he had a wonderful library—and articulate in his views about the occult, and what could be called popularly "magic." I'm fortunate to have known him, and I wish he was still around. He was a close personal friend, and the only lion tamer that I ever knew. The fact that he had a lion in the basement in his house, in violation of what you're supposed to have as a domestic pet, added to his allure. He got away with it for quite a long time, even though the neighbors were complaining about the howling in the middle of the night. Eventually his lion had to be donated to the San Francisco Zoo. He was a colorful friend, and the only kind of musician that I knew that could play all the old tunes that I love for me on his Hammond organ that he had in his home. I miss that aspect.

How do you see Anton LaVey's legacy, now and in the future?

He was one of a kind, and one of a kind don't repeat themselves. I don't see any successor to him coming along and displacing Anton's legend, his legacy of being a very colorful individual. I see Anton LaVey's legacy as a very personal one. He was one of a kind, and you don't easily knock out a duplicate of a one of a kind: they're one of a kind.

Blanche Barton, San Diego, 2018.
Photo by Carl Abrahamsson.

8
BLANCHE BARTON

"He wanted people to be the best human beings they could be."

As Anton LaVey's partner and biographer, Blanche Barton lived and worked together with him between 1984 and 1997. In 1990 she published the book *The Church of Satan* (Hell's Kitchen Productions), which was greatly expanded and republished as *We Are Satanists* (Aperient Press, 2021), and the authorized biography of LaVey: *The Secret Life of a Satanist* (Feral House, revised and republished in 2014). She is also the mother of Anton LaVey's son, Xerxes LaVey, and holds the position of Magistra Templi Rex in the Church of Satan.

How did you first hear about Anton LaVey? What was the actual instigation that caught your attention?

When I was a little girl I was always drawn to magic and the supernatural, psychic stuff, and UFOs, and it certainly was the time for it. In the 1960s and 1970s, you know, there were a lot of people exploring that sort of thing, and I had already been drawn to witchcraft and magic. I'd seen *The Satanic Bible,* and I saw this strange guy on the back that looked kind of intimidating. I thought, "Ah, well, you know, he looks

kind of full of himself." I thought that maybe he doesn't really understand that continuum the same way I would see it. So I took it, and I
put it back; I took it up, put it back. Finally, a book called *The Devil's
Avenger* came out in 1974: the first biography of Anton LaVey. It talked
about his lion; it talked about his history in the police department and
in the carnival and in the circus. He worked with a lot of lions; he had
a lion and worked with animals and tigers. It was also about his love of
life, and his disdain for the oppression and the prejudice that can grow
out of conventional Christianity, and I certainly understood that.

I read the "Satanic Statements" there, and I read about other people
who were aligned with his philosophy. It just seemed to make a great
deal of sense to me. For me, it was the awakening of this blending of
what I wanted in a religion. It was the first time I saw a religion that
blended the supernatural aspects; the emotional, poetic aspects; but also
integrated the brain and the head and reason and rationality, and in
which you enter the ritual chamber by choice. You're not deceiving yourself; self-deceit is not to be advocated. All of this just made perfect sense
to me, so I became a Satanist. I started self-identifying, as they say, as a
Satanist at twelve years old, after reading *The Satanic Bible*.

How did this then develop into your actually actively contacting the Church?

I became a member, an actual card-carrying member, in 1976, which
was a couple of years after I'd been identifying myself as a Satanist. I
was talking with my friends; I gave my parents the book so that they
would know what I'm into. They sort of raised their eyebrows, but my
father was an atheist, and he understood where Anton LaVey was coming from. My mother was always very supportive of me, so they were
fine with it. They knew that I was bookish and that I had all kinds of
strange ideas. I decided that I wanted to join a couple of years later—I
think I must have been fourteen—and my mom wrote out the check
for me: twenty-five dollars to join the Church of Satan. It was great.
I got the record, I got the Baphomet, and, you know, I felt that what
it provided for me as a young person was that I didn't feel alone. I felt

like there were other people out there, on an international level, who really understood what I was going through on a day-to-day basis. And that it was okay to feel angry and resentful and suspicious and disdainful and misanthropic sometimes. That was fine; it came from natural impulses, and I could use them, you know. I started working magic. I liked the ritualizing, because at that point I was ritualizing alone, and it was essentially meditation: you get into a meditative state. I would use a black candle, and I'd just sort of quiet my mind and connect with whatever was out there. I felt something responding; I felt myself aligning with other things going on, and seeing a direction.

I then went on my merry way; I graduated with the respect of my peers and teachers from high school; I graduated from college with a concentration in literature and writing, Phi Beta Kappa, again, with a wonderful relationship with my teachers and my professors. Then it happened that I was elected to Phi Beta Kappa on April 11, which is Anton LaVey's birthday, so I wrote to the Church, and I said, "I'm a member, and this is what's going on." They replied, "Well, if you're ever in town, let us know, maybe we can arrange something." After my graduation, my mother said, "Why don't we go to San Francisco?" She loved San Francisco, so we went there. I picked up the phone . . . Oh, my goodness . . . I don't shake; I'm not a nervous-type person, but I was literally shaking when I made that phone call. . . . They were very gracious, and I went out to dinner with Anton LaVey. I met him, I shook his hand, and as I've said before, I didn't know what to expect. You don't know whether he's going to be a pompous asshole, or really full of himself, sweep into the room in his long black cape and, you know, "Here, kiss my ring" or something. But he wasn't. He was pleasant, he was funny, he was genuine, he was joking, he knew music and references to movies that I knew and that I was familiar with.

We went back to his place, and he played music the way that I would hear it in my head. That was a gift that he had: he could connect with people through music; that was one of his magical abilities. He knew people, and he knew music. Someone would walk into the room, and he'd pluck a song that I knew he hadn't played since before I'd known him. They would say, "I haven't heard that song since I was ten years old," and they'd fall in love with him. I was mesmerized. He wrote me a letter: "You will be in San Francisco; you're needed here and you will come here." I said, "Okay."

I went back to my home in San Diego and rolled my eyes and said, "I don't have plans for that," but within a couple of months a friend from college called. She said, "Oh, we happen to be moving up to San Francisco. . . . Would you like to move into a house with us?" I just said, "Yes, please!"

I started working in the organization: writing letters, filling book requests, and eventually becoming Doktor LaVey's right-hand man. I didn't know it at the time, but he was going through the process of separation from his wife Diane. I respected her; I expected to meet her and be part of her world as well, but I didn't realize what personal things were going on. He was very discreet about it for a good six months to a year, and sort of kept things open for her to come back. He fully expected that. I mean, my goodness, they'd been together for so long, and he loved her and wanted to have her back in his life whenever she was ready, but that didn't happen. She was very resentful and very angry toward him, and things got very legally contentious as things progressed, unfortunately.

But I started working in the office and got to know some of the other people. The Satanic Panic was just starting. Some of the early accusations of Satanic child abuse and ritual abuse and the recovered memories and all of that was just starting. That was the beginning of our relationship. I found myself on national media within a year of moving to San Francisco and being part of the Church of Satan directly. A lot of us—the people that are in the organization now—that's how we sort of went through blood and battle together: going on these shows, radio shows, television shows, and just telling people, "No, we don't hurt animals; no, we don't hurt children; it's in *The Satanic Bible;* read *The Satanic Bible* instead of just waving it around on your shows, and you'll find out what real Satanism is." But that was opposite to "Joe Schmo" with his little band of seventeen-year-olds sacrificing cats down the street. That was a lot more interesting to the media, I suppose, than the real thing.

There was also something else that happened, and that was the amorous aspect. What was the seductive trigger for you, or the emotional enchantment? Your being involved in Satanism was one thing, but there was something more in this, too.

The attraction to Anton LaVey is undeniable. I mean, I'm certainly not alone in my obsession with him, from a very early age. I fell in love with him: physically, spiritually, psychologically, all of the above, from the time I was twelve years old. He was an ECI for me. I'd already gotten into that stream through Dracula and vampires. I was lucky, because there were a lot of movies out and available at the time; there was a context for that sort of dark, masculine, compelling archetype that Anton LaVey represented and personified. I had slept with his picture under my pillow for a number of years. I had thrown a lot of magical energy toward him as a person, as a man, and manifested him physically in my young, youthful, adolescent, burgeoning libido for a number of years. When we met, I suppose all of that Kundalini energy just sort of swirled around and exploded. We understood each other physically and were attracted to each other immediately.

As mentioned, we met and had dinner the first night, and then the second night we went out again together and we kissed in the sunset overlooking the Cliff House. It was always stimulating, romantic, dynamic, and devastating. He challenged me physically, sexually, intellectually, and he fulfilled me. We explored a lot sexually and physically together, as well as intellectually and emotionally. I couldn't have found that anywhere else.

One of the essences of Satanism is to just go with it. If you're attracted to something, you know, go with it. We're not going to judge what you do, how far you go; there are no parameters. You set those parameters by the consequences that you encounter. You can go as far as you want with drugs or alcohol or sexual escapades or food indulgence, but there are going to be consequences to that. You push yourself out of your comfort zone, and that's why it's dangerous. I mean, the Satanic philosophy, the "left-hand path," is not an easy one, because it's generally an individual path. There's very little guidance; you have to find your own way; there's a lot of conflicting information that will come at you. You have to find your way through that, and it's also not going to say "No" to you. It's going to say, "Yes, yes, yes, yes, yes," and you have to find your way through that.

How did these first meetings impact your life?

From that first meeting with Anton LaVey in San Francisco I knew that as long as he walked the Earth, that was where I wanted to be: at his side. I could be no other place. It had given me so much as a philosophy already; it had guided me every day since I read *The Satanic Bible* and *The Satanic Rituals* and *The Compleat Witch*. I threw myself into that world and that reality, and it had given me guidance for lesser magic and for greater magic. The reason I wanted to meet him and meet Diane and be part of the organization was that if there was anything that I could give back, I wanted to. I wanted to give back to that. I guess I'm sort of an idealist. I should be more cynical and more reserved, but I'm not: I've always been an idealist, and I throw myself into it. I should have been thinking, "Okay, what can I do now, after I've left college, what can I do to find a career or do something?" No, Anton LaVey said that I needed to be working with the Church of Satan in San Francisco, and so I was. I had some other gigs going at the same time, but they were all intertwined with my work with the organization. Eventually, I was the one that would be arranging his meetings with journalists, or clients that wanted to meet him; people that were asking for his help in various ways. It was 24/7. It was the Church of Satan and only the Church of Satan, and I was very, very happy to be there.

What would you say has been LaVey's greatest contribution to your life?

Wow! Anton LaVey gave me so much and continues to give me so much. I think most Satanists will find this to be true: that it knows no bounds. You start to unpack Satanism, and okay, yeah, maybe you start at magic, maybe you start at psychic stuff, maybe at the carny stuff, or cold reading or palmistry or psychology, but then you get into Jack London, you get into Lovecraft, you get into Dostoyevski, you get into Nietzsche. Any direction you want to go, there's a Satanic aspect; there's the pervading rebel in politics, economics . . . it continues to unpack itself for me.

For me, one of the reasons that I was attracted to the philosophy in the first place was that I already was drawn to animals and to the Satanic archetype as being the Lord of the Earth. At that age you're looking for a philosophy, so you're weighing a lot. Buddhism, maybe Judaism, maybe Christianity, you know, spiritualism, different things— you're evaluating as an intelligent person; you're looking for something to orient your life.

The reason I like Satanism was that it emphasized animals and the Earth and women. The power of women; the power of the witch to outrage, to make people uncomfortable, to demand, to destroy, to enchant—whether it's intimidation or bending the mind to your will— to bewitch; this was always in Satanism from the very beginning. It was long before the Wiccans started with their Dianic path, and the more organized neo-pagan ritual stuff. This was back in the 1960s; this was back in 1966 when he started the organization. Before that he had his witches' workshops: teaching women how to bend men's minds to their will, and owning your power.

I get frustrated with people now dismissing him as being "ancient" and, you know, heteronormative and misogynistic, which is a complete lie! He glorifies women. He was an observer of humans from the carnival, the burlesque, the circus days, and he saw the power that women have. Basil Zaharoff, whom he very much admired, saw how women could do what men could never do, and he understood that dynamic.

You can deny it; you can deny that sexual interplay and try to make yourself over as a man, and try to be something in that context, which is fine if you want to go in that direction.

He understood the power that women have, and he wanted to encourage that: to celebrate it as he celebrated, and as the Church of Satan celebrates, homosexuality, asexuality, bisexuality, transsexuality. Not as a tolerance, but as a celebration. That's a cornerstone; that's foundational in Satanism from the very beginnings. I can't see why people who have ripped him off subsequently, starting their own little groups, look back and say, "Oh, he's so old fashioned, and he has these strange ideas." Well, I'm sorry: he was a heterosexual male, and he liked presenting as a heterosexual male.

He told me that the whole dynamic that he felt—and that he described very well in *The Compleat Witch,* republished as *The Satanic Witch*—was that we all have our "apparent," and then we have our "demonic." You find a partner that can express your demonic, and then you're playing off each other; you are two halves of the same whole. He said, "I need a demonic woman who's fleshy and overblown and aggressive and gum popping; sort of like a gangster moll, and smart-mouthed." He said, "because I don't look good in high heels." He could do it himself, but he said it would just be ridiculous. So he was this pillar, you know: this dark menacing, silent, vampiric, Satanic character. And then he can be complemented by this bouncy blonde, overblown, smart-mouthed moll, you know? That was the dynamic that he really enjoyed and wanted to personify.

He was very creative in terms of the philosophy, and also in developing the philosophy. I wonder if there are any of his concepts that are still super vital, super resonant, with you now?

The keys to Satanism are essentially what antiauthoritarians have been saying in many, many different guises for many years, and that's to think for yourself. That's the interesting part about the Doktor's philosophy: not only can you keep unpacking it, but it keeps maintaining its relevance more and more every single day. Politicians will lie to you. Advertisers will lie to you. They want to sell you something. Is this news? Tell this to the people on Twitter; tell this to the people who voted the way they voted in America. Why is this a lesson that we cannot get in our brains, these little monkey brains of humanity?

That's one really important thing that keeps resonating with me: we're herd animals, we're easily swayed, and we have to really concentrate on questioning everything. Question authority and think for yourself! Do your own research. This whole tribalism stuff . . . he was way ahead of the curve on that. I hate to say it, I hate to use the word, but he's almost prophetic, you know? He started a religion, and lo and behold, fifty years after what he wrote, it's more and more pertinent, and more and more important, for people to just stop and see who is actually gaining. "Cui bono," you know? Who is gaining from you thinking this way, and what are they trying to sell you? Just that whole carny aspect of, "Don't follow what's being given you—look behind the curtain!" See who it is that's selling you this stuff.

I think the fact that people are still ripping him off and reselling, repackaging his philosophy, and selling it to a whole new generation of people; not using his name, not using Satanism, but some new package. . . . I think it shows that it's got legs and that it's still around, and it's still pertinent and more important than ever, actually.

What do you think was the greatest change for America, specifically, that LaVey, but also the Church, brought to the table?

I think Anton LaVey and the Church of Satan can definitely be seen as at the forefront of the counterculture wave that was happening at the time. What I appreciate is that he wasn't swayed. He got very irritated by the whole hippie movement, because people would come to him, and they'd try to give him beads or rocks or something to pay for his lectures. And they'd come in high or stoned or on LSD or drunk or something. He would slam the door in their face. Because you don't want to go into the ritual chamber without your full faculties, because it can be very, very dangerous what you conjure for yourself. Again, the left-hand path is not for sissies, you know? You can conjure some very dark demons for yourself, and they will pursue you, and it will take you to some very bad places.

He didn't want that disruptive element in the ritual chamber at all. He didn't feel that people should be out of control, whether that's through television, drugs, whatever you are vulnerable to, whatever addictions you are vulnerable to. He wanted you to recognize them and understand your limits with them. Saying no, no, no isn't going to help anything. Sometimes you have to fully explore: "Where did this come from? Why is this happening? What are the consequences?" Once you get through it, then you understand what the consequences were.

What was good about the hippie movement was the whole antiestablishment, "question all things," and also, you know, "live your life to the fullest." There was definitely that, too, but he would go down Haight Street, and he'd see these kids, these lost kids, being picked up by people like Charles Manson and other people. They were listless, they were high, they were vulnerable, and that's *not* the direction he wanted to take things.

I think what happened as a result was that the pendulum swings back and forth. There was the hippie movement, and then we got all the way back over here to the overspending, conspicuous consumption sort of wave. But one key to Satanism is that they're all the same sort of brew; just different lenses to see it through, you know? You can't be mesmerized by this shiny object any more than you can be mesmerized by that shiny object. Again, the truth lies somewhere completely different, and you can only find that from within. That's easy to say. Saying that to somebody, but then you say, "Well, what the hell does that mean?" What Satanism advocates is to read widely without prejudice, and try to seek the truth within yourself. Then you'll find a path going forward to be productive in your life. That's what a good philosophy will do for you.

Do you feel that LaVey has been misrepresented? I don't necessarily mean by the people who are trying to pick the cherries and repackage them, but on a greater level, a cultural level. And if so, why?

I think sometimes people don't know what to do with Anton LaVey, because they think, "Well, was he really serious? Did he believe what he believed, or was he just posturing to try to make money or something?" Well, if he was trying to posture to make money, he really wasn't very good at it. He didn't market the T-shirts and the posters and the . . . he didn't franchise like he could have.

He was a man of conviction and sincerity and integrity, and I'm not sure that people are ready to understand that about him yet. I think they will, eventually, understand that. History will judge him. His writings are funny and clever and have a great deal of insight. He was a lot like Jayne Mansfield in that way, you know? She came off, she presented, as the squeaky, bubbly woman, with huge "assets," and the way she used them would lead people to ask, "Well, is that an act? Is she really like that in real life?" Well, yeah! Was Anton LaVey really like that in real life? Yeah!

He was funny, he was personable, he was all the things that you would want him to be, but he was also a complex person. It'll take a while for people to really understand him. I think academics are all too willing to dismiss Satanism in general as a phenomenon of youth, of rebelliousness, associating it with black metal and some way to piss off your parents. But our generation, my generation, has been moving forward with our lives. We raise kids, we have jobs, we graduate with honors, we accomplish what we need to, we have crises, we lose our parents, we lose our children, we shift as any human life shifts. Not once have I ever said, "Gosh darn, I wish I was a Lutheran! I'm not getting anything out of this Satanism stuff anymore; I really am thinking about maybe, I don't know, Seventh Day Adventist or something." But no, it's always there. It unpacks, and it moves through life together with you. You pick up *The Satanic Bible* wherever you are. Whatever you need, you think about those archetypes, and it continues to guide you and enrich you and encourage you in your darkest times, in ways that other religions don't do for a great number of people.

That's the fun of being a Satanist at this time, because we're seeing this happen; we're seeing people apply it over decades of their lives. It doesn't just stop at adolescence, it doesn't just stop with slamming your bedroom door to the rest of the world and cranking up your music and defying and finding your way through that. Yes, that's part of it—I think that's a really important part of it—but it moves on from there. It gives you tools beyond that, which is brilliant. I mean, that's golden.

We have been privileged by having proximity to the source. But I also hear similar things from people who have just begun reading The Satanic Bible. **The philosophy still fulfills that function. It's there through all the phases and aspects of life. It's a working philosophy.**

It really is. I think when people reach beyond *The Satanic Bible* and get into the Doktor's essays and the interviews that he did, they find more: he comes across as very genuine, committed, and a no-nonsense person. That's what you get from him; that's what I got from him every single day that I was with him; and that's what you get from his writings. They're funny, they're very accessible and even simple.

You know, some people pick up *The Satanic Bible* and they say, "Well, that's just basic psychology, that's not intimidating, that's not scary." Other people, from another context, they'll pick it up and they'll be terrified and throw it across the room. You don't know how different people are going to react to it. I think an important thing is to read his essays and explore other avenues, and then you see a broader aspect of who he was. That's what I tried to do with the biography: enrich people's vision of who he was, because then you understand where he got all these ideas. They're in context. They're in the context of *Weird Tales* magazine and existentialism and Jack London and Maugham and the romantic poets, and all of these influences that were very strong in him. And the artists that influenced him: Reginald Marsh and, of course, *The Command to Look,* by Mortensen.

He was a photographer and he was a visual artist, as well as an amazing musician. All of this fed into his philosophy. He wasn't a religious scholar, and he never pretended to be a philosophical scholar. He just went from observation and knowledge of who people are; and basic psychology; and what people need, and how you can strengthen yourself. He wanted people to be the best human beings they could be, because he saw animals and insects being the best creatures they could be. Humans have such potential to be amazing creatures, but so few of us concentrate and get past our own fears and our own guilt. Whatever we saddle ourselves with to breathe and sparkle and shine the way we really should, the way we deserve to: *that's* what LaVey wanted people to be able to do.

What do you think is the main reason for people misrepresenting him? Is it the potential inherent in the philosophy or the symbol of Satan?

I think the reason that Anton LaVey intimidates a lot of people is because of that combination of the *S*-word—the dreaded *S*-word!— plus a philosophy of liberation and empowerment that you get from Satanism. It seems such a straight-line logic. I mean, he's not the first one. The romantic poets often brought up Satan as the archetype of liberation and defiance, and the fin de siècle diabolists, and, of course, the Hellfire Clubs. They all aligned themselves with the Devil, the Dark One, and secrets and cabals. Again, seeing through the shade that is presented to us as reality. But the combination of doing that in the name of Satan . . . no one had really done that before.

People had dabbled; people had gotten close. But just to stand up, and just balls to the wall, just give the sign of the horns in defiance, scream it, and publicly perform it . . . no one had done that with the gusto and the conviction and the drama that Anton LaVey had done. I think that's what disturbs people still to this day. It's one thing to have self-empowerment, you know. We've all got our little piles of self-help books, but to just kind of hold your fist up to God and say, "If you are the one running this show, you're not doing a good job, okay? The wrong people are dying, and there's conflict and there's destruction and there's devastating pogroms and destruction of the Earth and the animals. If you're in charge of this, I will defy you for eternity!"

I think that's what disturbs people about Anton LaVey, as well it should. It should disturb them, because it's a powerful, powerful continuum to be on that Satanic path. You just touch it, and you feel the electricity there; you feel the power, and it's the power of being a human being. Satan is the representative. His fall is our fall. We have that in concert: the expulsion from Eden and the expulsion from Heaven, for defiance and ego and individuality, for thoughts and pride.

People resonate to that a lot more than some guy hanging on a cross two thousand years ago. That has no context for people. It just doesn't make any sense. How would that have anything to do with us? But it's been used to control people for a great number of years. It's caused a lot of bloodshed, and it continues to cause bloodshed.

Getting back to the immediate relevance of Anton LaVey and his philosophy. . . . That's what Satanism is all about: the scapegoating and "us versus them" philosophy, it doesn't work. We cannot move forward with that kind of thinking at all. We are all on this Earth together, and it's all our responsibility to be responsible to each other and the Earth and the animals so that we can live together peacefully. Is that so difficult?

But when you have a single god who's the right and the only way, then you have every right to treat the others as less than human—as devils. You can kill them, you can harm them, you can rape them, any atrocity. Anton LaVey tried to start a philosophy that said that's wrong. He did it the best way he could: by taking the image of Satan, and instead of being cowering in a corner, and being used or abused because of your freakishness, because of your differences, he simply said, "Stand up! Use your differences! Be proud of whatever makes you different, and use that to your advantage. Don't be used by it. Don't let society take that from you, because that's what makes you unique, and that's what makes you powerful in the world!"

My impression is that his own views on the S-word as such changed over time. In the beginning it was great in its controversial aspect, meaning it gained attention in a time when he wanted that for the philosophy and the Church. But later on, in this more reclusive stage, it was more like the S-word became like a strict bullshit detector: a possible filter or a gateway into a more fruitful conversation with people. Would you say that's a correct assumption?

There were plenty of people that told Anton LaVey, from the very beginning—before he even wrote the book—"Well, yeah, I understand what you're saying, but why don't you just call it something other than Satanism? You know, that's going put a lot of people off. You'll get a lot more followers if you just call it even 'Luciferianism' or, you know, Belial or something, Leviathan, something not quite so controversial." But that's kind of the point! The *S*-word is loaded with a lot of baggage that's been given to you since you sat on your mother's knee in church. It's a loaded word, and he didn't want to use anything else; he didn't want to water it down. He wanted it to be a thunk over the head for people, because if you are reacting to that word, think of all the other trigger words that are being sold to you, or given to you, or you're being used by.

Language is a potent, potent thing, and you have to get beyond that and see what's really beyond it. He was always very serious about the use of Satan in his ritual chamber as well as in his life and in his philosophy. Of course it got attention in the beginning, but he didn't really have to look for it. He wrote *The Satanic Bible;* he started the Church of Satan as a true, honest philosophy and religion, because he felt the word best represented what he had to say. For hundreds of years before that, there's always the Satanic; there's always the one that defies; there's always the one that challenges. Coyote or Prometheus . . . there's always the one that dares to go outside, into the borderlands, and bring that knowledge back to the humans. Usually the sorcerer, the shaman, is treated as an outsider in the society, and that's as it should be. Because he walks, and she walks, a path that others do not walk, and should not walk. You bring that knowledge back to the people who can benefit from it. The borderlands are not a safe place, and you have to be prepared for what you will find there.

How do you see his legacy right now, and how do you think it will evolve in the future?

It's fascinating for me to see, after having been a Satanist for so many decades, and reading Anton LaVey's work, how his ideas are now being applied and promoted and expanded on in the wider society. Artificial human companions, total environments, seeing through the film of religion, and not respecting the Catholic Church or Christianity and the machine that has represented it for two thousand years as sanctified and holy and the only giver of life and truth. On the contrary, we're finding out more and more and more despicable, vile, disgusting things that have happened in the name of Christianity, and that have been protected! Protected by the hierarchy that was supposed to be protecting and inspiring and enriching the people that it was their mandate to tell the truth to, to bring to spiritual enlightenment. What a betrayal! I mean, there's no worse betrayal. I give my children to a priest, and I want him or her to learn from that person; to learn strength and inspiration and be closer to God, and instead that trust is betrayed in the most disgusting way that it possibly can be.

I think it's important for Satanism to be there for people. I see these changes in society as a whole as a direct result of not just Anton LaVey or the Church of Satan, not only that, but also of a wave of understanding that power depends on manipulation. Power depends on manipulation, and the more power someone has, the easier it is to manipulate people. You have to be responsible. No one else is responsible. The doctors aren't responsible for your own health. The pharmaceutical companies are not responsible for your health. They have something to sell you, they have surgeries to sell you, they have pills to sell you, to solve all your problems. Don't give your power over to other corporations or other entities just without even thinking about it. That's what we see: a message that's coming forth more and more. I see that as Anton LaVey's legacy, certainly.

And the artificial human companions are moving forward apace, which is great. The total environments: that's exciting and stimulating. People have more control of the sort of expressions they like: the Renaissance fairs and the meetups with similar-minded people, people getting into costumes and exploring different sexualities; S&M and different expressions of sexuality. That's all glorious, that's wonderful, it's magical, and I am so glad that I was part of the organization that was at the forefront of that dazzling display of the best that humans can be: imaginative, creative, driven, exciting, life-loving people.

He conceptualized the "Invisible War," but for some people back then, I think it was quite abstract. It's much more apparent now, because both reality as such and the media flow are so malleable. It's almost like the invisible war is now completely visible, because it's being brought up to the mainstream surface. That's yet another idea and concept with which he was ahead of his times.

Right. Another concept that some people don't understand is so integral to Satanism is the cult of victimization. Anton LaVey wrote a lot about it, especially in the 1980s, in his essays. He saw that people were wringing their hands and making a lot of to-do, and gaining political power, and societal power, through the "poor me syndrome." We see this manifesting everywhere now, worldwide, and people are acknowledging it as the cult of victimization. Anton LaVey was the one at the forefront, recognizing it, along with the Invisible War. That was another sort of sociopolitical concept that he had and that he pioneered: there are people trying to manipulate you, there are people trying to get at you in so many different ways, and now, with the internet, it's no longer an invisible war, it's right out there in front of us.

People are still vulnerable; they're still being used by it; they're still being manipulated by it. You would think with the tools that we have, and the awareness that we have, that that would not be possible. But it's insidious, and people have to be ever watchful of people that are being marketed to you as trustworthy. He talked a lot about the good guy badge. They have their little good guy badges on, invoking trust in people because they do good works; as Satanists we don't have that. We're not good guys; we're never going to be good guys. We're always going to be the ones that tell you the truth and tell you the bad news. That's why we're Satanists. We're cynics; we'll see behind the smoke and mirrors and try to keep telling people to be vigilant.

I think that's why Satanism will survive, and needs to survive—in the body of the Church of Satan, specifically—because there needs to be a body that says, "Yes, this is Satanism" or "No, this is not Satanism; this is not what Anton LaVey intended." The reason that we have this sort of organization for nonjoiners is so that we can continue to define and protect what Anton LaVey originally said and move it forward into new contexts as society and as technology move forward. And also to be able to reach out to people who are just new to the philosophy: the twelve-year-olds, the thirteen-year-olds, the fifteen-year-olds, the twenty-five-year-olds who are seeking something real and substantial that makes sense in their lives.

We will always be there, and I'm glad that the Church of Satan is there to touch the people in the way that I was touched when I was young—and inspired and strengthened—because I would have been a very different person had I not had the Satanic philosophy. If I had tried to be a Christian, and I'd tried to reconcile what happens in the reality of the randomness of life, and I really believed that there was a god who pretended to love me, but made all these bad things happen, I think I would have become homicidal or suicidal—had I not had the option of knowing that what I perceived in my heart was true.

No matter what society told me, no matter what my teachers told me, no matter what religious or political leaders tried to sell me, the way I perceived it was truer, and that made a world of difference in my life. I can work with people. I mean, I'm a very friendly person. People meet me, and I'm not snarling and yelling. If you treat me well, I treat you in kind. If you cross me, then it's less pleasant. But I'm not looking for a fight. I'm not going around with a chip on my shoulder, because I know what humans are.

I expect humans to be humans, and a lot of times they're very cruel and heartless and unthinking and shortsighted, but that means that I have to be involved. I think there's an element of activism, by definition, in being a Satanist. If I wasn't—if it wasn't activist—then I'd be an atheist or a humanist, and I'd be fine with what's going on. But as a Satanist I am saying, "I take a stand. This is a line in the sand, no more bullshit, it stops now, and I'm not buying it from you or anybody else." So I do take an active role.

I'm a vegan, and I table at vegan events; I take a political role in certain things that are important to me, certain issues that I think are important to me, environmentally or for certain human rights, and certain animal rights. I am actively involved. I think we're the best people to do it. I like to see people that are Satanists out there, politically involved, because there's a lot of people out there whose philosophy is built on sand, and I don't want them making decisions for me.

I like Satanists to be politically involved, and I don't care whether it's right or left or middle or whatever it is, as long as you're taking a stand, and it makes sense to you, and you have conviction. Then we can talk. We can talk respectfully about certain issues. I'm not stuck in a pigeonholed box of "these are the people I'm aligned with, and I have to swallow, whole cloth, everything that they say, or these people over here, this is what's getting us into trouble." It's this emotional investment in an identity, what they call "identity politics," I guess. You have to vote the man or the woman, and you have to vote the issue, you know.

Don't get stuck in tribalism! I mean, again, this little monkey brain, it can only handle so much, and it's easy to be tribal; it's easy to be up in the trees and squawking at the guys over in the other trees, but it's not moving us forward. Our technology has moved forward so much. It's outpaced our society and our thinking, so that we have responsibilities that we shouldn't really have at this stage in our physical development.

But lo and behold, we do have them, so we have to step up and live up to what we've invented and how we've moved forward and the consequences of that. And we can. I'm very hopeful.

Again, I'm an idealist, so I'm very hopeful that we can, but only by taking back the rhetoric and looking each other in the eye, shaking hands, hugging each other—even if we don't like each other. Communicate, just communicate. It's not that hard. Don't build walls, don't build walls. I have friends that are Christians, I have friends that are Buddhists, I have friends that are all, you know, nature religion philosophers. I'm fine with all of that. Just don't create a box that is so hard for you, as a Satanist, as a Christian, as anything, to get out of that you can't talk to people or communicate with people. Participate in the world; let your light shine. That's what being a potent Satanist is.

What would you say were the reasons for his gradual seclusion? You came in at a point where there was already a trajectory of not engaging so much with media. Was he just tired of it or were there actual traumas from threats and incidents?

I think that people perceive that there was a time, maybe in the 1980s, when Anton LaVey backed out of the spotlight a little bit. He did, because there was a lot of media stuff going on. But he did it purposefully, because although he was no less excited and committed to his philosophy, he felt that he had been around long enough. He'd written enough books, and he'd gotten his word out so that other people could step forward and address a lot of what was going on in the Satanic Panic days, in media and television. The internet was nowhere to be seen yet, but it was just beginning.

People like Peggy Nadramia and others that were very active in the early days of the internet were making strong statements as Satanists. He didn't want it to be just a one-man show, you know. He wanted to step back a little bit and let these other lights shine forward, to show that he wasn't the only one having these thoughts, that other people could articulate them boldly and just as capably as he did. Plus, he didn't want to give Oprah or Geraldo the satisfaction of the high priest of the Church of Satan sitting on a stage next to, you know, some kumquat brain, talking about what he thought Satanism was, and then giving Anton LaVey five seconds to explain his philosophy.

He'd done enough tap dancing. He did all of that. He did the Joe Pyne show, he did Johnny Carson, Phil Donahue; he did endless amounts of talk shows. He was a tireless representative for his philosophy, and there was no reason for him to go and be a performing monkey for people anymore. We reached out to animal protection, to law enforcement—national law enforcement, international and local law enforcement—and gave them the truth of what Satanism is.

I wrote the *Church of Satan* book. I wrote the history of the Church of Satan, but as a little pamphlet book that we could hand to people and say, "This is what we believe; this is how we practice. Anything else that you're investigating, it's not Satanism." He was very accessible to law enforcement people.

An exciting thing was that there was a big zine revolution, so he gave a lot of time for free to people that had excellent zines; you know, like *Answer Me!*, *Rollerderby*, and things around the world. He would give time and attention to people who deserved it. He felt that that was very Satanic—that he wouldn't just give time to people that were offering him $10,000 [or] $20,000 to get in front of the cameras, which they certainly did. He wanted to spend time with young people, especially, who were on the cutting edge of new filmmaking or music, or exploring the old cult films, or exploring bachelor pad music, and a sort of a revival of the 1930s, 1940s aesthetic. That's when he got excited, and that's where he wanted to spend his time.

As a consequence, I think there was a great deal of influence that he had in the creative arts because of that. So I don't really feel like he was in seclusion. He never lost his verve or his enthusiasm or his energy. He slept like two, three hours a night. It was almost as if he knew that he only had so much time. I know it's a cliché to say that, but he was doing a lot of writing, he was recording and finally getting his music out, and he was making great inroads with the right people; that was what mattered to him.

I love the essays, his shorter writings that are much more personal, but they also contain a lot of really super inventive stuff. It's obvious that he was coming up with these magical concepts all the time, and some of these things trickled into the Cloven Hoof.* *But I'm curious whether he discarded a lot of material. Did it all get to be used or did he actually discard things?*

Another thing that was happening during that 1980s period was that he was making contacts with people who would become very important to him. One of them was Adam Parfrey, who was excited. He was doing his own outrageous publishing even then. He had met Anton LaVey and wanted very much to see his writings out there. He wanted to, first of all, republish *The Compleat Witch,* to repackage it as *The Satanic Witch,* and that was great.

Adam and Doktor LaVey hit it off immediately, because both of them had an encyclopedic knowledge of strange people and strange groups who had been innovators or oddballs of the previous two to three hundred years. They both collected those kinds of stories of that kind of people. So he and Adam really were partners in crime, encouraging each other in many, many ways. They could just spend hours talking to each other.

One of the things that came out of that was that the Doktor finally got a chance to publish *The Devil's Notebook,* which was a collection of his essays that he'd been writing for many, many years—since the publication of *The Satanic Rituals.* He'd been doing that for the *Cloven Hoof,* so he'd been getting his stuff out. But it was sort of an opportunity to put all these pieces in a book. Then they also did *Satan Speaks!*, which came out after the Doktor's passing.

There's a lot of richness in his essays, and he was always coming up with new ideas. There was never a silent moment between us. We'd

---

*The official newsletter of the Church of Satan.

BLANCHE BARTON ☞ 111

watch movies, he'd play music, we'd yak and yak and yak, and he'd come up with these ideas. He loved the laptop; he got one of the first notebook computers, and he could take that with him and jot down ideas and develop them into these very readable short essays, which was his gift. He really liked that format. He got it from other people, previously, who had written these delightful little essays that he admired. He was always exploring, right up until his death.

I think most of the essays saw print; there might be some essays that never got into print. There were some in the *Cloven Hoof* that have not been collected yet, but I'm sure that'll come. As things are archived, as things move forward, these things will come.

One thing he was exploring just before he passed, was this whole "Plotzville" idea. He was publishing things in the *Cloven Hoof,* these sort of news items about a place called Plotzville. He'd never really explored fiction before. He was building these wonderful characters, and these ne'er-do-wells, and these sort of slovenly women, and these sort of, I don't know, kind of carny guys, and these movers and hustlers and kind of making this whole world up. Then there was this other place that he was just beginning working on: a Lovecraftean area outside of town, where weird things had happened. He was just getting to that part before he passed. His brain was always active; he was always coming up with new concepts.

Was there a lot of creative ping-pong going on? Did he expect or want feedback from you also?

Yes. I think what people need to understand is that certainly, within the leadership of the organization, there's a lot of back and forth that goes on. I think it's essential for there to be two people at the head of the organization. Anton LaVey certainly would bounce ideas off me, and we'd talk about the essays he was writing.

I learned a great deal from him as a writer. That's something that has hardly ever been touched on as a topic of discussion, but I think it would be a good thing—to write about his writing technique. He was a wonderful writer. He would enter any topic with sort of a twisted perspective, and he'd throw in interesting anecdotes from his past, and he'd throw a side light on something or put a little bit of humor into his writing. It's just so much fun to read his essays. I learned a great deal about pacing, about content, about throwing people off, putting something in that's a little bit unexpected.

He was one of the last raconteurs. We don't have people like that anymore, that would talk about Milo & Roger, or people from the Magic Circle, or people that he'd known in the circus, or Rubber Bubber Johnson, the *Weird Tales* writer, and his escapades with him. He loved characters, and he could engage people for hours, sharing stories of people that he'd known, but very little about himself, you know. For all the context about Satanism as an egotistic religion, a lot of times he would spend more time talking about other people, not about himself.

He made sure that I was in the position to take over the organization after he passed. I had Xerxes, and I wanted to devote myself to helping him. I felt that the two legacies that Doktor LaVey gave me were the Church of Satan and Xerxes. I took his education and raising very seriously. I wanted to homeschool him, which we did for a number of years.

I could have kept the organization, but it wouldn't have been the same. I didn't have that other person to work with. You need that. I think it's good if it's a man and a woman, because you have different perspectives; you complement each other very well. Anton and Diane complemented each other very well when the organization was just starting, and then he and I bounced off each other.

It's not a nine-to-five job. You've got a lot of things on your shoulders; you've got a lot of people and events and interviews and issues that you need to talk about—sometimes late into the night in bed, or over breakfast. Or when you're walking, or when you're having dinner, these things come up—it's a flow that's going through you both all the time.

I knew that Peter and Peggy had been very good for us, as far as public representation. They'd certainly proven themselves, both professionally and personally, to be very supportive of me and of the Doktor and of Xerxes. When the time came for me to make certain decisions about the organization and where we were going, there was very little reflection—because I didn't really have anybody to discuss it with—about who would be best to lead the organization. Peter Gilmore understands Satanism. Both of them do: Peter Gilmore and Peggy Nadramia. Both understand the shadowed ritual, the dramatic aspects of the Church of Satan and of Satanism, the historical context of magic, and the evolution of ritual magic. They also understand the carny, the colorful, the cold reading, the basic psychology aspects, and the fun escapades of Satanism at the same time. You can't have one without the other; they're all a part of what Satanism is. They understand that in their bones; they always have.

Interestingly, we came into the organization at about the same time. I believe they sent in their applications for active membership in the same year, in 1984, that I came into the organization. Not long after that, we met them, and they became representatives in New York and did a lot of media stuff. Peggy Nadramia, our high priestess, was already making great inroads on the internet, the burgeoning internet, and clearing up a lot of misconceptions about the Church of Satan there.

They have guided it and weeded it and been responsible for an amazing explosion of really top-notch people being attracted to the philosophy, as a consequence of their diligent conceptualizing and protecting and moving forward what Anton LaVey originally conceptualized as the Church of Satan.

In terms of planning for a legacy, would you say that there was an increase in his planning and strategizing and conceptualizing for what was going to happen after he passed? He had already had a few incidents that indicated that time would be up soon. Was there an increase in his thinking about things concerning the Church and the administration?

Doktor LaVey knew what was coming, as far as his death; we'd had a few incidents before then. He was a very prideful man, and for very good reasons, he didn't want to share any vulnerability. There were people who would have delighted in seeing him in a compromised situation. He didn't want to enrich other people with his death or his discomfort, and also he just didn't want to be seen as vulnerable. He came from an era when there was a certain amount of pride that a man kept in himself, and he felt that it was not for him to be seen in public in that way. He was never physically compromised a great deal. He needed a cane at the end, but it's not like he needed someone to feed him, or that he was physically incapable in any way right up until the end. But he was aware that things were happening.

We dreaded it—I think I'm fairly intimate in my portrayal of that in the biography—and it was painful for both of us. He was rather superstitious about a will—he didn't really want to make a will. But after he had an incident of what they called "sudden death" at home in 1995, he wrote out a little will for me in his own hand, so that I would be able to be his executor and take care of things, largely for Xerxes, so that Xerxes would benefit from whatever he had, whatever legacy he had. He certainly wanted the organization to be protected, and he knew that I would do that, that I'd be responsible for that.

He had already appointed me high priestess in 1990, and I had a lovely scroll documenting that. I was acting in that capacity, and we had become more intimate as a couple at that point. But then, after this incident, he gave me another scroll, again appointing me to high priestess, because we weren't sure where the other one was, and he wanted to make sure. Because according to our bylaws, our articles of incorporation, it was important for me to be able to say, "Yes, I'm the high priestess; yes, I can move our organization forward and act with the authority of the Council of Nine." I was well prepared to do that.

We didn't have explicit talks about who should do what, or where anything should go; he knew that he'd done what he could to get his philosophy out, and he knew that there were people working on his behalf that would continue the philosophy and would keep on doing what they were doing. The people in the right places were there, and they would keep doing what he wanted them to do, which was move the philosophy forward. He recognized that the Church of Satan was not a building. It was never a building; we don't have to build buildings; we don't have to own property; we don't have to tithe and give to the Church—it's a different way of thinking about spirituality and a church.

The Church is us: all of us moving forward in our lives, being joyous, and accomplishing things, and having children, and building lives and careers, and being fulfilled as human beings. That's our church; that's what we do. We don't need a lot of people to do that. He didn't want to attract a lot of people; he only wanted the right people to be influenced and touched by what he did. I think he would be distressed if it appealed to too many people, because then he'd think he's not doing his job, you know?

So yes, there was a certain amount of conversation about his legacy and what would come after. He loved being with his son; he was very happy to have a little boy. He loved his daughters very much. As far as Zeena's decisions that she made in her life . . . of course he was hurt.* But at the same time, when people would ask him, he'd say, "Well, you know, we raise our children to be independent beings, and she certainly is doing that." He could understand that and support all three of his children. He loved watching Xerxes, to be with him in his little world, and sort of invest him with whatever he could. He was a wonderful father, and the time that they had together, he made it very valuable. He spent a lot of time with Xerxes, and just rejoiced in his life and his passion and his giggles. He was authentic in his love of animals and children, because they're the most natural magicians on Earth; they're so true and pure, and yeah, the more we can connect with that, the better. So that's how he would spend his days: with his music and his son and his writing.

---

*In 1990 LaVey's daughter Zeena officially distanced herself from her father and the Church of Satan.

***There must have been a huge both emotional and existential blow at the
time of the actual demise. How the hell did you cope?***

When the Doktor passed, it was devastating. He was my world, he was
everything. I remember when the incident happened in 1995, going up
and down the hallways, and the doctors told me, "We don't know how
much functionality he will regain." Physically and mentally, it was a
hard, hard blow. I was wheeling Xerxes back and forth in his stroller
and thinking, "What was the last joke he told me? What was the last
piece of music that I heard him play?" These are the things that are
important to you: his voice, his smile, his touch; holding me, being with
me . . . just what we shared.

There's a phenomenon that happens—I think probably a lot of
people who have been close to someone who passes know this—where
you hear their voice once in a while. I'd be in a grocery store or walking down the street, and all of a sudden I'd hear, "Blanche!" I'd turn
around, and I'd look for him, and . . . it was devastating. I had my son;
my son saved me.

There was a pull, of course, to just go right over after him. I think
there is that, with any couple who's tightly bonded. But I had Xerxes,
and I had the organization, and I had wonderful friends, Peter and
Peggy and Ruth. They made sure that I wasn't alone, that we weren't
alone. Xerxes's birthday is around the same time as the Doktor's passing, so around Halloween they made sure that I was in New York or
Texas or somewhere with friends, surrounded by friends. I just couldn't
have made it without that support.

That's what people expect from their religions, you know, their
church, right? And so that's what I got: I got a lot of love, and it humbled me; I was humbled.

My one regret is the house. I really tried to save the Black House;
I loved that house. It was an icon for me before I ever stepped through
the door, and I know it was a Mecca for so many people. I would peek
through the peephole, and so many times people would drive past, and
they'd sit on the street outside across from the Black House and just

look up at it. They wouldn't intrude; they wouldn't come and knock at the fence or anything; they'd just hang out, and I knew they were our people—dressed in black and heavy silver jewelry, lots of tattoos. Maybe not always, but sometimes.

It was a blow to all of us, but they were determined. I understand it was purely business, that they could make more money with the property torn down than they ever could trying to save it. Karla and I both tried to reach out to historical preservation societies, and we did our best. One of our members even offered a great deal of money, but it wasn't enough. We tried to raise money to save it, but other people within the organization said it was time.

When the Doktor passed, the Black House passed, and now it's as much a mythology. It's interesting that the icon of the Black House has almost as much potency as Anton LaVey himself. There are little pins of it and T-shirts of it, and it's still enriching us and strengthening us; that little house is where it all started. Even though physically it's long gone, its shadow is still there in our souls.

The Doktor said, "Its roots go all the way to Hell; I made sure of that: all the way to Hell." It's still with us just as he still is, you know. When he passed, I had this idea that now he's transformed into something else. He's not just a body, he's not constrained by this body, but he's our dreams, he's our nightmares, he's everywhere and everything. And also the people that he's exposed us to—the artists and the musicians and the writers—we can go to them, and we hear him.

He gave us so much in the bibliography to *The Compleat Witch*, the writers that he admired and that he respected: H. L. Mencken, Twain, Ben Hecht, Maugham, and Nietzsche, and all the people that he drew from to create what has been codified as Satanism. It's all part of it; it's showmanship, and it's dedication, and it's romanticism, and it's idealism, and it's everything that a Satanist is.

I've met some amazing Satanists. I've been blessed—if a Satanist can be blessed . . . I'm looking for a word that means Satanically blessed. I've been fortunate enough to have amazing people around me. The most consistently intelligent, driven, exciting, open-minded, imaginative, beautiful, rich people that I've ever met have been Satanists, and that continues to be true. The younger ones that come up, it's the same thing. That's how I know we're still doing what we intended to do, and what Anton LaVey wanted us to do. We're still attracting the best and the brightest, the most imaginative, the most driven, the most creative, open-minded, no bullshit kind of people, and those are the people that he wanted. That was his legacy, and that continues to this very day.

I was thinking maybe a good word would be blissed.
Yeah, maybe! Blissed, yeah.

To have a comprehensive list of books and films that were an inspiration to him was and still is very valuable. I think that was one of the things that made us click on my first visit: satellite TV had just started, so there were these channels dedicated to old movies, and I also used to go to the Cinemathèque in Stockholm almost every day. I was just a young Swedish guy, but I knew a lot about American movies, and I think that was one of the reasons we could connect.

Definitely, yeah, and it's interesting, too, that a lot of times when people would meet him they'd expect to maybe talk about Satanism or something. But nine times out of ten he wouldn't start yammering on about Satanism; he'd talk about guns, or he'd talk about movies, or he'd talk about cars, or he'd talk about style, or clothing styles. There was very little direct occultism; you know, "Let's get out our magical robes and compare Enochian pronunciations," or things like that.

Magic is a tool, and that's the way he wanted it to be presented in *The Satanic Bible*. When he was looking into it originally, and when he wrote the book, magic was still protected within groups; it was secret, occult knowledge that you had to pay extra for, and it was inherited—you had to have a grandmother who was a witch, or you had to have somebody that was important in your bloodline. He just said, "This is the way it is; I've experienced it."

He got some wonderful collections of black magic material together in *The Satanic Rituals,* and it's very potent stuff that he tracked down because he had started the organization. People started sending things his way: the most wicked stuff, the stuff with the darkest reputation. It was sinister stuff, and he started using that, and he wanted to collect it, and put it in a context of Satanism, so that people could use it in their ritual chambers. He saw magic as a very potent tool. Lesser magic is basic psychology, nonverbal cues, everyday magic. In greater ritual magic, you work with that as well, hand in hand. It's like I was saying about the *S*-word, and the concepts of defiance and liberty and freedom blended together. The lesser and the greater magic blended together is absolutely unstoppable.

Did you frequently or actively use the ritual room at that time? Or was it more or less like a museum of the Church in a way?

The front ritual chamber we used from time to time for rituals. I think at that point in his magical development, he had more expression through his music, so wherever his keyboards were was a more active place for ritual magic for him. But we did go into the front chamber from time to time—very rarely and very carefully—because the atmosphere in that room was so charged. It was dark, it was palpable, it was electrifying to be in there.

I wouldn't say that it was a museum, because a museum sort of doesn't give the true impression of how charged it was from all the rituals that had been performed for so long. The actual time when he was performing public rituals wasn't that long. He'd been doing stuff with the Magic Circle from the time he moved in, and then from the beginning of the organization until, I don't know, 1972. In 1972 he was pretty much not performing public rituals anymore. I think he did it mostly for outrage, but also to legitimize his religion: that we could marry people, that we performed funerals, that he baptized his daughter into something that he respected, and it wasn't just to piss people off.

Again, I think people get confused about who Anton LaVey really was. He really did feel that Satanism was a true philosophy, and that it would have lasting influence, and, if properly applied, that it could very much have positive results in an individual's life. It was never just performing; there was always connection and magic and truth.

During the time that you lived and worked together, would you say that he was self-generating in terms of the magical ideas and concepts that he used in his essays, for instance? Or was there at some point or in some phase some magical influx where he said, "Blanche, I read this wonderful old mystical stuff, and I'm going to use bits of this and bits of that." Tracing things back in a way, or was it all coming from his mind?

One of the many wonderful things, as far as his magic went, was that he was always aware of the legacy of black magic, and of the magicians that had been practicing and exploring hand in hand with Satan and the Devil and the demons and the darkest, purest continuum that had previously been explored. He felt very much in tune with that. For me, he was a channel for a lot that had been developed magically through the eons up to that point. There is a very rich, fulfilling essence that he vibrated to very honestly, and conjured effectively.

Every time he sat down at the keyboard, every time he sat down to write an essay, those were his rituals. He had performed rituals with the Magic Circle. From the time he was a child, he'd connected with those forces, and he'd developed a relationship with them. I think that's what doing magic is all about: developing a relationship with those ethers. We struggle for language when we talk about magic at this point, because so much protomagic is now confirmed by technology, and scientists are getting better and better at understanding psychic phenomena and ghostly phenomena. The only people that have been able to talk about it have been spiritualists or ghost hunters or magicians, warlocks, sorcerers, and witches who have used and formed this magic.

He figured that he wanted to give people laboratories. That's what a ritual chamber is: it's a laboratory. He said, "I didn't create the telephone, I use a telephone." These days we use the same metaphor with a cell phone, you know? You don't need to know everything about how it works to be able to work it and utilize it effectively in the world. That's what he felt with magic. He couldn't explain all of it, because we just don't have the language for it yet. But he knew it worked, and he was practicing and refining techniques, not just in the ritual chamber, but in everyday life. Feeding things in, weaving things in—in your conversation, in what you think about, in the things around you.

That's where total environments come about too; it's all about feeding your conscious and your unconscious mind, your subconscious mind, to achieve your goal. That goes on thousands of times a day, not just in the ritual chamber. He definitely felt connected to the legacy of black magicians that had come before him and used those principles. He drew on those principles, as well as certainly inventing and blending in. He resented that this information should remain secret. That's where the *S*-word comes in. You have to be able to walk that path and own that path, and to be able to utilize it to your own benefit.

What were your first reactions to The Compleat Witch? Had you also read that book before you met LaVey?

When I was first exploring Satanism, my first entry into Anton LaVey was *The Devil's Avenger*. But then of course I wanted to read anything there was by him, and so inevitably I found out about *The Compleat Witch*. I ordered it from the Church; they had them available at the time. It was really my first exposure to Anton LaVey's humor. He had funny little jokes, and he was very accepting of women using what they had; whether you're heavier or slimmer, it doesn't really matter, you can be a complete witch no matter what your body type. He had a way of using sex, sentiment, or wonder.* If you were an older woman, maybe you could use sentiment, and maybe you could have wonder. If you were extremely ugly by most standards, you could use

---

*A concept stemming from the image-composing theories of American photographer William Mortensen (1897–1965).

that as a fascination; you can still attract people to you and have people bend to your will. I thought that was perfectly sensible and very Satanic.

Did the resonance you felt in The Compleat Witch *just enhance other things that you were already familiar with? Or did you feel that "this guy really understands me as a woman"?*

In *The Satanic Witch* I really got a glimpse of his carny background; he really understood people. He understood fetishes, he understood smells, he understood just the way that people can get very keyed in on one particular aspect, and ways to find out about that. If somebody really likes long hair, or if somebody likes a particular scent, use that. And don't cover up your body scents. He wrote another essay, I believe it's in *The Devil's Notebook,* "Don't bathe!" He was a big believer in people being natural. If you douse yourself in perfume, not only is it going to stink and alienate a lot of people, but it's not . . . any woman or any man could wear that scent. If you're trying to establish a relationship with someone that's an exclusive attraction to you, you don't want to smell like thirty million other people; you want that unique scent to be associated with positive things in you.

Many will argue that the book came to fruition as a kind of backlash to, or as a provocation against, the kind of unisex feminism that was going on at the time. Would you say that that's correct?

Some people see *The Compleat Witch* as a backlash. It was all about Twiggy and women dressing in their fathers' oversized clothes, and trying to be men, trying to own masculinity. The Doktor saw that that was not the way to go. Women have power, and they should utilize what power they have; women always have power; it's the women who make the decisions; it's up to them how much they want men to feel empowered.

From that very outset he said that a leader's best friend is always a woman, and that "my right-hand man will always be a woman, because a woman can do what a man cannot do." And he, in his description in *The Compleat Witch,* or *The Satanic Witch,* of the demonic, he said that that's an expression of the male's, or the female's, other self. You are attracted to someone who expresses some demonic within you that you can't express yourself.

For example, he himself, being a very sort of dark, mystical, "Ming the Merciless" sort of affectation on the exterior, he liked a very curvy, a very gum-popping moll type. You know, sort of a bouncy blonde, smart-talking woman that could take charge and really call it as she sees it. He even said, "I would be that woman, but I look terrible in heels!"

So it's a complement. He saw that there was a potential for a partner. In *The Satanic Bible* and in *The Compleat Witch,* he's not judgmental about people's fetishes or their sexual expression; he just sees that there is a dynamic between the masculine and the feminine that is an immortal dance that we do; people should take advantage of that.

How do you see our contemporary times from this specific perspective? Is the book still relevant, in the sense of a provocation, or have times caught up? Are these times more Satanic in that sense, or less so?

It's really interesting when I look back, as I do from time to time. When I'm writing an essay or a review, or I'm working on a book, and I pick up Doktor LaVey's writing again, *The Compleat Witch,* or some of his essays . . . I'm flipping through, and I'm rereading a lot of it, and I think, "Wow, this is today, this could be written today, this is very relevant." This process of things will go out of favor and then come back in, but his truth is always there. The nub of the truth, it doesn't change. He was very aware of what makes something immortal. I think it goes back to Mortensen, and his having an eye for the Law of the Trapezoid: the focus.* He didn't just leave that at being

---

*The Law of the Trapezoid is a metaphysical-psychological concept formulated by Anton LaVey. Taking his cue from the geometrical figure of the trapezoid—basically a pyramid with its top taken off—LaVey wove it into a theory about the impact of nonharmonic shapes on the human psyche. LaVey's precursor to the Church of Satan, emerging from the Magic Circle, was even called "The Order of the Trapezoid." According to Barton, in her LaVey biography *The Secret Life of a Satanist,* "the Order of the Trapezoid continues today as the directing force within the organization" (Port Townsend, Wash.: Feral House, 2014, 302).

an artist, or being a musician, or being a photographer; he transferred that into human nature—he was able to magically translate that—and he wrote that in a way that would be perceived in an immortal sense. So yes, I think it's very relevant still. If you look at it and go, "Well, this was a product of the 1960s . . . it was just a backlash," you're only seeing the surface of it. You're not really seeing the deeper, magical implications of what he was seeing.

I find it interesting how his ideas seep into mainstream culture, given enough time. I mean, for instance, this thing that's been going on for quite a while now: this neo-burlesque movement. It's a very interesting manifestation of "Satanic Witchcraft"—the reclaiming of a flaunting femininity, which is in a way exaggerated and has to do with proudly showing off, but that obviously strikes a chord of resonance in young women. I think he was behind the scenes of that particular resurgence.

Doktor LaVey luckily lived long enough to see the emergence of a sort of "bachelor pad" music, as well as the neo-burlesque culture, where all of the things that he had advocated for so long and tried to push forward actually reappeared. He got to see that coming to fruition, and that's something that a lot of people don't get a chance to see. When you're an innovator or a pioneer, a lot of times you're gone before people even glimpse where you were going with all of that. So he was able to see the revival of the music that he really liked, and the fashions, especially from the 1930s and 1940s, and the artists that he liked. Even now, a lot of stuff that is emerging are things that he was interested in decades before anyone else was. He didn't want to reach a lot of people; he wanted to reach the *right* people. That is the key to his longevity and his survival.

In my opinion, one of the key things that made LaVey unique was his active integration of his own life experience into fields that are traditionally "established" and that newcomers simply adapt to (occultism, philosophy, religion, etc.). What are your thoughts on why this was? How would you define the character traits that made him such a creative developer?

One fascinating aspect of modern Satanism is how it flowed so organically from the personality and talents of Anton LaVey. From childhood, Anton perceived and appreciated those moments of authentic magic, enchantment, and active imagination that all of us experience—but he held on to that sense of wonder into adulthood, intuitively linked it to his moments of most intense creativity, and saw that his thoughts sometimes had a very material result. If he had not been such a musician, such a visual artist, spending hundreds of hours in intense concentration, allowing his imagination free rein, he would not have had the opportunities to perceive this shifting of reality, this warping of space-time that sorcerers and witches had experienced for centuries before him.

LaVey didn't wake up one day and say to himself, "I want to learn how to be a magician, so I will follow the instructions for conjuring set down by practitioners of ceremonial magic." On the contrary, he observed he was already altering his life, creating desired results, and asked himself, "What am I doing right, and how can I refine this?"

He was always drawn to the darker corners of humanity, to the eerie, the haunted, to the taboo—this, too, shaped his magic. With Jung, LaVey understood that we can never run from our demons. We must embrace, explore, and be strengthened by what is most abhorrent within us; this is where the psychodrama of ritual comes in. In developing Satanism, LaVey stripped magic down to its foundations, analyzed it in human terms, and rebuilt it in his own image, supercharging it as an artist and a musician.

On the same topic: one of the quintessential traits was his active integration of pop culture that had been forgotten or discarded, and thereby contained a force that could be tapped into and used. Do you have any memories of songs, films, et cetera, that he displayed for you as being such magical works? Have you woven in similar explorations and practices in your own life?

Doktor LaVey exploited and encouraged time-shifting as a source of magical power. By this I mean, he understood that interacting with houses, cars, songs, movies, physical items, activities, and diversions that were once commonplace and popular but which have now become rare, neglected, is energizing for both the participant and the viewer. Glimpsing a sleek car from the 1930s driving down the street, for example, is arresting! In the most elemental way, such anachronism fascinates us. These are applications of Mortensen's theory of the command to look.

Listening to old music, in old formats such as vinyl records, or typing on a manual typewriter, is satisfying in a tactile way. One could pick apart why these moments are energizing—both viewer and participant are disoriented in their perception of time; one is stimulated by the visual lines or aural sensation in unfamiliar ways; such an encounter requires increased concentration to mentally sort out this unexpected sight (increasing blood flow and alertness). What it adds up to is being lightly shoved out of your comfort zone in a eustress kind of way. Anton saw this friction as potent energy that can be harnessed and utilized by the competent witch or warlock.

LaVey also created a concept he outlined in *The Compleat Witch* that he called Erotic (or Emotional) Crystallization Inertia, more commonly abbreviated to ECI. This he defined as the point in time and experience during which a person's emotional/sexual fetishes are established. It is often the historical time of an individual's youth, when he is most vigorous, open, optimistic, and sexually excitable. Anton, for example, was a teenager in 1940s America, so he was most energized by music and movies of that era, as well as styles of dress, automobiles, and other elements that he surrounded himself with in order to maintain a youthful perspective and vigor. This is another form of time-shifting magic—a way to reconnect with your own potency and pleasure.

When I was with Doktor LaVey, I dressed in the period of the 1940s, complete with appropriate hairstyles, painted nails, and heavy makeup. This created erotic sparks for both of us! Since Anton's death, I find myself drawn to the Victorian period—I feel sexy and formidable in my corset and layers of petticoats. Must be all those Gothic horror and romance novels I read as a child!

When it comes to creativity, I get the impression that LaVey was happiest when playing his tunes, telling his stories, and writing his essays; that is, being immersed in his own expressions that he mastered so well. But these usually also require a second party: a listener, a reader. Did you ever get the impression that he expressed himself mainly to have that second party, or was the expression in itself, for himself, the most important aspect?

Speaking of the performance aspects of Doktor LaVey's creative pursuits, I never got the impression he played music or wrote books solely to impress an audience. Anton practiced on his keyboards for several hours every day, often when no one else was around, nor was there any guarantee anyone would read all the essays he wrote. There was satisfaction in maintaining and refining his technique, creating the musical phrasing or sounds he longed to hear, almost like visiting with old friends. The music he chose was yet another opportunity for LaVey to dash through his various time corridors, playing songs that evoked specific memories to him alone. With his writing, a seed often came through conversation. We'd be talking about something, or he'd be reminiscing with a colleague, and as he spoke, he'd already be shaping arguments, making observations, or exploring topics he found worthwhile, testing whether there was enough of a thread to justify putting pen to paper.

LaVey understood and appreciated the dynamic relationship between audience and performer. That energy exchange is vital, with a reciprocity that benefits all involved. While ego gratification is encouraged in our religion, it certainly didn't seem to be Anton's primary interest when sharing his arts.

Can you see any similarities between LaVey and other notable creative people at the time (regardless of their particular expressions or views)?

Meaning, would you say there was something distinctly zeitgeistish about him?

While there were a number of creative counterculture leaders gaining attention at the time of the Church of Satan's founding, LaVey was unusual in specific ways. Anton could be compared to Timothy Leary in the fact that both were advocating exploration into areas that most people at the time would consider taboo. But LaVey was antidrug. Many leaders were emerging in the context of dramatic social and political change, but LaVey was largely apolitical.

I suppose the person I could see as something of a parallel to LaVey, in that he was a lasting, defining artist of his medium, rose to prominence in the 1960s and was an unashamed practitioner of what most in polite society still considered distasteful: Kenneth Anger. He was also a good friend of Doktor LaVey's, and they encouraged each other's blasphemies.

It would be improper to say Anton LaVey was part of a zeitgeist of his times. By the time he died, LaVey had become so influential through various avenues seen and unseen that it would be more apt to say he had helped create the zeitgeist in which he found himself.

Inside the Black House, which was your favorite room, and why?

That is a difficult question to answer; I'm not exaggerating when I say I have deeply positive associations with every room in the Black House. We spent most of our family time in the purple room and kitchen (with occasional forays into the front ritual chamber or the Den of Iniquity). The kitchen was also the Doktor's laboratory, where he had his keyboards, so that was a room of delight.

We kept the Front Chamber closed most of the time to protect the palpably eerie, rarified atmosphere that had been fed and refined through thousands of hours of rituals and lectures. It was always transporting to spend time there. The room was muffled and cold, no matter the season.

The Den of Iniquity had something of that rarified quality, also, though not so grave and solemn as the Front Chamber. We spent many hours of debauchery there, with Doktor LaVey playing the Hammond organ . . . the one with the multicolored lights under the keys and the Leslie speaker whirring to life. Anton's artificial human companions were lounging about, glaring, slumped, and flipping us the bird, adding sparkle to the roadhouse scene.

Off the Den of Iniquity was the Cornell Woolrich Memorial Hotel Room, a cheap, tawdry affair where the rain was constant outside the window—Doktor LaVey had rigged it, Disney-style. Red neon lit the room from that same false window. There was a shoulder holster hanging within reach of the bed, stains on the carpet, and a bottle of scotch on the peeling desk.

Most of the rooms in the Black House were designed to defy time and space. Blended with the effect of an evening in the company of Anton LaVey, it's little wonder most people left the Infernal See at daybreak thoroughly bewitched.

Were there any quirks or habits that you found odd in LaVey? Meaning, unexpected expressions of moralisms that might have seemed un-Satanic and perhaps stemmed from the times or the religion he grew up in? Things you sort of didn't quite see coming?

I can't recall any surprisingly un-Satanic quirks. . . . He never allowed smoking in the house or anywhere near him. In this, he was ahead of his time. He was against overindulgence in drugs or alcohol, largely because they befuddle the brain and require relinquishing control over your own life. We had our cocktails before dinner and wine with our evening meal. LaVey's operative phrase on the topic was "indulgence, not compulsion." A competent witch or warlock must be able to recognize the difference. I don't see that as particularly prudish in a man who built a religion of self-mastery. There were some sexual horizons we chose not to explore together, but that was a matter of personal taste, not condemnation or repulsion. He didn't grow up in a religious household, so I never caught any odd moralistic attitudes from LaVey.

In the LaVeyan encouragement of fetishizing objects and environments (working with ECI, creating total environments, for instance) it's not that far-fetched to talk about an ensouling of these objects (or spaces) that one has an intimate relationship with. Did he ever give the impression that he felt that way about human beings? Meaning, that he could feel OK with using the word soul *or* ensouled *or* spirit *or* spirited *when talking about humans? I guess the extension of this question is whether you ever saw signs of his not being a 100 percent strict materialist?*

I don't believe Anton presented himself as a 100 percent strict materialist. He had seen too many strange "coincidences" and had practiced successful magical workings for the majority of his life. While he always began any inquiry from a foundation of cynicism—challenging and rational—he also intimately understood the power of the poetic mind and left room for the paranormal.

LaVey felt, and had ample evidence, that there are many avenues for supernormal abilities and events within human grasp of which most people remain blissfully unaware, even stubbornly ignorant. Undeniable weirdness happens. Through Satanism, through experimentation and observation, Anton attempted to discover and refine methods to harness that weirdness for greater happiness and achievement, and then to communicate these methods, inspiring other like-minded Fortean pioneers to romp boldly in those sinister borderlands. Most Satanists worldwide who practice LaVey's methods of both greater and lesser magic combined would judge his efforts to be a resounding success.

Did you ever feel that LaVey put on a show at times because he felt it was expected of him rather than because he was genuinely in the mood himself?

No. Anton never put on a show for others. He was self-driven from childhood and never lost that as his True North, prizing self-satisfaction above pleasing others. Judging from the reaction many journalists described regarding their first meeting of LaVey, that element of honesty, of almost self-deprecating good humor, was one of his most disarming attributes. I can say with authority that he was exactly the same man when we were alone as he had been in the company of others.

I once asked him a similar question about Jayne Mansfield—what was she like in private. Did she drop the squealing, breathy charm? Anton said that she was pretty much the same person as she was on-screen—very sweet and genuine, intelligent and positive. He said that was an aspect of their personalities they felt were similar. Both had strong public personas that some thought were acts but that truly weren't.

Did you perceive him as being sensitive to what others thought or felt about him?

Doktor LaVey wasn't thin skinned; he didn't care much what people said about him. If they said he looked odd or smelled bad, fine. That his teeth were crooked, or that his ideas were outlandish or offensive, great. But he didn't like to be misrepresented, for people to put words in his mouth he didn't say. To purposely alter aspects of his philosophy—saying he advocated animal sacrifices, as an example. That precisely contradicted what he wrote, and that angered him. And he didn't like people who tried to say he hadn't lived the life he had led—that he really hadn't worked in the circus or as a police photographer or as a musician in various places. These things were easily verified and have continued to be verified as years have gone by and people have exerted the effort to track down some of the details he mentioned. But for their own ego needs or to somehow denigrate the philosophy he developed, some people—both while he lived and since he died—have questioned events in his past. As if that will make Satanism go away.

It is somewhat laughable to me, the degree to which people will go to deny LaVey's past. In the first place, I wrote his biography! I saw the pay stubs from the San Francisco Police Department, I handled correspondence from people he had known in the circus or carnival who still kept in touch with him, I saw the cute notes from Jayne, we hung out with his old theater organ buddies late into the night. I put nothing in my book I couldn't independently verify.

Secondly, Satanism was very much a product of Doktor LaVey's varied life. Every element of cynicism, imagination, ritual, realism, enchantment, and sophistication that is hardwired in Satanism directly emerged from various paths in LaVey's life, combined with his wide-ranging reading. He was, himself, a product of all those jobs, events, and experiences, and the influence from people he met along the way, such as Dr. Nixon and Robert Barbour Johnson and the upstanding businessmen who started Las Vegas. Satanism evolved organically from exactly who Anton LaVey was; remove one piece of that intricate puzzle and Satanism is missing an essential element.

Do you think there was something or some things that he would have done differently in his life, had he had the chance?

I don't think there was anything LaVey would have done differently in his life. There are other paths he could have pursued—professional music, maybe. Or later, acting or screenwriting. But Anton was destined for a much more individual path and had no regrets about closing the door to other possibilities. He sometimes joked about an aunt, I think it was the one in Pasadena, who remarked on more than one occasion, long after he'd started the Church of Satan, that he was such a good musician, he could have been a wonderful organ repairman!

Could you tell me a little bit about the writing projects he was working on toward the end of his life?

In the final months of his life, Doktor LaVey continued to write his insightful essays, and to play the keyboards as his energy allowed. To my great delight he started exploring fiction. I was always drawn to writing fiction and had shared some bits of novels and short stories with him that he encouraged me to pursue. But he maintained he preferred writing nonfiction. He liked reading fiction, and certainly saw its value. However, he didn't think it was something that he would enjoy working on. He started writing these little sketches, some of which were published in our newsletter, the *Cloven Hoof*. At first, they were in the form of little newspaper articles from a fictional middle-American town he called Plotzville, accompanied by pictures of ladies fighting and being naughty, which he'd created on Photoshop.

I featured as Blanche Beerbower, who was slutty but fierce! That led to writing intricate character profiles and mapping out the town itself, where everyone lived and what their relationships were. In many ways, it brought his creative energy back full circle to when he was a little boy, sitting on the floor of his bedroom, making an elaborate city with model railroad houses, buildings, grass, trees, cars, tiny people, and other elements he fashioned by hand. Anton was just getting to the point where he was introducing darker notes into his stories, a foreboding borderlands area on the edge of town where no one dared wander after dark called the "Tawse." We were both looking forward to where the stories were going, but unfortunately, we'll never know.

Becoming involved with LaVey, in CoS, and eventually leading the organization is a big responsibility, and a visible one. How did your family react along the way? Did they meet LaVey and get along?

My parents knew that I'd been passionately admiring of Anton LaVey and his philosophy since I was twelve years old. I'd had them both read *The Satanic Bible* soon after I did—I was so enthused! They never forbade me to read anything I wished. My mom signed the check for me to become a member at fourteen, and we were on a trip to San Francisco together years later when I met Doktor LaVey for the first time. When I moved to the Bay Area without a job prospect, they must have been worried, but they never discouraged me. They knew there would have been no stopping me.

My mom and dad both spent significant time with Doktor LaVey through the years and felt very warmly toward him. There was never any friction or conflict. Well, during the Satanic Panic, my mom did get a bit nervous and looked in to having me kidnapped by one of those cult deprogrammers. But she didn't follow through on it. I think she was mostly responding to pressure from brainwashed friends. Dad helped a great deal with the actual running of the organization toward the end, when I had a lot of work, processing general information requests and helping publish and distribute the *Cloven Hoof*. Both my parents were loving and consistent in their encouragement of all my eccentricities and were especially supportive after Doktor LaVey died. I chose them well.

Is there anything that you feel that you want to add?

I think the final legacy that Doktor LaVey left for all of us was to fully manifest yourself in the world. He did that. He was born one person, into one kind of family, and then he created Anton Szandor LaVey, the leader of the Church of Satan. All his experiences blended into a whirlwind of intelligence and heart and music and art and photography, and all the strains led to his being who he was. It's this whole idea of, this is your party; if you're not having a fine time, then change something, do something. It's up to you; it's not anybody else's responsibility to provide you with good health or happiness; that's all in your power. You have that power. I think that was what he wanted to give us, and I think that's what people are drawn to about him: that freedom.

He was a man of deep conviction, and for all of his misanthropy I would have to say he was an idealist, or else he never would have done what he did. He believed that. As he said, "I'm a happy man in a compulsively unhappy world." He did his damnedest to try to point people in the right direction: toward celebration and happiness and enjoyment of this life here and now. Because as far as we know, this is all we get, and you'd better make it a damn fine party. I hope that that will be his legacy.

He was very generous in pointing us in directions where we can enjoy movies and books and artists and musicians. We can celebrate and continue as we unfold in our lives. As I become an older person I can understand things better, and also the directions that he pointed me in—that continues to enrich me. It becomes this dialog with the

universe that's going on all the time. You need to be aware of that dialog, and when the universe winks at you, you know, laugh! Laugh, and
enjoy it! Those are our moments together; those are our moments with
each other, and with those ineffable things that are rare, beautiful, and
inspiring. That's what he wanted: he wanted us to have those romantic,
beautiful moments.

9

MARGIE BAUER

Margie Bauer, San Francisco, 2019.
Photo by Carl Abrahamsson.

"It was very freeing to be around him, because you could be exactly who you were."

During the last years of Anton LaVey's life, Margie Bauer worked at the Black House as his and the Church of Satan's secretary. Today, she works as an artist and costume/clothing designer.

How did you first hear about Anton LaVey?

When I first met my husband, I was sixteen, and I had always been interested in metaphysics. He was very involved, and he had a huge library of books. I've always been a voracious reader. Three of the books that he had were *The Satanic Bible, The Satanic Rituals,* and *The Compleat Witch.* That's how I first heard of LaVey.

What were your impressions then, after having read them?

Like a lot of people say, it was more of an "aha" moment. This is somebody that thinks the way that I've thought my whole life, you know. More than a discovery, it was sort of a recognition of a kindred spirit. I read all of those books, and then I read *The Devil's Avenger* by Burton H. Wolfe, which is another book that my husband had. I became fascinated by the Doktor himself and the amazing life that he had lived.

How did you first get in touch with him? What was the background for that?

That was quite a while later. Unlike a lot of people, I guess I didn't feel the need to become a member of the Church of Satan. I really didn't even know at the time if you could become an active member anymore. I knew that he had sort of gotten reclusive after a certain point, and I didn't know about that side of it—I just practiced the philosophy. I guess I was about twenty-three when I decided to just write him a letter. I felt that I really wanted to sit down and let him know how much his writings had meant to me, and I did. I bought a card that I thought was perfect. I forget the name of the artist at this moment, but it's a satyr, and it has nymphs dancing around. It's one of my favorite pictures, and I thought that would be perfect. I wrote the letter and I put it away, and then it got shuffled in a drawer. I forgot about it until about a year later. I was going through the drawer and I found it. I reread the letter and I thought, "Well, you know, I might as well still send it." I put a picture in there and a contact number. I didn't really think that anybody would ever contact me: "Oh, they probably get thousands of letters and this probably won't ever even be seen." I just popped it in the mailbox and forgot about it.

About a week later, I was sitting at home, and the phone rang. This was back in the dark ages, so you didn't know who was calling you until you picked up the phone. . . . There was a woman's voice on the other end: "Hello, this is Blanche Barton, and I just wanted to call you because the Doktor and I received your very lovely letter, and we wanted to know if, possibly, you had a time in the next couple of weeks where you might come by and meet with us." I'm sure she was smiling on her end, because if she had read the letter, she knew how important this would be to me, right? I pretended that I wasn't as overwhelmed as I was and, you know, sort of checked my schedule. I said, "Well, yeah, I think I have a free night next Friday to come by." So we made an appointment for me to come by there at midnight, and that was the beginning.

How did that meeting impact your life at that time?

It was amazing; it was everything that I hoped it would be. I've met heroes of mine in the past, and a lot of times you meet them and they're a little too human, or a little disappointing in one way or another, in real life. They're not quite as you would expect or hope that they would be. But that wasn't the case with the Doktor. He was every bit what I hoped he would be.

This thing that developed, in terms of your working as a secretary and dealing with practical things, how did that come about? Was that on the agenda from the beginning, or was that something that emerged after you had gotten to know each other?

I don't really know from their side of it, if they were looking for some-body to help with that kind of work; it seemed to happen very quickly. When I went over there the first couple of evenings, we spent a lot of time talking and, as you know, he would play keyboards and tell won-derful stories. At some point in the evening we'd watch a movie, or several movies, and we just all got along really well; it was a really good fit. I don't remember exactly when it became an official thing that I was to work there, but probably after the first few times that I went over.

What was the nature of the work? Was it like dealing with incoming mail and sorting things?

At the time when I first started going over there it was 1994, and they had had a period where there was a lot of backed-up mail. I would typi-cally show up around midnight, and we'd work in the kitchen, where the keyboards were. I'd sit with Blanche, and we'd either work on writing, or we would work on processing memberships. The Doktor would play key-boards and tell jokes and stories, and after that we'd always watch films. I was also a student of the Doktor's, so that was part of the evening as well.

I think in the general mind frame, people say that those years, or that final decade, were just reclusive or isolationist. But if you care about your

business and the things that you're doing, you also care about the mail.
Did he say that specifically to you? Meaning, did he care about keeping
the vital communication of the Church alive?

Oh, of course he did. I mean, I think that's one reason I was there; I think that's one reason that everything came together when it did. There's an interesting story about the letter that I wrote, and the fact that I had kept it for so long before sending it. The first night that I went over there was very magical. I remember standing outside the gate, and it was very foggy out, and you could hear the foghorn in the distance. It was Tony that let me in, but I didn't know at the time. The door just creaked open, and this whispery sort of voice was saying, you know, "Come in, come this way, come this way, come in, come in." I'm teetering up these stairs that have no handrails, and they're all slick from the fog, and I'm in three-inch heels. I'm going up there, and it's all dark—I think there was just a red light in the hallway. I couldn't see the person who was talking to me. When he let me in, we walked a little way down the hallways, and then he unlocked the door on the left, which was the ritual chamber.

Blanche was in there, and she introduced me to Xerxes, who was just a little over a year old at the time. We exchanged pleasantries, and then she said the Doktor would be with me in a minute and I should go sit down. And so I waited for him. When he walked in, it was exactly as I had imagined he would be, you know? He sat down and talked to me, and he said, "Well, I'm at a bit of a disadvantage, because you seem to know everything about me and I know nothing about you." So I started talking a little bit, and he said, "Blanche and I noticed that you wrote the letter on my birthday a year ago." I mean, of course I'd read it in the books, I had seen his birthday mentioned, but I wasn't conscious about that on the day that I wrote the letter, that it was his birthday. And I said, "Oh, no, I wasn't aware of that." He said, "Well, I thought that, because you don't mention it in the letter." So that was an interesting point. Then he also said that the card that I wrote the letter in was very interesting, because it was the same card that Blanche wrote her letter in when she first wrote to the Doktor. Both he and Blanche thought that was quite a coincidence. He asked why I had not mailed it for a year, and I told him that it just got shuffled away. He leaned back and closed his eyes for a minute and said, "Yes, timing is everything." It felt very fated.

When you started working on a regular basis, did you experience any kind of negative response from people in your surroundings?

No. Well, I'm always very private. I know that some people like to show their alignment; it's very important for them to be open with it. It was never important to me to make a show of it, because it was something that was so deeply, personally important to me. I don't really share it with people that I'm not very, very close to. That's why this is the first interview I've ever done. But my boyfriend at the time, who became my husband, was already interested in it, so there was no problem there. He was more patient than anybody would have been. I worked as a cocktail waitress at the time at a supper club downtown, and I would work there from like 4:00 to maybe 9:30, and then he would pick me up at work, and we would go have dinner, and then he would drop me at the Black House at midnight, and I would be there until five, six, seven, eight, nine, ten the next morning—more often later than earlier. He was just very supportive. Doktor actually noted this as well, and did want to meet him. Unfortunately, he passed away just around the time that we were talking about it, so that never got to be. I don't think my parents understand it, but they've never given me a problem about it, either.

What would you say has been the greatest contribution to your life, in terms of these meetings and getting to know him?

I just love that family; I love Blanche and Xerxes and the Doktor, and just the wonderful friendship. That is the most important thing to me. I loved being there. It was unusual for people to treat me this way at the time. He assumed that I could do anything. They would give me tasks and projects to do, and it was just assumed that I was intelligent enough and capable enough to carry it out, and that really led to a sense of confidence. When somebody that you admire that much treats you in that manner, with that sort of respect, it is a confidence builder. I was very young at the time, in my early twenties, so that was a big deal. Also, another gift that he gave to his friends was that, however you were, if he liked you, any of your little idiosyncrasies, and any little personality traits that other people maybe were irritated by, or thought you should change, those were actually the things that he loved about people. It was very freeing to be around him, because you could be exactly who you were. And he just seemed to love every minute of it, so it was really wonderful.

You also mentioned that you were a student of his. What did that entail?

Sometimes that just entailed discussions; there were a lot of things that we would talk about. Sometimes it entailed more practical applications of magic or magical principles, a lot of tutelage in lesser black magic, you know, *Compleat Witch* stuff. Yeah, it varied.

In all of these things, whether personal or teachingwise, is there any idea or concept that's still extra special and relevant for you today?

All of it is relevant to me today, as relevant as it was when I first discovered it. Because it was a philosophy that aligned with the way that I was anyway.

What do you think were the greatest changes that he brought for America? What can you see that he changed in America?

In a way, everything. He was part of the decade that changed everything. I was speaking with my husband about it earlier today, and we actually started looking at it in the larger picture of the times. America's history at that time, and in the decades just previously, was very intense. You had the events of the stock market wealth and everything of the 1920s, and then the crash, and then the desperation of the 1930s. And then you had World War II, and you know, people were very simple.

No matter how open we seem on top, with all the media and outrageous stuff, it's very puritan underneath. I feel it continues to be so. And especially during those hard times, people appreciated simple values, such as God and religion—they always permeated this country.

To add to that, you had World War II, and many of those men who went away didn't come back. The ones that did come back, they just wanted things to be even and normal. So you have the 1950s, where everything became very tight and very predictable. But that's what people wanted; it was very important to them, socially, and again "God" was a big part of that.

And then the 1960s exploded. People always liken the Church of Satan and the Summer of Love, and lump it all in there, but actually he was before that. He was doing his workshops and the Magic Circle long before 1966, and the Summer of Love wasn't even until 1967. LaVey kind of turned everything on its head, you know? I don't think we can have a concept of it now, the way that things are, just how much he did so. Because he stood out.

It's an interesting occurrence of the third position, because he was neither free love, nor was he an arch conservative. You know, he was in the middle, and no side could really come to terms with what the hell it was. That's the power of it, of course.

It is the power of it; it is. During this time period and just after, you had JFK and you had Martin Luther King, and you had all these social changes. JFK came in, and everyone thought he was just amazing. He did all this stuff for America, and then he was shot. And Martin Luther King was shot. It was just a time where everything was suddenly turned; everybody's values, everybody's ideas that the safe world that everybody thought that they had constructed and were a part of, it actually wasn't. It wasn't safe anymore. The Doktor was in a unique position because he came in and told you that basically you'd had the wool pulled over your eyes and showed exactly *how* you've had it pulled over your eyes, and *how* this is exactly what you can do about it. "And you know what?

You don't need God, because you are your own god." It was part of a decade that just changed everything in America. It still has its ramifications today; it's still going on—echoes of what happened then.

What was the key to his controversy, according to you? Was it merely the S-word, or was there also something else?

I think that was part of his formula: 99 percent respectability, 1 percent outrage, right? That was the outrage. Because he was well spoken, and he was obviously intelligent, and he was personable, and anyone who met him liked him—he was very charismatic. And yet there was that S-word. I mean, that is the thing that everybody has a problem with. "Why don't you just call it humanism? You'd reach so many more people." But that isn't the point. I think the S-word is part of a stratification, if you can get past that. Only a certain kind of person will.

What do you miss most about him?

He was really fun. He could be demanding, and he could be totally unreasonable, and he could be very difficult when he wanted to be. But that was the thing with him: he could be all those things. Then he could also be very sweet, and very caring, and very fun. One of my favorite things that always caught me off guard was his smile. Here you had this man who could look very serious and very imposing, but if you made him smile, or something made him smile or laugh, he suddenly looked like a ten-year-old boy. It was always disarming, you know. There's nobody like him. I think that once you've had somebody like that for a friend, you don't ever stop missing them. I cherish the time that I spent there, because he was an exceptional human being, and an exceptional friend.

You mentioned that The Compleat Witch was one of the trio of his books that you discovered in the beginning. It's an incredibly advanced book— way ahead of its time—and it popped up in the bland 1970s when everything was unisex. It's a radical book.

I think its ideas are even radical now. In fact, I think it's especially radical right now. For me, as a woman, that book was probably the most important to me, more than all the blasphemy. For me it was the philosophy itself that was so sound, and I agreed with it so wholly, and right away. For me, it was never very hard to accept it, and with *The Compleat Witch,* that was a natural for me. I had always gotten criticism because I've always been very feminine, and then when I became a teenager, there's a whole other dimension to that. "Why do you have to look so sexy, why do you wear your dresses tight, why do you wear all that makeup?" I was doing it just out of my natural way of being; that's just the way that I was.

My parents were sort of, not the hippie generation, but just after, and their aesthetic was very different, and they didn't really understand me. So when I cracked open that book and I read it, I was like, "See, I'm right! I'm right, this is me!" A lot of it was very natural for me already, and the Doktor recognized that. So anything that we talked about in that respect was just something extra, you know? I found it to be an empowering book. I don't understand why feminists have an issue with it—unless they haven't read it. It's basically saying that no matter what type you are, no matter what you look like, it's great, it's fine— you're perfect for somebody, for some situation. It also teaches you how to manipulate. They complain about men manipulating women, but I mean it's a great book for teaching women how to manipulate men. I still think it's ahead of its time.

The entire philosophy amplifies what's already there. Use it to your advantage, don't decrease it; just amplify. And that of course brings the train of thought to a whole different area, like the fascination with freaks, and with people who are outsiders: it's never about being invisible or decimated. On the contrary! Would you say that this kind of celebration of differences, that that is something good for feminism? If I look at it from the 1970s and onward, I can't figure out what feminists want—the main problem being that certain women have taken on the role of spokeswomen for other women who have not given them that right.

We haven't given them that right, and we don't really want them speaking for us. It is a problem that I've come up against again and again when discussing it. I remember one of the first times I came up against the kind of feminist you're talking about. She believed that to be a strong woman was something more like turning yourself into a man. I think she was the wife of somebody that my husband was playing music with. They were playing music, and so the wife and I hung out and talked, and she had to go run some errands and I went with her. At the end of the day she said, "I don't understand it. You're very intelligent, you're very well spoken, you're deep, your thoughts are deep, why do you do this?" And I asked, "Do what?" She motioned to my clothes, and I answered, "Because I enjoy it, because I like it."

Somehow, in her mind, if you were an intelligent woman, you weren't supposed to show off or exploit your femininity, because that was somehow buying into what men liked, or what men thought of you. That kind of thinking is very backward to me. To be a strong woman is to be a strong woman. You should express your femininity; you should be strong in your femininity. Some women may not be as feminine, and that's okay, too. But to be told that my expression is wrong . . . I just think that a lot of the time, those women turn themselves into exact copies of the kind of men that they dislike the most. They take on all these traits that are traits of the most boorish kind of guy, and they think that's strength?

LaVey really made me aware of Ben Hecht, and at that time I just couldn't figure it out. I couldn't figure out why he brought Ben Hecht up, specifically. I've heard other people having been presented with other things, and other key people. Do you have any of those memories? Did he present stuff to you that you realized, perhaps later on, that "oh, so this is what this is about."

He probably recognized that in you, and that's why he was showing that to you. There was a lot of that. I don't put on a front anyway, but I knew that it would be impossible to do there. Whatever I wanted to seem like, he was going to see right through it. So I was always very genuine. I did have the sense of being scanned or being watched. I was also, like I said, in my early twenties, so everything had major significance. Everything was possibly very significant. It was just a very magical situation.

There were certain films or certain books that he would present me with, both because he recognized that they would be something important to me, but also sometimes it was something that he wanted to show me; almost like a lesson. That's why I said the learning was really varied, because it was never standard; you know, "Now we go into the ritual chamber!" We did do that, but sometimes it was just talking. I feel sometimes it was just sharing these books with me, or sharing these films with me. A lot of times these held a greater message.

After we'd been going over there for a while an apartment mysteriously appeared open. We had been living on the peninsula in Millbrae—about twenty minutes outside of San Francisco—for a while when I was first going over. So aside from working and then going over there all night, I would have to take two buses and a train, and walk about a mile uphill to get home to my bed every time. I was dedicated! I don't know if I could do it now, but I was dedicated then. Anyway, the Doktor talked about us moving: "What if you moved closer?" And I said, "Well, yeah, that would be great, you know, I'd love to live right down the street, I'd love to be able to just go home and go to my bed, or be able to come here maybe not so scheduled, like if you guys just called me up and needed me for something."

And lo and behold, no real surprise, a few weeks later a friend of ours that had an apartment about six blocks away announced out of the blue that he was getting married—we didn't even know he had a girlfriend at the time—and he was moving out, and did we want to take over his apartment? We jumped at it, and the Doktor was very happy to hear that I lived closer. Around this time, I was going over there three, maybe four times a week sometimes, and I'd always come home in the wee hours of the morning.

Well, one morning I was coming home, and it was about 6:00 or 6:30 in the morning. But it was wintertime, so it wasn't light out yet. I took a taxi because it wasn't light out yet, and I had a weird feeling. But I had the taxi driver drop me on the corner, because of safety reasons, so he didn't know where I lived; maybe I felt paranoid. Then I was walking to my house, which was maybe half a block away. A car came around the corner as I was walking across a dip for a garage, and then just turned into the garage, pinning me between the car and the garage door. My mindset wasn't immediately that there was something wrong. I just thought that the idiot driver didn't see me. So I walked around the car, and at this point I was maybe three doors down from my house. I heard the car door close, and somebody was running up behind me. It was very foggy, so I couldn't really see them. I turned around, and they said something to me, and it was kind of jumbled gangster stuff. It was a woman, too, which threw me off. I still didn't understand what she said, and I asked her to repeat it. Then I realized she had a knife, and I realized what she wanted. So I threw my purse at her. Luckily my house was right there, and I had my keys in my pocket, so I ran in the door.

I was very angry. I think I'd just been paid that day and gone to the bank before I went to the Black House, so of course I had a bunch of money in my purse. The next time I talked to Blanche on the phone I told her about what happened, and we were making a time when I could come over. We talked about that a little bit, and the next time that I came over everything was as normal, you know. I came in, played with Xerxes a little bit, we went in the kitchen, worked a little bit, listened to music. Then, later in the evening, when Blanche went to set up the movie for the evening, the Doktor came over and sat at the kitchen table with me, and he asked me about what happened. But he asked me in a way that he wanted me to describe everything about what had happened: what the car looked like, what the morning was like, what the person looked like, what their voice was like, and he just sat there with his eyes closed and he listened to me. Then he'd ask questions every once in a while and have me describe some more stuff.

Then he said, "You know, there are so many ways that people like that can meet their end." And then he described in great detail so many bad things; the different bad things that could happen to people like that. We probably did this for about an hour, and then he stood up all of a sudden and said, "Well, Blanche is waiting; we should go in the other room and watch a movie." I very much believe that right there, at the kitchen table, what we were doing was a destruction ritual. I wouldn't want to be those people. I'm sure nothing good happened to them. I don't have anything else to say about that.

That's another example of his brilliance, in weaving in psychological aspects into old, sort of, occult concepts. When you talk about cursing traditionally, there would be theatrics and formalized behavior.

Right, but this was just us. This was the energy that we were building between us; there was imagery in the sensory [aspect] of describing the situation. He was angry that this had happened to me, and of course I had emotion, because it had happened to me. All of this was present as well. After we had talked about it, we just cut it off; we just went and watched a movie. We never discussed it again. Doktor was very earthy, he was very practical, he was very no-nonsense. But he did believe in magic, and he did utilize magic. He believed in magic as that force, that electricity that you could generate, either on your own, if you were emotional enough over something, or with other human beings, in that simplest form of building up that energy and then just throwing it out. As Blanche has said, at the very least it makes you feel better. But those of us who have done it and utilize it often recognize that it actually has very real results beyond that.

It's been twenty-two years now since his demise. But there is always something going on: new films, books, anniversaries.

He's very much still around. I think this is a very important time. I think the film that you're making now, and several other things that have been coming out or that are in the works, either by people in the Church of Satan, or even by people that have been estranged from the organization . . . it's all coming together in a very interesting way, all at the same time. We'll see where that goes.

I'm just overjoyed that all of us who were part of his life in some way can actually formulate these things and compare stories, and leave something behind. As we can see, time moves on. That is why I'm so fascinated with his behavior at that time . . . feeling scanned, but happily so. I also felt that he dropped these things on my lap; it was like sowing little seeds— Ben Hecht here, and Eddie Cantor or William Seabrook or William Lindsay Gresham or "freaks" there—secrets that later on bloomed.

I think that he planted things in people; that he saw that they could appreciate that they could bring something to fruition. He often said that he never was going to live long enough to do all the things that he wanted to do. And so by having these different people that were doing all of these different things . . . maybe even people like me who at the time, you know, I was just starting; I was just figuring out exactly who I was, and what I was going to be doing. Because of his influence, and things that he planted in there, later on I could draw from that. When he did that, it wasn't anything that would be alien to who you were; it was something that he recognized in you, that you could appreciate, or that maybe you would have found on your own, sometime, perhaps. I think he planted different seeds in different people, and you see a lot of it flowering now, so many years after he passed away. Maybe that was his evil plan.

One of the quintessential traits was his active integration of pop culture that had been forgotten or discarded, and thereby contained a force that could be tapped into and used. Do you have any memories of songs, films, et cetera, that he displayed for you as being such magical works? Have you woven in similar explorations and practices in your own life?

So many! For me, this is a very essential aspect of Satanism and of Doktor LaVey's teachings. Music and films were so important. Certain films and music. They instantly convey a time, an aesthetic, a quintessentially Satanic way of thinking. Because many of the films and musical pieces he showed me were things that had once been incredibly vital and then forgotten; they were an instant source of energy and power to tap into. Precisely because not everyone in the world was focusing on them anymore, it gave you something that immediately set you apart from the herd. A perspective those around you did not have, that you could utilize.

When it comes to creativity, I get the impression that LaVey was happiest when playing his tunes, telling his stories, and writing his essays; that is, being immersed in his own expressions that he mastered so well. But these usually also require a second party: a listener, a reader. Did you ever get the impression that he expressed himself mainly to have that second party, or was the expression in itself, for himself, the most important aspect?

Both! I do think he enjoyed performing and sharing his creativity with an appreciative audience. But I also know that, like most creative individuals, he would have done these things anyway and did, for his own enjoyment. I had the feeling that the most important thing was the expression itself—and if other people enjoyed it as well, that was great.

Can you see any similarities between LaVey and other notable creative people at the time (regardless of their particular expressions or views)? Meaning, would you say there was something distinctly zeitgeistish about him?

While there are always similarities between creative individuals in any particular time period—I feel that everything in life moves in waves and creative people in particular are sensitive to that—I think LaVey stands out as a true individual among his peers. During a time when much of the world was going through social, political, and religious upheaval, and while he was definitely a part of that, he took it in a very different direction. I can't think of anyone I would directly compare him to.

Inside the Black House, which was your favorite room, and why?

Hmmm . . . that's a tough one. I don't know that I had a favorite. They were all distinctly unique, and I enjoyed each of them for different reasons. I loved the kitchen for its coziness. Most of our hours of music, general casual conversation, and storytelling were spent there, with coffee and cats and baby Xerxes toddling in and out. The purple room was where we would adjourn for movies. The evening almost always wound up with Doktor LaVey and Blanche sharing a favorite film (or two) with me. Sometimes I even got to show him one he hadn't heard of before. So there were many fun and instructive hours spent there as well. The ritual chamber was of course wonderful; it was special because that's the room I was initially taken to when I was invited into the Black House the first night. It's also where I would spend time with the Doktor as a student, learning magic. So that is a special room for me.

Sometimes I would work alone in the downstairs of the house, in the room adjacent to the Den of Iniquity, with the low light, and all of LaVey's "people" inhabiting it, the mannequins that he created. That was always an evocative and delightfully creepy experience. His characters really did seem to come to life if you stood in that room and looked at them a little too long. All the little details! The women had earrings, chipped nail polish; there were half used matchbooks near the ashtrays on the bar—it was wonderful. The bathroom itself was memorable— old and dusty, with mannequin limbs stored in the old disused shower, one bare light bulb, and a poster on the wall advertising a Tempest Storm performance.

Off the Den of Iniquity, a door opened into an amazing recreation of a 1940s hotel room, complete with neon sign flashing outside the "window," a dress hanging on the door, photos on the nightstand. It felt as if the occupant had just stepped out on an eternal rainy noir evening. I loved it!

Next to this room was another smaller room that housed many of LaVey's books and old magazines. And yes, there really were secret passageways! Not just the ones that have already been written about—the rotating bookcase in the purple room that opened into the bedroom, or the faux fireplace that had a ladder behind it—but all throughout the actual walls of the house as well.

The upstairs, which had been at one time the main living quarters, was beautiful, with stained-glass windows at the top of the stairs, and Uncle Einar's Room—the entire house was fantastic. One got the feeling that it had seen so much that it was now a living and breathing entity of its own. An Old Dark House straight out of the old films. You certainly could feel its history.

Were there any quirks or habits that you found odd in LaVey? Meaning, unexpected expressions of moralisms that might have seemed un-Satanic and perhaps stemmed from the times or the religion he grew up in? Things you sort of didn't quite see coming?

I would say not moralisms as much as unexpected vulnerability? He was always very human, but certain things would seem to get to him emotionally in a way that was sometimes surprising to me. But again, this is what made him such a multifaceted, interesting character. I would not say un-Satanic. To me it was very Satanic. Little insights into the very real humanness of this larger than life man. I think it made him even more remarkable.

In the LaVeyan encouragement of fetishizing objects and environments (working with ECI, creating total environments, for instance) it's not that far-fetched to talk about an ensouling of these objects (or spaces) that one has an intimate relationship with. Did he ever give the impression that he felt that way about human beings? Meaning, that he could feel OK with using the word soul *or* ensouled *or* spirit *or* spirited *when talking about humans? I guess the extension of this question is whether you ever saw signs of him not being a 100 percent strict materialist?*

This thing of seeing LaVey as a strict materialist seems to be a viewpoint that has sprung up since his death, a sort of misunderstanding of his writings. I never thought of him as a strict materialist, and I would never, ever describe him that way. Why bother starting an occult organization if that were the case? Just call it atheism, or philosophy, and be done with it. But he didn't. Because he understood that there is a basic human need and draw toward the spiritual, the mysterious, the unexplained. Before the organization—before the early classes, even— he sought out the strange, unusual, and arcane on his own. He was a ghost hunter at one point! Just because he never came across a ghost he believed to be a real spiritual presence didn't mean he wasn't intrigued by the possibility.

In the early Magic Circle, and in the classes he gave that eventually led to the creation of the Church of Satan, many of the things studied were mystical or occult themes—of course, mixed with psychology and a firm study of human nature. That is in fact what made Satanism unique, that combination of everything that we are, spiritual *and* material. It wouldn't have been nearly so intriguing if it were just another materialist philosophy. I know in my own studies with him, we used magic. Real magic that worked. The building up of energy and its release toward an outcome you wish to happen. That invisible energy that connects us all, that you can push around to make things happen; what do you call that? Is that strictly material?

We discussed often how you could lavish so much love and importance on an object or a space, put so much of your personal energy into it, that it would come alive in a very real sense. So in that way, you are ensouling that object or place. And also, the ability to effectively time travel by creating a total environment. All of these things are tapping into a "something" outside of what we accept as the strictly material. One of my favorite sayings of Doktor LaVey's was that these things were not supernatural; they were supranatural. Meaning, rare, but not outside of nature or of the real—rather a heightened part of what was real, very much a part of our natural world and abilities.

Did you ever feel that LaVey put on a show at times because he felt it was expected of him rather than because he was genuinely in the mood himself?

Yes. Sometimes. Because he knew the importance of an image. He knew how people wanted to see him, and how essential that was for them. Also, that there are certain kinds of people you cannot show aspects of yourself to, because they will take them as weaknesses. Like any good performer, he was always "on." And I don't mean this in a way that insinuates he was performing something that was not sincere. This image was of his own creation, taking his natural personality traits into account, and an entirely real aspect of him.

Did you perceive him as being sensitive to what others thought or felt about him?

Yes, but not in the way most people are—not as an insecurity. He didn't care what people thought, on a general level, of something he wanted to do or say. One of his favorite sayings was, "If you don't like it, fine. Don't let the door hit you on the ass on your way out!" However, again, he realized the power of an image and was very aware of how people wanted to see him, and the importance of following through with that.

Do you think there was something or some things that he would have done differently in his life, had he had the chance?

I feel that ultimately Doktor LaVey was a very satisfied, deeply happy man. He had lived an incredibly full, interesting life. The only thing he ever mentioned along those lines, to me anyway, was wishing he had more lifetimes to do all the things he would like to do! But as far as the life he did have, I know he enjoyed it to its fullest. He never expressed regrets over anything to me. He was a man who truly appreciated the things that he had, and the people he had around him. He always referred to himself as an extremely happy man in a compulsively unhappy world.

Is there anything that you would like to add; something that you think should be mentioned?

I think the most interesting part of Anton LaVey was his human side. I remember him telling me that he had to be very careful who he showed certain aspects of himself to, because people had an expectation of him in a certain way. If you weren't careful, and you showed yourself as being too human to the wrong person, a lot of times they would use that to their advantage and see it as a weakness. I feel honored that I think that with me, he recognized that he could be himself. I felt very much a part of the family there. Before I met him, I always envisioned we would be great friends. And then when I met him and we all became great friends, that was pretty amazing for me—it was an honor.

I was there on the night he passed away. I knew something was different. He was just a very strong man, and he had a very strong will to present himself in a certain way. He knew how he came across, and his personal strength was very important to people. But he did have health issues for a long time. He had a long-standing heart condition that he'd had for almost his whole life, and you couldn't tell most of the time. He told stories, too, of a couple of deaths and coming back to life experiences that he'd had already.

I had not seen him for a few times when I went over, because sometimes I'd work upstairs, but then we had also worked it out that I worked in the downstairs area as well. This may be because he wasn't always up to company at this point or whatever, but I would work down there, too. And it was right next to the Den of Iniquity, and it was really creepy. I'd be alone down there, and if I had to use the bathroom I had to walk through the Den of Iniquity to get to the spiderweb bathroom that had mannequin parts where the shower stall had been, and the Tempest Storm poster on the wall, from some strip club in the 1940s, or whatever. It was great, but it was also totally, completely creepy, because those mannequins in the Den of Iniquity, they really moved if you looked at them too long. It was wonderful.

So anyway, I worked down there, and I had not seen him the last few times that I had been there. This night I was down there, and I hadn't been there very long, just maybe a couple of hours. All of a sudden Xerxes came running down there, and he had his coat on. He was little, he was four maybe, and he just sat in the chair with his little coat. I didn't know what was going on. I asked him, but he didn't say anything to me.

Then Blanche came down and said, "I have to let you out." She was an amazing actress, like nothing was wrong. "I have to let you out; we've had some things come up." She gave me a hug. My husband was waiting out there in the car for me. I got in the car, and I told him what had happened, because it was odd. As good an actress as Blanche was being, the whole thing was very odd. We just sat there for a moment. Then there was an ambulance coming. We stayed where we were, and the ambulance pulled in front of the house. We watched and waited, and we saw them bring somebody out. We didn't even go straight home. I went straight to a pay phone and called Blanche, and yeah, that was . . . yeah . . . unreal, unreal. I didn't find out for certain what had happened until a few days later.

Did you perceive, like on a day-to-day basis of normality, that he was aware of a potential demise?

There were certain things that he said that, at the time, I maybe didn't understand in the way that he was trying to convey them to me. But when I think back on it now, it's clear to me that he knew. If he didn't want to show you that he was feeling badly, you would never know that he was having any difficulty at all. I mean, he could pick me up with one arm; when you'd give him a hug, he could pick me up with one arm, even that late in life. He was very strong, and I think his will was even stronger than he was physically. He just stuck around for as long as he could.

Peter Gilmore, Poughkeepsie, 2018.
Photo by Carl Abrahamsson.

10

PETER GILMORE

"He needed the S-word in there to really make the impact."

Peter Gilmore is a composer, conductor, and musician. He is the high priest of the Church of Satan and is married to Peggy Nadramia, high priestess of the Church of Satan. He is the author of *The Satanic Scriptures* (2007).

Let's begin at the very beginning. How did you first hear about Anton LaVey?

I first heard about Anton LaVey when I was shopping for books, when I was about ten years old. I was a big fan of science fiction. There was a bookstore in the Port Authority Bus Terminal called The Book Bar, and I was in there after a trip to the Museum of Natural History. I was buying some Asimov and some Clarke and some Harlan Ellison, too, and on the rack as I was going in, I noticed this book, *The Satanic Bible.* I thought, "Well, I read the Christian one and thought that was pretty awful, and I've read some Eastern texts and thought they were kind of nebulous and interesting, but not particularly relevant." So I picked it up, looked at the back, and saw that very dramatic image of Doktor on there. I thought, "Wow, that guy looks like Ming the Merciless; that's

157

kind of cool, but it's also a little hokey. I'm not sure I'm going to be into this." So I flipped through it briefly and then set it back and said, "Ah, well, you know, I've got another mission here; there are other authors I want."

But when I got in line to pay, that book rack was there and *The Satanic Bible* was turned toward me. So I picked it up again and looked at it and then started reading some of it. I immediately felt not only an excitement at the tasteful drama that it had, but the principles resonated with me just in this cursory glance, looking through "The Book of Satan" and then reading a little bit of the other essays just as I'm standing there, waiting in line. So I said, "I've got to take this home; I've got to read this whole thing because it makes me very curious, and it's certainly not like other religious scriptures." When I got home, I read it that night. Beforehand I considered myself a skeptical materialist atheist, and then I now added the much more appropriate definition of Satanist to myself. That was the beginning.

From having bought the book and integrated it, how did you first come into contact with him?

I actually couldn't find an address to write to the Church of Satan. I felt when I was young that it would be inappropriate to try to approach them. I hadn't really accomplished that much yet, and I felt that I really should bring something to the table. When I felt I was ready, I went down to the city; I went to Rockefeller Center, and there they had these beautiful racks of phone books from all across the country. They were in these beautiful brass backings; you kind of lifted them up like they were tomes of sacred magic. I found the Yellow Pages for San Francisco, and I found an address for the Church of Satan—it had a Baphomet in there, and there it was! I wrote a letter and posted it.

A few weeks later it came back, stamped, "not at this address." I called Information for San Francisco, and they only had the same old thing that was in the phone book; they didn't have any kind of updated address. So I waited for rather a while until I found a notecard that somebody had put up in Herman Slater's Magickal Childe bookstore. It was from a guy who was saying he was interested in the Church of Satan and Satanism and was interested in being in touch with other people. I think he was in Baltimore at the time.

So I wrote to him and said, "Hey, yes, I read *The Satanic Bible* when I was ten and felt I was a Satanist, and I've never met anybody else who actually considers themselves to be a Satanist. I was trying to get in touch with them and don't have an address." So he said, "Oh, I have their address" and gave it to me. That's when I wrote another letter; I sent it out there, and I got a very positive response, and that started my route. I was still not eighteen, but I was told that when I got to be eighteen I could become a member and participate in things. They said that "at this point we can certainly help teach you about things and give you reading material lists and all that sort of thing."

They turned me over to the local grotto, which was the Lilith Grotto, in Spotswood, New Jersey. This was in the early 1970s. So I actually have letters from Lilith Sinclair, being very cordial and saying, "Well, you do seem very intelligent and you understand this, so maybe you can come and witness a ritual or two." And then she fell out of contact, because the whole Temple of Set thing happened.*

But then I was older, and I found other ways of researching. I found another address and got back in touch. It was a kind of on-and-off struggle, because you had to go look up something physically or call somebody; it wasn't necessarily so easy to really get something that was going to function. But ultimately I did, and was happy to get the information for how to join. I joined, and Peggy did, too. As we were in college, we waited a little while, to really feel again that we were getting through our studies, and that we could then have something more serious to bring to the table.

Then we gave our active applications, which were accepted, and

---

*In 1975 CoS members Lilith Sinclair and Michael Aquino left the organization and founded their own group: The Temple of Set.

then we were invited to come out and see Anton LaVey. We'd never been to California before, but with that cordial invitation, how could you not go? So we did. We booked a flight and made arrangements and went out and visited the man himself.

How would you say that this first meeting affected you and your life?

One of the things that I was concerned with when going to meet Doktor was, "Would he be the man that I experienced in his writings?" Because I really admired that fellow; I loved his wit and his humor and his earthiness, his candor and his erudition. Often you meet people that you've heard about and you admire what they do, but in person they're really kind of disappointing—sometimes even really off-putting. I had read the *Washington Post* piece,* which wasn't necessarily that complimentary to him, before we had gotten to go out there. So I was definitely a little trepidatious; and not sure what it was going to be like.

But we were corresponding with Blanche at the time, and she was very chipper, wonderful, and welcoming. They had already appointed me as a representative—pretty much right away—because they saw that I understood everything. They said, "You can go out and talk about our philosophy to people and media and whatever." So even before meeting me in person they had taken that leap of trust with me.

So we went out there, and our first meeting was to meet at that wonderful restaurant: Izzy's Steakhouse. We were staying at the Press Club because Blanche had suggested that. She said, "Oh, it's very reasonable, and it's old and musty and has history; you don't want to stay in just any regular hotel; this would be very cool." And it was; it was really kind of awesome. It had a stinky old pool, and the cat clock on the wall, and our room had the map of the world behind the headboard that was old, yellowed, and peeling; it was just amazing. It was like being in some kind of Indiana Jones film.

---

*Walt Harrington, "The Devil in Anton LaVey," *Washington Post Magazine,* February 23, 1986. Available at ChurchofSatan.com (website).

We got dressed and went into Izzy's, and when we went in the door, suddenly we heard a voice boom out, "Peter Gilmore and Peggy Nadramia!" And there he was: Anton LaVey, with Blanche perkily perched on a stool, sipping, I think it was a martini. That was how we got started. We had a drink, and then moved to a table, and then started a conversation that didn't end until the next morning.

He also actually drove us around San Francisco, to show us the city in the middle of the night. Then we went back to the Black House to continue really in-depth conversations. It was a fantastic first meeting. During our conversations he showed that he was that guy that I saw in his writing; that he was charming, and he was witty, and he was friendly, and he was curious. He'd ask questions of me about things that I knew about, and we shared topics that we had of mutual interest. We'd kind of suss each other out to see what we each knew about these topics. It was always fun to see that we had very similar information about a lot of things. We left that evening—well, the next morning!—feeling as if we had met the best uncle you could possibly ever have.

You and Peggy are special, because you got so involved that you're now running the show, and that's a big deal, of course. But on a strictly personal level, did things change in your life or your perception after he died in 1997?

We felt that he died very early. It was kind of a surprise to us. We had known Anton LaVey's health was deteriorating, and he'd even had some experiences. . . . He once got on the phone with me and kind of pretended he was a feeble old man, and acted like, "Arrrrgh . . ." We were just going, "Oh, good heavens, what's going on?" But he was just pranking. He was just laughing; he liked to prank you, he liked to have that kind of fun. But at that point we had really been working ever more closely with him, and with the organization.

We were handling materials, we were creating materials, we were redesigning things to update them to the current desktop publishing—which we had the facility for, and which he didn't. I was trying to freshen up everything and make it all look professional and spot-on. He was really happy with that. We would be talking about where the organization was going to go, and that we had a role in that. He made it very clear that we were part of where it was going to go when he wasn't around. So that happened suddenly, and faster than we thought. It was definitely kind of an upending thing, because suddenly our responsibilities were multiplied.

Without him, where to look for direction, or any kind of guidance if we had a question? Suddenly it was really on us. Another thing that he told both Peggy and me is that he felt we understood and could apply his philosophy equally to him; that he really felt that our understanding was the same as his; that we had the same exact perspective. We had also the depth of perception: our understanding about the individualism of the organization, and how it had to be able to embrace many different kinds of people and how they applied Satanism.

Even though it was a little frightening that he wasn't there, we did have the confidence to say that, well, he had that trust in us, that we would be ready to shoulder that even without him. He told us that we could. At the time, it was kind of amazing and thrilling, but with him passing, it was suddenly a real responsibility on your shoulders. It really was Blanche, Peggy, and I who held on to things and kept it focused and going. That was the change: we were the ones doing everything.

On a personal level, what would you say has been LaVey's greatest contribution to your life?

I think Anton LaVey's greatest contribution to my life was giving me a proper definition for myself. Before I found *The Satanic Bible,* I really didn't have a specific moniker for what I was—I was just me. I never lost any of what I was, because I'm a diverse person: I do art, I do music, I do research, I do all kinds of different things. My creativity is in all these different realms, and I never lost that. But when I read *The Satanic Bible,* I suddenly had a framework in which to put a lot of the things that I was questioning.

Because I was an atheist, I had rejected the idea of there being any kind of god when I was eight years old. It became obvious to me when reading about past civilizations. I was very interested in archaeology, and of course you learn all about the temples and the gods that were there, and immediately it struck me that they weren't real; and the current ones that are being held up now are also not real. It's the same; this civilization will be gone, and there will be other gods, probably. My atheism was set.

The kind of aesthetic focus that Satanism brought was important. That you can be misanthropic, that you can really be very brutally honest about the human animal and its condition, and understand the worst and the best, and focus on the best aspects of yourself in that framework. And that it supported it without any kind of contest: it's there in the literature, in the principles, that you can be the best you possibly can, and then you make your choices about whom you're going to deal with, and where your direction is going to be . . . that kind of focus was invaluable.

It directed me so that I could continue to be an artist, and become more of a philosopher, too. I think that was always part of my thinking, but it was never so focused. But now that I'm representing a philosophy, I have to really concentrate on that. I had read philosophy and such; now it was being put into practice. And to become a practical applier of philosophy—not just in how I do things, but also in conceptualizing it and putting it out there for other people to understand. So that aspect of my life became crystallized after his death.

Is there any idea or concept that he gave you personally, or through his writing, that's still relevant to you in your life?

We used to discuss past ideas about how Satanism was applied and compare them to where we were at the current time. I think one of the focuses that we played around with was the idea that a Satanist is born and not made. When he created the Church of Satan, he originally was much more interested in its infiltrating society in general. I think he felt that anybody could look at Satanism and say, "This is a rational choice; why shouldn't I be a Satanist?" He really thought that, in some way, a lot of people would leave many other religions to become a Satanist.

He had found out, by the time we had met him, that that wasn't the case, and that it was going to be kind of a niche philosophy. One of the things that I brought to the table was the idea that there are very different natures of people; that not everybody is the same in that sense. Of course he knew that there were different natures of people, but I felt there was a major divide between people who were spiritual and who were interested in things that were ephemeral and placed all that above themselves, and people who are carnal and self-focused and were really dealing with the life that they were leading and were concerned about the people that they cherished.

I said, "I don't think that's something that one can change. I think one really is one or the other, and the person who is carnal is one who is a self-authority, and the person who is spiritual or ephemeral is somebody who is looking for some other kind of authority, whether it be a religious figure or a political figure or whatever." That was an essential divide.

And LaVey agreed: he really said that he hadn't quite seen it that way, but he then started working it into his interviews; he liked that focus that I brought to the table and discussed. If you're a carnal person, you still don't necessarily have to be a Satanist, but on some level you're a de facto, because we talked about de facto people in history, and I was always pointing them out. It wasn't something that they had to have forced on them; it was their nature, and that nature always wills out. We came to agree to a meeting of minds and a sharing of ideas that I think energized things; to make it all even more sharply focused.

What do you think were the greatest changes that he brought to the bigger picture for America, or for the American culture?

Anton LaVey affected pop culture very specifically, in bringing out this idea of the devil as having some kind of active symbolic presence. He'd wear the horned headpiece, and his red-lined cape, and would cavort with nude altar women, and say occult words such as *Shemhamforash,* and then say "Hail Satan!" No one had said "Hail Satan!" before; that was not part of the culture. That suddenly became part of the culture. He gave a context to a sort of ritual that was literally Satanic; not just "Our Father" backward, or some kind of simple blasphemy, or blasphemous inversions of Christian practice. He created a positive Satanic practice that hadn't existed before. And that inspired so many people!

You can find the way Milton handled Satan, and you could find Byron's dealings with that. You can look through art imagery: Doré's images of Satan, and Blake. All of these people in the past—all of these romantics of sorts—were Satanic in that they would look at the figure of Satan as something positive, and being about self-liberation and self-glorification.

LaVey tied into all that, but he brought it into a contemporary American setting. It wasn't always looking at some musty old thing, looking at some old etching, or reading some old poem. Suddenly, here was something fresh and very active. By his doing interviews, and doing films like *Satanis,* and appearing on these different interview shows, suddenly there was this man who looked like the Devil to the popular culture and was talking about Satan as this positive role model. That affected everybody; it became worldwide.

Suddenly musicians were doing albums that were more Satanic, and using a positive symbolism of Satan was suddenly becoming more and more rampant. And his imagery found its way into horror films. The Sigil of Baphomet, which he named, was just a drawing in a book, in several books. The various variations of it had no name. He gave it a name: he called it "The Sigil of Baphomet." That suddenly became the representative of Satanism because of *The Satanic Bible* and the Church of Satan. You went and saw a horror movie; if it was about devil worshipers of some sort, there was now a Baphomet. Before, it was an upside-down cross, and they might have a goat statue.

I always have fun looking through horror movies, to sort of

say, "These are pre-Church of Satan and these are post-Church of Satan." Because that was a change. The imagery that he created for the pageantry of his rituals suddenly became the standard for what was Satanic and Satanism, and it remains so. He aesthetically totally pushed a whole new paradigm into the culture that hadn't existed before. His interest in film noir, and his wearing a fedora was another thing. First it was the carnival, and the capes, and the tombstones, and the stuffed rats. He got tired of that at a certain point and wanted to bring an elegance to Satanism. Bringing it to the film noir paradigm, but also that of successful people; that, too, became part of Satanism. Not only the sort of carny, sideshow aspects, which he began because he knew it would be very easy to get attention with. But then it became more sophisticated. So that's his second wave of influence on pop culture, and other culture, too: of the Satanist as the sophisticate. The epicurean who is so successful that their control and enjoyment of the world is unfettered. That is a very powerful paradigm, and that, too, was something that he created.

What do you think is the main key to his misrepresentation? Does it mainly have to do with the S-word, or was it just that the philosophy was so controversial?

I think that misrepresenting what Anton LaVey put out there became easy for people because they didn't want to accept the reason that he was offering. His original concept was to create a philosophy that, even though it used sort of garish carnival trappings, provided an alternative that any rational person would want to adopt. That is terrifying for some people. They might be happy with whatever they had before but would also feel threatened, because *maybe* they weren't actually so happy with it. I think a lot of people, especially in the 1960s, were disgruntled with conventional religions, and they were often looking toward Eastern philosophies for some kind of new avenue.

LaVey came up with a third side, of course, that was shocking intentionally, and also meant to drive away the wrong people, because the outrage of using Satan as a main figurehead is of course going to chase a lot of folks away, absolutely. That was by design. But the misrepresentation, I think, was on the part of people who actually could look at the philosophy and realize that it was something that could be attractive beyond the trappings, and that that actually made them feel threatened; they really didn't want to see that supported or communicated clearly, because it could undercut what they were doing. I think the evangelical Christians always felt that if you gave the Devil a polite face, you were letting the real Satan in. Because they really do believe that Satan is around, so they were terrified of it for that reason.

Other people who were atheists and humanists didn't like to be tarred with Satan, because they wanted to have a wider audience and to bring people in. Suddenly, here's a guy who's actually more articulate and getting more attention than most of them, and they felt that he was stealing their show, and they didn't want to be associated with it. So they'd be happy to misrepresent him as well, to sort of get him out of the picture.

He faced a lot of adversaries because his ideas were threatening to people. It's not, I think, one specific thing; I think it's the whole package. He presented this rational philosophy that antagonized people both from the religious and the secular aspects, and they really didn't want this guy horning in on what they were promoting. They felt that here was this new act, and that on some level they couldn't really compete with it, and they were angry and jealous and just didn't want that to continue. So I think they were all very happy to try to put out ideas that certainly wouldn't be a clear representation of what Anton LaVey was trying to do.

What do you think his impact would have been on American society and culture if he hadn't used the S-word?

Anton LaVey's impact without Satan might have been much less. I think that what galvanized him as a philosopher was the passion that the imagery evoked. Satanism is about passion; it's about people being passionate. It wasn't just some empty symbol. Look at American Atheists, for example. Madalyn Murray O'Hair was a very brave woman; she challenged so many people, and she stood for atheism. She came up with this lame little symbol of a sort of atom swirling or something—it was like an "A." That didn't fly; it wasn't very aesthetic, and it wasn't exciting.

Satan is exciting, either pro or con; Satan is exciting. You throw a boulder into the pond with Satanism. If you are just an atheist, it's a pebble. That was the impact that was necessary. There are so many people who are different kinds of atheists and humanists, and very few of them had the kind of immediate worldwide impact that Anton LaVey achieved just by putting on that horned headpiece, and standing in front of the Sigil of Baphomet, and raising a sword and going, "Hail Satan!" That shattered everybody; it blasted the doors open and demanded to be paid attention to.

Some people thought it was funny and hokey and stupid. But then, when the literature started coming out, this was a whole other story. He was an erudite gentleman. When he did interviews, sometimes he would wear his cape, and other times he was more subdued, but he always spoke intelligently. The doors had been broken open, people started paying attention to him, and then he could bring the ideas in rather than just being kind of lost in the sauce—this morass of just sort of wishy-washy humanism of various sorts, which would tie into different kinds of politics; some were leftist, and some were more rightist. None of it had any kind of focus, especially on the individuals. Anton LaVey decided that was going to be his primary foundation. He needed the *S*-word in there to really make the impact.

What do you miss most about him, on a personal level?

What I miss about Anton LaVey not being around is being able to share all the things that I think that we both would enjoy together. When we'd be out there, we'd go to gun shows, we'd go to reptile shows, we'd talk about how we both would have loved to have had fruit bats as pets. . . . There were just so many different kinds of things that we shared an interest in, such as submarines and zeppelins.

He was like a little kid; his eyes would light up, and he'd just be thrilled, and we'd go off into rapturous discussions about all these different details of things that he knew or I knew, and we could share things. That kind of sharing that we had, that I thought was just so warm. I miss that so much. I still come up with things I've seen, going, "I just wish he was here, that I could just let him see this or let him hear this." I think that he would have been so happy.

And more so now that the Church of Satan has grown. All of the people that we have, all the amazing individuals that have come into it who never got to meet him—this is something I would like to share with him. Because I think he'd be so elated with where the organization has gone, and the kind of people that it's attracted, and the impact that it's having. Again, as always, even on a broader level than ever before. That is something that I think would make him feel justified, proud, and satisfied.

How do you see his legacy now and, more specifically, in the future?

Anton LaVey's legacy is definitely something that has been my crusade, to use an ironic term. Bringing that legacy forward for other people has been a major part of my life. I feel that my communication of it, in ways that I know that he would appreciate and agree with, is affecting so many people. I think that is going to continue. When I finally lay down my reins on this and have other people take over that job, I know people are going to be prepared for that, because we have so many articulate spokespersons at this point. More people come forward all the time who are amazingly intelligent, productive, creative, and accomplished. Those are the kind of people that he always wanted.

When you look through the archives, they got a lot of nut letters and a lot of people who were not really interested. We get emails like that every day, but we also keep getting gems. We keep getting people who understand Satanism and see it for the galvanic force that it is;

that it can work for them, and that it's going to heighten their life experience; it's going to heighten their creativity. More and more of those people come to us. Seeing that what he intended has flowered and then borne fruit in such a copious way, that is something that I think will continue.

We do have people that are trying to purloin the term *Satanism* and turn it into something else, and water it down, or make it somehow palatable to the masses. I do think that those people will come and go; they always have. We're over fifty years old, and there have been so many people who have tried to set up imitations or tried to usurp what's here. I think that Doktor LaVey created a real bedrock that serves a certain kind of person exceedingly well as the ensign that they can put their life under. Those people are always going to appear, regardless of what culture they come out of. We will be here, I'm sure, into the future to offer them that kind of set of principles that will focus their lives, so that they can better themselves, and in doing that enrich all the other people that they cherish, and all the people who are lucky enough to encounter them.

I see this as something that gets stronger, and I don't think the kind of people that are really Satanists are going away. I think there are more and more of them. We have this outreach that's absolutely global at this point, and that's going to continue for many centuries to come.

When you got actively interested and found the Satanic Bible and became interested in the philosophy, were you also aware of his musicianship?

It didn't really say much specifically about music. You kind of got these ideas about how it could be integrated into things, rituals and such, and he'd make mentions, but I had no idea of Doktor LaVey's absolutely intense study of music and his great performing skills. It was delightful to learn in time that he was a wonderful keyboardist. *The Devil's Avenger* was really the opening into that, because the first version of Burton Wolfe's book really took you on a journey with him. You found out that he really had quite an experience from a youth up until an adult. And of course, when we first met him, that was one of the things that he was very delighted to do: to take us into the kitchen and sit down at the keyboards and just play amazing things for us.

It was a shared interest between the two of you. But did you also talk about music? And listen to other musical things together?

We talked about music. Particularly, he knew that my expertise was in classical music. One of the things that Doktor LaVey would do is that we'd sort of hang around and talk until very early in the morning. Then we'd go to bed, and then we would say, "Well, later on when we all wake up, we'll all get back together again." But sometimes I would hear that he would sneak down to the kitchen while we were all supposed to be asleep, and he'd practice things. When I was there he'd be practicing Wagner and Liszt and Beethoven, because he knew I liked those composers. He really wanted to satisfy me and show me that he knew them and could play them with the sort of gusto that he brought to the Tin Pan Alley tunes and other old popular songs that he'd discover and would want to play. That was so sweet of him: that he really felt that much of a kinship.

We would talk about those composers: Sousa and his marches, Strauss and his waltzes, and then the other Strauss and his tone poems; it would be a really wide-ranging discussion of all kinds of music. He had a lot of facility with so many things. The first thing that he played for us was the *Danse Macabre* by Saint-Saëns, and his arrangement of it is unique and wild and wonderful. The way he played with the rhythms to it was also not exactly as it's in the score, but it was his own kind of quirky take on it that was really constantly reshaped. It would be surging forward and pulling back; he had really flexible tempi with it; it really worked and was quite amazing!

His renditions were always personal. He really could mix and match and put a personal touch to it.

Oh, absolutely. Anton LaVey was a consummate musician in that he would absorb the music and digest it and bring it back out through the lens of his own experience and feelings, so that you've got these passionate performances that were completely unique. Again, very flexible tempi, very bombastic; he could really stretch things out, and he would just make it broad and big, and then he could pull something way down, and be very quiet and sneaky about it, and he'd kind of look at you and smile. And then do other wild things, because he knew what you'd be expecting, if you knew the piece. He'd kind of play with it in ways that you wouldn't expect. Then he'd give you a big smile; we'd just have a blast; it was so much fun. He loved to show off.

What were your impressions after the first "kitchen experience?"

It was fascinating that he played for us so quickly when we went out to visit the very first time. We went back to his home and talked until three or four in the morning, and it was when we went back that he was ready to regale us with all of his musical abilities. I'd seen the pictures in the *Washington Post* article that Walt Harrington had done; you saw him at the keyboard. To actually have him there, playing and bringing it alive, was fantastic. It was pretty loud, and he had the foot pedals for the synthesizers, too, and he would just be very Doctor Phibes-y, you know: he'd be swooping his hands down to really get into, and make it like the "Phantom of the Organ." Peggy has a really amazing memory for lyrics for songs, so he'd play popular songs that she'd know the lyrics for that were kind of old and weird. So he engaged us both very purposefully, and in a way that he knew would charm us. He was always a charmer. His lesser magic skills were so operative through his musical performance. That was a very powerful aspect of his personality. That is something I truly miss.

In what way would you say that music is a magical tool or language?

I see music as the art form that communicates directly with your emotions. It is an emotional journey, even though it is also an intellectual one in an architectural form. Especially in classical music, you have very elaborate forms that one can follow in the structure. Music can be something that is very architectural, in that it could represent a small, jewel-like structure, or it could be something like a cathedral or a skyscraper for people who think about it that way. Anton LaVey under-stood that, and he understood that that was something that interested me as well. So we both would discuss how that kind of magic of music was powerful, that it could really reach in and touch your emotions.

He would talk about the suicide songs, such as "Gloomy Sunday"; there would be chord progressions that could be really affective of one's emotion. Either it might be cathartic or it could lock somebody into emotions that they are surprised that they get stuck in; it's such a direct touch. That kind of power he found when he used to play in The Lost Weekend.* People would be there for whatever they're trying to forget; they're drinking, they're having fun, they might be miserable. He would basically play different tunes to see whether he could push them into maybe more joyous or more morose states. It was this experiment that he would really test and see how people behaved when different music and different chord progressions were played at them, and he found some fascinating results. It was totally a laboratory for him to work that way.

How would you say that his playing in bars and clubs in the 1950s and 1960s influenced the philosophy?

Anton LaVey was always observing the human animal in whatever cir-cumstances he could possibly do that in. When he was younger and he did some circus work; when he worked with the big cats and saw how people reacted to them; and then when he played for circus performers; and then later more freelance kinds of gigs for people and at nightclubs, he found that humans were always very carnal. They're very reactive. The kind of idealism of music could make them feel that way, but it would be something that was more artificial and, with a lot of peo-ple, placed upon them; they were being manipulated; their emotional streams could be very easily manipulated.

So seeing how the human animal could be toyed with in some ways, or given catharsis, and given actual cures, or inspiration—that became

---

*A bar in San Francisco where Anton LaVey played the organ.

part of the way his philosophy worked. Understanding how ritual can work as catharsis, because music for him was his ritual.

He later brought in the idea of all the formal ritual trappings that other religions had, when he had decided to create something that was a religion. But for him, whenever he did ritual in his house, the music was one of the most important aspects; that informed everything that he did. His design sense, how he learned things from Mortensen and his ideas of how space—negative and positive—would affect something aesthetic. LaVey felt that that could be applied to a larger aspect of human consciousness, and music certainly does that too. So all of these aspects totally percolated together to be the foundation of Satanism.

Did you ever get the feeling that he wanted to compose more music himself?

I think that for Anton LaVey, composition was not a primary concern. He really enjoyed what people had done and how he could interpret their music. He did do a couple of pieces, but basically because he had some ideas, he felt, "You know, these are good, I like them, I'm going to put them down and have fun with them." But most of the time he was aware of this wealth of music that was forgotten or wouldn't be interpreted in the way that he would do it. He was so happy to just take something old, because already, this stuff had cues in people. These were signs that he could pull out: like the sign for this and the sign for that, this chord progression, these words. He felt that that was the magic: taking things that people might have had in their deeper consciousness. He could weave that all together in such a way that it would impact people in really fantastic fashion. He didn't really have the need to do a lot of original composition; finding actually obscure things and reviving them in his own unique way really followed that impulse in him. Whereas for me, I'd be looking, trying to write something fresh. He was more like, "I'm going to take something that nobody remembers and I'm going to play that in a way that nobody ever would." I think that was how his genius manifested.

Do you think that LaVey played alone a lot, or do you think that he actually needed an audience?

I know that he would certainly practice alone to work out the ways, and his fingerings. Because he had really unusual fingerings of things; they weren't what you would consider the standard that they'd teach you if you had a keyboard teacher. His fingers were long, but they were fat, you know, kind of sausagey. So he couldn't do a lot of typical fingerings for things. He always had his own unique way of doing it, which, again, I'd watch and go like, "Whoa!"

So I think he spent a lot of time working that out on his own; that was part of his way of gestating the pieces. I think he'd really think about them; it wasn't something that he'd just completely do off the top of his head. I think his interpretations were very well honed. He would spend a lot of time, especially with his synthesizers, because he could create so many different orchestral timbres.

He would say, "I want this to sound like this shabby band that's at this club in this year. And by the way, the percussionist is kind of a drunk, and the clarinetist is pissed off." He would try to make these instrumental sounds. He'd tweak the patches on the synthesizers so that they really had unusual aspects to them; they were definitely not something just to be pretty or typical. Then he'd play this whole thing, because he'd have a kind of fantasy in his head about who was actually performing. He was pretending to be this ensemble with the way he performed it, which is kind of an amazing thing. Because . . . who does that?

It was really a unique concept that he would indulge in when he would do this. When he had his audience he would be so pleased if you caught on to all these things that he'd be doing. He'd play little funny bits, like some little licks on a clarinet or the snare drum, and it would be kind of "off," because it's that time of night, and the guy's really had one too many, and he's not really quite keeping up with the rest.

He was conjuring so much. It wasn't just playing a song or a piece of classical music; he was conjuring this whole almost cinematic or literary experience of where people were. And then afterward you'd discuss that with him, and he'd kind of want to see what you caught out of what he did, and then he would just be happy to go on, and then do a different one. He would conjure something else; a whole other time frame, some moment and some fantasy of what might have been going on, and who might have been involved.

It was really a ritual for him in that sense of creating a time out of time, and a unique space, where things are happening that were magical, and there were various personalities melding and blending and dancing and fighting and making love in all of these musical ways he depicted. It was really extraordinary.

Indeed. I'm thinking of it like he was creating these inner total environments, that were sort of immersed with, perhaps not necessarily ECI, but definitely something emotional. He was like a sampler. He went back in time and could sample stuff that he had experienced.

Yeah, he would be pulling memories. But also it was raw material, because he would try to recreate something he might have experienced, but then what he would do is try to come up with something new. It's like being a novelist. You might have experienced different people, and those are characters, and you're going to meld them into these new characters; you're going to create a new plot for them, and then see what they do with each other. I think sometimes his creativity would be, as he was playing, running through his head. New plots would occur to him, so that would influence the way he played things. For the most part, he wouldn't play things the same multiple times.

Later, one of the things that Anton LaVey liked to do was have his friends sing with him. Blanche had done singing with him, and Nick Bougas had done singing with him, and he knew Peggy and I could sing, so he insisted that we did, too. Peggy sang some popular songs. At one point he played Beethoven's Ninth Symphony, the "Ode to Joy," which I sang in German for him. He was so thrilled to be playing that, and I was singing along. And then we did "Stout Hearted Men," and I actually prepared that before we came; I kind of took the lyrics and tweaked them a little.

Plate 1. Carl Abrahamsson visiting Anton LaVey in San Francisco, 1991.
Photo by Blanche Barton.

Plate 2. Anton LaVey and Blanche Barton in the Black House, San Francisco, 1989.
Photo by Carl Abrahamsson.

Plate 3. Blanche Barton in Merano, Italy, 2019.
Photo by Carl Abrahamsson.

Plate 4. Current heads of the Church of Satan, Peter Gilmore and Peggy Nadramia, in front of the infamous Hell Hole thrill ride at Coney Island, New York City, 1993. The ride was decommissioned after a freak accident in 1995.
Photo by Carl Abrahamsson.

Plate 5. Anton LaVey surrounded by books during a late night visit to the Black House, San Francisco, 1989.
Photo by Carl Abrahamsson.

Plate 6. Peter Gilmore and Peggy Nadramia at home in
Poughkeepsie, New York, 2018.

Photo by Carl Abrahamsson.

Plate 7. Peter Gilmore in Poughkeepsie, New York, 2018.
Photo by Carl Abrahamsson.

Plate 8. Carl Abrahamsson in front of the Hell Hole ride
at Coney Island, New York City, 1993.
Photo by Peter Gilmore.

Plate 9. Film director Beatrice Eggers with Anton LaVey
and Carl Abrahamsson at the Black House, 1991.

Photo by Blanche Barton.

We did it three times, and each time his accompaniment was completely different.

The funny thing with that was that he didn't want you to sing well or professional; he wanted you to feel world weary and worn. We were there for, I guess it was maybe a week, or a week and a half, and we were staying in the house. This was our last night, and we actually didn't go to bed; we were just going to take a cab to the airport that morning, and everything was packed and ready to go. Then, in the wee hours of the morning, he says, "Okay, now it's time to do the songs." And we were like, "Oh great, we've been up all night, every night, for like a week and a half, and now we have to do this?" He was chuckling.

So we did it. You felt a little strained, a little rough, but for him that was the kind of character he wanted. He didn't want somebody to come in and be professional. I had done something like that with him, and that's not what he wanted. He wanted something a little more world weary, or pushed, or forced, or just something in which there was another story going on. He always wanted to have that sense that there's some other story.

We did three takes of "Stout Hearted Men." But that kind of shows this sort of magic that he had, the wild arrangement that he came up with. I'm hanging on for dear life, because he's getting louder and louder and doing different things every time around. We had plans on doing so many more things, but he passed away, and we never got to it.

How would you describe his sense of humor?

Anton LaVey's sense of humor is something that is very sly and canny, because it's based on a real thorough understanding of human behavior. He found the foibles of humanity something to laugh at. Instead of something to be frustrated at and something to get angry with, which are expected reactions, he would try to find them to be things to use for his own amusement, because he could manipulate people and enjoyed doing that.

Sometimes when people would do stupid things, he would want to make them do something even more stupid, and then enjoy laughing at them. That was his way of readjusting the balance of experience; his sense of justice was one that was very finely honed. And he also just liked to enjoy himself. He liked to tease people—especially pompous people—and if anybody was all stuck up or silly or pretentious, he would always throw something at them.

He said he used to do that even to his earlier Church of Satan members. He brought this guy in once who was like a short-order cook at a diner. He made hamburgers—they were kind of greasy—but he called them "hamboogers," and he talked kind of funny; he was an odd character. So Doktor brought him into one of their evenings, when people were hanging around the house, and he kind of presented him as this sage—this guy was just a short-order cook, and barely that. He would be talking about the hamboogers, and how he made them, and then everybody was sitting around, going, "Why is this guy here, and is there some significance to this? Oh, this must be symbolic of something."

Doktor would just sit back there and be kind of chuckling, while this guy is just prattling on about his greasy hamboogers, with everybody sitting around thinking there's some kind of occult meaning to this. The occult meaning was that Doktor LaVey was enjoying the hell out of teasing them. So that's Doktor LaVey's sense of humor!

I think he talks about that in Speak of the Devil, *also, where you not only create justice; you also have fun and mock at the same time.*

Exactly. Well, mockery is always the Devil's game, and he enjoyed doing that. When people would make themselves into his enemy, he would often have a lot of fun mocking them. He used to send us faxes with some really funny things on them. He'd make cartoons of people that were really devastating, and he'd give them crazy titles. This thing would come through the fax machine: "What the hell is this?" It would be something like that. It was just him, sitting around a little pissed off at somebody, so he'd scribble something out. He did that for years. That was one of his ways of working off his annoyance with people.

That would make him feel much better. He had captured and dealt with them in a way that was appropriate. He felt that there would be a lot of people who had opinions about him, and they'd be people that he didn't care about and that his life didn't really impact, and he'd always feel like, "Why the hell are they focusing on me? What is bringing this on? I don't have anything to do with them, I don't care about them, why are they trying to rain on my parade in some way or another?" So he would release his frustrations and annoyance of them through this kind of humorist sensibility.

Did LaVey change how you looked at magic as a potentially transformative tool?

Anton LaVey is the one who gave me the idea of magic as something other than stage magic. I didn't believe in, you know, the "magic-y" kind of hocus-pocus stuff. I always thought that was just fictional and fun. Using magic as a tool to manipulate myself and others was a concept that directly came from Anton LaVey—in his writings and then in conversation with him. There were so many ways of approaching my creativity, and my interactions with people, that could be defined as magic, and it certainly became more productive and effective when looked at in that sense. I completely owe that to him and his perspectives. That was why I felt his brilliance was something that I could be interested in, because he brought this to me that was something very new in my way of approaching things. These were great tools that enhanced my way of doing almost everything that I do, and to him I'm very beholden for that wonderful revelation.

In my opinion, one of the key things that made LaVey unique was his active integration of his own life experience into fields that are traditionally "established" and that newcomers simply adapt to (occultism, philosophy, religion, etc.). What are your thoughts on why this was? How would you define the character traits that made him such a creative developer?

Anton LaVey was raised in a secular Jewish family, one that left behind old-world traditions of dress and observance to become Americanized, and part of that background was an encouragement of freethinking, of valuing the arts, sciences, and education. James Yaffe's *The American Jews* was put on the Church of Satan's reading list so that one could see how a religious group evolved into an ethnic group that would be seen by other groups to hold certain valuations and aesthetics—what Doktor thought might be the path forward for Satanism in the centuries to come.

His parents encouraged his youthful attempts at drawing and music making, and they cultivated his voracious curiosity, which was fulfilled by reading copious and diverse books. He also was a bit of a psychologist and anthropologist as, through firsthand observations of the people with whom he interacted, he began to ponder what motivated their behaviors. Some articles have called him a "junkyard scholar" while one might more elegantly refer to him as an autodidact. But he was never coached to separate or denigrate his own observations and experiences from those enshrined in books; to him all of what he took was fuel for his evolving perspectives on what it means to be a human animal.

On the same topic: one of the quintessential traits was his active integration of pop culture that had been forgotten or discarded, and thereby contained a force that could be tapped into and used. Do you have any memories of songs, films, et cetera, that he displayed for you as being such magical works? Have you woven in similar explorations and practices in your own life?

Doktor knew my musical focus was on classical music, so our discussions concerned composers we both enjoyed—Liszt, Beethoven, Berlioz, Wagner, Sousa—and I would bring to him composers that he might not have explored to the extent I had, such as Mahler, Bruckner, and Shostakovich. The works of these masters were magical in their skilled evocations of such a broad range of human emotions and aspirations. We both enjoyed a wide range of films, so we'd watch what he had in his VHS collection during our visits.

We similarly enjoyed crime films for how they dealt with human desire and how far some desperate people might go to fulfill their needs beyond societal boundaries, so we spoke about *Key Largo* and *Murder, Inc.,* amongst others. Peggy and I had not seen *The Gangster* from 1947, wherein Barry Sullivan's character, Shubunka, contends against the hostile world around him, only to be gunned down in the rainfall to expire in the gutter. We enjoyed viewing that in the Purple Parlor, and Doktor expressed how he felt there was a sense of Luciferian grandeur to Shubunka, who did not cease in his struggle, essentially trying to reign in the hell that his life presented to him.

For me, the pop culture of science fiction and horror films have played deeply in my ruminations, with Godzilla becoming a powerful icon for me from my youngest days. This avatar of conscious natural forces that shows man's folly and insignificance has always been an essential idol for me. Of course, the classic monsters—Dracula, Frankenstein and his creature, the Wolfman, the Creature from the Black Lagoon— they were always sympathetic outsiders with whom I could identify, as each had varied characteristics setting themselves apart from the masses who feared them.

When it comes to creativity, I get the impression that LaVey was happiest when playing his tunes, telling his stories, and writing his essays; that is, being immersed in his own expressions that he mastered so well. But these usually also require a second party: a listener, a reader. Did you ever get the impression that he expressed himself mainly to have that second party, or was the expression in itself, for himself, the most important aspect?

Doktor enjoyed being a showman, but he preferred to have a discerning audience. I think he thoroughly enjoyed exercising his abilities to create, or interpret, as so much of the music he played was not of his own composition, and he delighted in practicing as a means to evolve unique performances. That process was a laboratory for arranging the sounds to suit what he wanted to capture—often offbeat ensembles fulfilling a narrative impulse to his conceptualizations. He might feel he was replicating the seedy band playing for an Elks Lodge event, or the jaded, tired, and possibly inebriated musicians at a strip club in the wee hours of the morning. His writings were intended to be published and read, though some of what he crafted took years to reach people. He seemed to revel in the process but also enjoyed the communication of what arose through his efforts to those he deemed worthy of grasping and enjoying what he had wrought.

Can you see any similarities between LaVey and other notable creative people at the time (regardless of their particular expressions or views)? Meaning, would you say there was something distinctly zeitgeistish about him?

The general tenor of the times was to question prior social structures and authorities in a search for greater liberty and diversity, so LaVey was comfortable with the opportunities such an evolutionary time offered. I always get the sense that he saw very little of anything going on that he would endorse or support fully, hence his drive to offer something that he'd personally find satisfying, and then see if others might embrace and find fulfillment in the unique perspective he offered. There was an occult explosion, as some have termed that period, but Doktor was repulsed by the neo-witchcraft figureheads and what he saw as essentially just a relabeled form of Christian values but with Lunar Goddesses and Horned Gods displacing Jesus. He despised the hippies and the rampant drug culture—he felt that one didn't need substances to expand one's consciousness, that willpower and intelligence alone would be sufficient. In fact, he felt that experiences that were had using such means were not genuine, but illusory, something for dropouts, not the sorcerers and sorceresses he felt to be his kindred.

That it was a time of asking questions and reviewing past thought edifices served him well, but his guiding sensibility was to revivify the sense of the earlier romantics who embraced Satan as the avatar of self-direction and iconoclasm—the one to inspire one to be one's own savior and not be beholden to others. Hence his movement was not like the religious cults that arose then, with autocratic gurus enslaving their sheeplike disciples. That, he noted, was just Christianity repackaged, so uniquely, he embraced Satan as the archetype for what he felt was a healthy stance in dealing with the turbulent societal currents.

Inside the Black House, which was your favorite room, and why?

I enjoyed the entire house, with the various rooms being inspirational when partaking of time therein for differing purposes. The Purple Parlor was an essential space for conversation; watching films; and discussing the past, present, and future of the Church of Satan. Its walls were filled with significant books, many replicating my own collection, but with others of tantalizing rarity. The keyboard corner in the kitchen was a performance space, and I was encouraged to use the keyboards when visiting, so it was where music was played, voices raised in song, and thus an invigorating studio for musical magic.

The Ritual Chamber was deliciously intense, a place to focus and feel the timelessness of Satanism, for the shades of past thinkers and the cultural stream of diabolism in human endeavors presented there offered a view of the deep past. It sparked our in-the-moment greater magic, offering vistas of those to come who would be moved via resonance with the vibrations we set in motion in that unhallowed room.

The Den of Iniquity, with its odd bathroom—the shower stall filled with disjointed mannequin parts, its wall-mounted urinal and toilet perched on about-to-give-way flooring—was perhaps the most redolent space of all. The LaVey-crafted figures of "damned souls" inhabited what was a hellish reflection of the human condition, also a palace for earthy music, and for our female companions to dance sensually. All of these chambers conjured reflection and spoke to us, bidding one to stay in their embrace, while the mad throngs in the outside world moved on to their sorry fates.

Were there any quirks or habits that you found odd in LaVey? Meaning, unexpected expressions of moralisms that might have seemed un-Satanic

and perhaps stemmed from the times or the religion he grew up in?
Things you sort of didn't quite see coming?

Actually, no, none at all. He was the man I expected from the portrait he painted of himself in his writing. He enjoyed using what some consider blasphemous by emphatically saying "Jesus Christ!" in a way that you knew was meant ironically—there was always a twinkle in his eyes when he'd spit out that name.

In the LaVeyan encouragement of fetishizing objects and environments (working with ECI, creating total environments, for instance), it's not that far-fetched to talk about an ensouling of these objects (or spaces) that one has an intimate relationship with. Did he ever give the impression that he felt that way about human beings? Meaning, that he could feel OK with using the word soul *or* ensouled *or* spirit *or* spirited *when talking about humans? I guess the extension of this question is whether you ever saw signs of him not being a 100 percent strict materialist?*

He would speak of an "essence" or "quintessence" when addressing the idea of intangible aspects of people and places. As musicians, we both shared the metaphor of seeing ideas functioning like fundamental tones on which other ideas arose as overtones. Those who are perceptive might experience more of them than others. We spoke of how one's consciousness could be sensitive to people who have passed, and that, from our deepest consciousness and memories, we might conjure them subjectively for contemplation, but not that any sort of independent soul or spirit existed apart from the one doing the contemplating.

He handed me the original printing of Fritscher's *Popular Witchcraft,* so that I could read his interview, wherein he spoke of an externalized projection of Satan based on one's own needs and sensibilities. We discussed that idea, of an externalized godhead that is self-sourced, and I mentioned how I found that to be one of the most radical ideas in his formulating of Satanism—that such phenomena arose from those having the experience, so were varied but were not independent spiritual entities, was a new vista in religious thinking. So, to me, he always affirmed that there was nothing outside of nature, but that nature itself was quite complex and a long way from being completely understood, so that examining experiences and happenings that were atypical—supernormal—was part of keeping one's skepticism intact and one's mind open.

Did you ever feel that LaVey put on a show at times because he felt it was expected of him rather than because he was genuinely in the mood himself?

He was an old hand at being in the spotlight, and now that I am as well, I see that at times one might have to take the stage, even when tired, but that "the show must go on," and we both fortunately have the chops to offer our audiences what they came to see. It is not a question of mood, but of engaging the processes one has mastered.

Did you perceive him as being sensitive to what others thought or felt about him?

He certainly was aware of what critics and detractors expressed about him, and he could become quite vitriolic about what he considered to be willful misperceptions and misrepresentations of his actual personal history, his opinions, his concepts. But he also didn't want blind adulation. He appreciated being given the approval of those who were fellow connoisseurs of whatever subject, object, or activity was under consideration.

Speculative question: Do you think there was something or some things that he would have done differently in his life, had he had the chance?

He mused about having a different life, wherein he wasn't a public figure, but simply pursued his interests in the company of fellow aficionados. But he also saw, once he threw down the gauntlet of taking on the cause of Satan as an ensign of liberty, that there was somewhat of a destiny that he'd set in motion.

You already had a distinct musical taste and interest, which has since grown even more. Were there any composers or pieces of music that LaVey opened your ears/mind to? And vice versa?

His devotion to the Tin Pan Alley composers, in that they could reflect quite well the lyrics they selected both melodically and harmonically with deft instrumental arrangements, showed me that there was a stream of popular music that had subtle inflections. Most popular music I find simplistic, so he pointed out songs and their creators that had more to offer for my own musical perspective.

We both shared an interest in Russian composers, though I knew more from the Soviet era than did he, so I mentioned pieces I knew he'd enjoy—less popularly known works by Prokofiev, Shostakovich, Khachaturian, and their fellows. And he knew little of Bruckner but responded well to a piece of mine that was a pastiche of that Viennese maestro's work, and I brought more of the scores of Bernard Herrmann and Jerry Goldsmith to his attention, as I cherished music they'd written for some films Doktor had not yet seen.

Were there any other expressions that were massively influential for you, such as films, art, or books he showed you and Peggy, that then became influential?

We weren't that young when we first met Doktor, and what made us all simpatico is that we had seen many of the same films, art, and photography and read the same books and reacted in a similar way, independently. Reading *The Satanic Bible* at a young age led me to read about occultism and the history of witchcraft and chronicles regarding those who persecuted "witches," none of which had been a focus for me beforehand. But so much in that book seemed like it came from a kindred consciousness, that it was more a sense of knowing that another compatriot was "out there," and that was an exciting thought!

Becoming involved in CoS, and eventually leading the organization is a big responsibility, and a visible one. How did your family react along the way?

My family members had always seen me as rather an oddball. They knew I was intelligent, and I was a responsible person, so they had no worries. I was bored with school and pursued my own studies, but it was easy for me to take tests and do the required school assignments, which to me was often just child's play. So when I read *The Satanic Bible* and affirmed that I was a Satanist, it was another part of the offbeat progression that was always mine. I never sought anyone's approval, and to my good fortune, nobody in my family tried to impose their thinking, beliefs, or values upon me, so there really has never been any conflict between me and my family.

11

MITCH HOROWITZ

Mitch Horowitz, NYC, 2018.
Photo by Carl Abrahamsson.

"The price of using the term is being misunderstood, but the payment of using the term is that it's uncorrupted."

American scholar Mitch Horowitz is the author of the best-selling books *Occult America*, *The Miracle Club*, *One Simple Idea*, and *Awakened Mind*.

Where would you place LaVey in this bigger picture of occultism in America?

I think one of the great tributes to LaVey is that it's actually very difficult to place him within the larger mosaic of occultism in America. In fact, one my regrets—perhaps my only regret—in writing *Occult America* is that I did not include LaVey in the book. At that time, I made the mistake of feeling that LaVey was more of a showman, a media figure, a performance artist, and less a purveyor of occult philosophy. I was wrong. That would be one of the very few things I would change in the book if I could go back. In fact, I expect that I'll probably issue a future edition where I may have a new afterword, for example, paying tribute to Anton.

He is so difficult to fit into the pastiche of occultism in America, because he didn't really belong to any clear, identifiable, intellectual family tree. He created his own family tree, in a sense. He reached backward to primeval philosophy; he reimagined the idea of the Satanic in a way that had historical integrity but was also new, I think, in terms of the Western, modern, media-saturated world. He embraced aspects of carny culture, he embraced aspects of performance culture, he embraced aspects of the horror movie and the Gothic cultures, and he brought his own aesthetic sensibility to it all and wrapped it up in this neat, wonderful infernal package.

He created his own persona, his own philosophy, his own perspective. All of it had some relation to things that had come before. I think he has some aesthetic relation to Aleister Crowley; I think he has some ethical relation to Ayn Rand and objectivism; he has a connection to the countertradition of Satanism as it has been misunderstood and expressed by romantic and rebellious figures throughout history. He has a connection to all of those wellsprings, but what he created was entirely his own. He's one of the very few people, I think, who emerged on the late twentieth century scene, who created his own background persona, rule book, philosophy.

What Anton did with the Church of Satan and *The Satanic Bible* was in so many ways unprecedented, and that's why it's very difficult to plug Anton into any category. As soon as you say, "Well, he belongs to ceremonial magic . . ." there are too many differences. As soon as you say, "Well, he's objectivism with pentagrams . . ." he was so much more than that. As soon as you say, "Well, you know, Anton was kind of a performance artist . . ." well, he was also a social thinker, he was also an occult thinker, he was also an esoteric thinker.

There's no category that will hold him, so he has always remained this outsider in the American occult scene; he's almost this satellite off on its own, revolving around what's going on, drawing in other people and ideas and movements. But he was very much, it seems to me, a freestanding figure—very unclassifiable, very difficult to categorize—which in a way is the ultimate tribute to what he accomplished.

By his own will or design he brought in the symbol of Satan. How do you look at the S-word? Was that in a way a smart thing to use, or was it not?

There's a lot to unpack there: Is the *S*-word a barrier, does it block communication, does it facilitate communication? Ultimately, I believe Anton was right to use the term *Satan* and to deem his organization and his literature Satanic in nature, and the reason is this: first of all, one must never discount that Anton was a genius at communication, and he knew how to get attention. If he had simply used terms such as the *dark side* or the *left-hand path,* everybody would have gone to sleep.

But when a bald-headed man with a goatee and a cape comes on the scene and uses the word *Satan,* people pay attention. Anton knew how to get people to pay attention, but that was only the cracking open of the door, it seems to me. I think he made use of that term in a way that had cultural integrity, because [of] the reason that throughout human history, across all different cultures, we have these different myths of an opposing force, an upending force, a rebellious force, a force that goes against the grain, a force of ultimate nonconformity.

Many of these different ideas of foreign energies, outsider energies, and upside-down energies got grouped in one way or another under the label of the Satanic in the West. There are, of course, other terms in the Veda cultures and in the East and so on, but we, as a human species, have in common this basic myth of an opposing force.

Anton performed a brilliant and penetrating resurrection of this idea, as one that wasn't evil or maleficent in any traditional sense, but was an idea that embodies the energies of the rebel, the revolutionary, the romantic, the usurper, and even the emancipator. You can certainly make a reading of the serpent in the garden in the book of Genesis as being Eve's emancipator. Why was a tree erected in the garden that would give the individual universal insight, but the individual was told that "you must not eat from that tree"? It seems almost a cruel prank to play on humanity—a cruel cosmic prank—that the tree of knowledge is in our midst in so-called paradise, and yet we can't touch it. So how could it really be paradise? How can it be paradisiacal if you're blocked from attaining ultimate knowledge that's an arm's reach away? Something called the serpent comes along . . . was it Satan? Was it Eve's subconscious?

It was this universal spirit of opposition to prevailing power, opposition to conformity, opposition to arbitrary rule making or unjust authority. We, as a human species here in the West, came to call it the Satanic, and that's what Anton seized upon. It seems to me that Anton brought himself a great barrier in using that word, but also a great battering ram to blow open the doors of conformist attention, to get reporters and the media and college professors and social nags to pay attention to him, and he succeeded. I mean, here we are, talking about him decades after his death. We're not talking about his critics; we're talking about him, and for that reason I'm inspired to use the term *Satanic* myself, and to not run away from that term. I feel it's very important that we don't permit our critics to define for us what terms we use. I embrace such terms as Occult, New Age, ESP, Satanic . . . terms that run the gamut of disreputability but that have historical integrity, that mean something, that stand for something. I'm keenly aware that it's very difficult.

Several months ago I conducted a workshop, a talk, here in New York City, which I called "Satanism: The Dark Alternative," and everything was going just great. But one day I heard from a new marketing director at the venue where I was delivering the talk that people had been grumbling and complaining about it. There was one beloved astrologer, as she put it to me, who said she would disassociate from the center altogether if this talk were delivered. It's always disappointing, but I'm sure Anton would recognize it as a constant of human nature, that people who have the most to lose from clampdowns on free communication and free exploration are the very first ones to throw stones; they're *always* the first ones to throw stones.

You would think that the New Age folk, and the alternative spiritual culture, would be the ones running to my side saying, "Right on, you go for it, and when we get in trouble we know that you'll have our backs." I certainly would have their backs, but it turns out that this person and that person within the New Age culture were objecting, at least at this particular time and place. So the person said to me, probably in the spirit of compromise, "You have to change the title." I said, "I will not change the title, and if need be, I will cancel and I will do it somewhere else." Because I thought to myself: What do we have if we don't have the clarity of intention?

I wrote back that I would be giving a talk on the Satanic as a counter-tradition, as a tradition of usurpation, rebellion, nonconformity, and I explained that in the copy to the talk. I'm very capable of explaining that to whoever asks, but I don't feel that I should sanitize my message by using default terms, such as "the dark side." This term can be very easily misunderstood as entertainment; you know, we think of Darth Vader as coming from the dark side, or something Jungian in nature, such as the shadow side. I respect that body of work and thought very deeply, but that's not precisely what I'm talking about. If you use a term such as "the left-hand path," it's a perfectly good, serviceable term. It means something, but a lot of people simply don't know what that is. By the same token, a lot of people don't know what Satanism is either, and it does provoke, and it does push buttons. I'm not here to provoke for the sake of provocation itself, but I do feel that a person should stand up and very plainly state his accounts; state what he or she stands for.

One of my heroes here in America was the social activist Michael Harrington, who was a great socialist figure. Mike was a very charismatic, mainstream persona, and people would often say to him, "Mike, why do you use the term "socialist"? That term is poison here in America. Call yourself an economic democrat, call yourself something else; that term is a barrier to you." He would say, "Look, it's the truth, and all we have is the truth." I was always so proud of him for that, and again, people are still talking about Michael Harrington today; they're not necessarily talking about the people who said, "Mike, cool it." Those were the same voices who told Buddy Holly to not wear those funny glasses. I feel that one should never listen to those voices. The magnetic north of the herd is always the wrong direction.

Anton signaled that and signaled it with a sledgehammer, by using the term *Satanic*. He was doing it to be provocative, but what's wrong with being provocative? He stated, "You're going to take notice of me; I have a message." And sure enough: reporters, television journalists, and college professors did take notice of him. Anton's voice rose above the din, so I think he was right to use the term both as a provocation and for reasons of historical integrity.

I'm inspired to use the term today, and I do realize it can be a barrier. I have people, including people very close to me, who all the time ask me, "Are you a Satanist, do you worship Satan?" I answer them in the affirmative, but I say, "It means something different from the way you've framed your question." It's not difficult, it seems to me, to explain what that difference is. It's not difficult, and yet we are so conditioned to associate the Satanic with a kind of very commonly held conception of evil or maleficence, that as easy as it is to explain what this counter-tradition is about, people still have trouble getting their arms around it.

And yet, there's also no question in my mind that there are wonderful, wonderful kids growing up in the United States, in Europe, in other parts of the world who are just burning with the spirit of rebellion and nonconformity, and who feel that there is something Potemkin, something fake, something ersatz about this world of ours. They're trying to break through to something else, and for some of those kids or older people, when they hear that term Satanic, they feel they've found something; they feel they've found something pure, and something that's not compromised, and I think that's true.

So the price of using the term is being misunderstood, but the payment of using the term is that it's uncorrupted, it's pure; and it's so ironic because people think of it as corruption, and it's the ultimate uncorrupted term, because it will *never* be safe and sanitized by the corporate media; it will *never* be safe and sanitized by all the forces of consumerism that try to repackage rebellion for money. You can't touch this term. So in that sense, it's very pure; it has remained pure. It's untouchable, but that's what's kept it pure and uncorrupted.

What do you think LaVey's legacy will be?

It seems to me that LaVey's legacy, at this moment in time, has been the creation of a broadened space for us to think about human possibilities, and the energies and philosophies by which we want to define ourselves, and to which we can avail ourselves to find out a way in life; to gain power in life. For me, personally speaking, the greatest inspiration I've found in Anton's work is that he called out the spiritual culture, the religious culture, and the occult culture, and the alternative spiritual culture, and the culture of Wicca, witchcraft, neo-paganism.

He called out all these cultures, and he said to them, in effect, that what you're really seeking is power; what you're really seeking is a sense of personal agency in the world. You want to enact your wishes and your will in the world—artistically, commercially, sexually, in all the different ways that we participate in life. You, the individual, want to behave with agency. You're seeking power, and yet you thwart this search by hiding from it, hiding behind hypocrisies, by saying, "Thy will be done," when you really mean, "My will be done." You're really hoping that whatever higher power you're praying to has the same will; that his or her wishes run synonymously with your own. What you're really praying for is, "My will be done," and why not say that? Why not be frank about that? See what you find, see what you discover.

Anton was capable of seeing through New Age folk, witchcraft practitioners, alternative spiritual folk who would engage in spells and rituals and ceremonies and insist that this was white magic—as if there was something they had to juxtapose themselves to. Anton would say that white magic is just one more way of hiding from what you really want, which is power. I think Anton helped open me up to that in a way that felt very relaxing, ultimately, because suddenly there was this sense of honesty in the air, and that was helpful.

There's a British historian I like very much named Richard

Cavendish who wrote a book called *The Black Arts*. It's really, as far as I'm concerned, one of the great journalistic, historical classics in exploring the retinue of occult ideas and philosophies. He published it in 1967, roughly the same time of Anton's ascendency, and a lot of people approached Cavendish with the same complaints that they approached Anton with and said, "Why would you call your book *The Black Arts?* It just seems to return us to all the stereotypes we're trying to escape from," and also, "My style of magic isn't dark; I'm one of the good guys."

Cavendish prefigured these arguments, and he responded brilliantly in the book and said, "What I mean by black magic, essentially, is the assertion of one's will." Every magician thinks he or she is a so-called white magician; everyone thinks they're the good guy. It doesn't have to do with good guy or bad guy; it has to do with an honest reckoning of what your will is. Cavendish made the case in his book, I think very persuasively, that all of the magicians, going back to antiquity, up through the Renaissance era, up through the modern era, were really trying to figure out ways of harnessing energies to heighten personal agency, and he called that the black arts. He felt like, "Yes, I'm making a judgment call here that every magician, in a certain sense, is a black magician," insofar as wanting to summon powers that uplift the self; not that do someone else's will; not that do the will of the higher, so to speak, but do the will of the individual.

It seems to me that Cavendish and Anton and others have opened up a space for that discussion, and it has helped me in my own studies. I'm dedicated at this point in my search to the area of New Thought, or mind metaphysics, and this is—and has been for decades—a very hot question in the area of New Thought: the philosophy that thoughts are causative. Then of course people ask, "Well, whose thoughts? Am I a vessel for something higher? Am I enacting my own energies? Is my consciousness simply a metaphor for god? Whose thoughts are we talking about?"

I've talked about this in public, I've written about it, and I'll write about it more. Anton helped me bring a certain sense of relaxation into my own mystical studies, because I could come to grips with the fact, and speak frankly about the fact, that it is my will that I'm seeking to enact. That doesn't mean that I'm not part of a human community, and that I don't have obligations to other people. I have children; I have a family; I have coworkers; I have a pack, a tribe that I run with; and I do have obligations to those people, and I've written about that.

I wrote a piece called "Satan's Honor Roll" recently, where I talked about my perspective on Satanic ethics. I don't see myself as being or acting in isolation, and I do think there is a code—call it a code of honor if you like—that is very much in harmony with Satanic tradition, or in harmony with the left-hand path; I don't see myself as this isolated actor just behaving out there on his own. But at the same time, it has allowed me to speak and to think more clearly, more bluntly, more plainly, more honestly that my search is a search for personal agency—a search for personal power. The spiritual is part of that, and there are other things that are part of that, too.

My wish is to demonstrate excellence in my art, demonstrate excellence in other areas of life, to maintain my household intelligently, to manage finances intelligently. There's lots of things I want to do well, and my spiritual search is very much a part of that wish, that passion for power, for personal agency, the capacity to get things done in the world. An artist wants to complete his or her work with excellence; an artist wants his or her ideas or work to find a constituency, to find an audience.

We're all searching for that, and Anton, I think, gave us a language to express that, to marry that to the inner search, to the spiritual search, or the mystical search, however you want to put it. He allowed the individual to seek and to self-seek while employing mythical objects, terms, rituals, ceremony, aesthetics, and the feeling that I could be a part of something greater; I could be a part of something bigger than just myself, while still seeking personal agency. He gave me that language, he gave me that permission, he gave me that opening.

So at this moment in time, I think that's his greatest legacy. His legacy will be different for different people, but for me personally, he married the language of self-seeking to the search, whether you define it as a search for meaning, or an inner search, or a mystical search. Whatever language you want to attach to that, he revealed the connection between power seeking and the individual search, and that, for me, has been a real opening.

12

BOB JOHNSON

Bob Johnson, Poughkeepsie, New York, 2018.
Photo by Carl Abrahamsson.

"He gave America the right to pleasure."

Bob Johnson is a writer, editor, and publisher. Among his works is
The Satanic Warlock (2016).

How did you first hear about Anton LaVey?

Well, I guess my very first recollection of that, and it was a long time
ago, was probably when I was maybe thirteen or fourteen years old,
and I discovered *The Satanic Bible*. To me it was, "Who is this man,
where did he come from, and how did he get the balls to write such
a blasphemous, incredible work?" That was my first notice of Doktor
LaVey. Then followed a little bit of research, which today would be
simple doing on the internet. But it was quite difficult: trying to find
publications that he was involved with and where he was interviewed.
Fortunately, my penchant for men's magazines led me somewhere.
Those were really the only magazines that would kind of take him seriously; except for maybe, I think it was *Look* magazine or *Life* that did a
cover story on him. I was following the bits of information that I could
find on Doktor LaVey as much as I could.

What attracted you to it?

Any religion that has naked girls as altars is 100 percent for me. It's that combination of carnal enjoyment, indulgence without being obsessive. He codified the way I think that many people—probably most people—actually live but won't admit it. He codified that in this concise, slim book and wrapped it all around with occult mystery; it was an intoxicating combination. Probably like most men, or like most people who are Satanists, we gravitated to the dark side, to the macabre, to the esoteric, to the mysterious in all ways when we were young—through comic books, through movies, through Broadway shows, through music. It's innate, that interest in the macabre, and Doktor took that and made a religion out of it. It was something that resonated amazingly with me, and many of the people I knew were interested in things like that. I didn't know why; anything that had bats and vampires and witches . . . I remember Disney's *Fantasia,* the *Night on Bald Mountain,* and the gargoyles. . . . That was my favorite part of the whole thing.

How did you first come into contact with him?

Over the years, that interest in LaVey and the Church of Satan grew and grew and grew, and it was always in the back of my mind. I dog-eared the original copy of the book I had and would refer to it all the time. I knew I was a de facto Satanist whether I joined or not; I knew that was the path to take; everything just felt so right.

I was the editorial director of a group of men's magazines: *High Society* and *Cherie* and even *Playgirl* for women, and a bunch more. That kind of fits with everything. I decided that I wanted to do a feature story on Doktor, so I wrote a note to the P.O. box in San Francisco. They responded, and then I met Peter in New York, and we chatted quite a bit. I was vetted to do an interview, and apparently they liked what they heard and saw, and they granted me the interview.

So I get the date settled, and I get on a plane to San Francisco from New York. I get to the airport, and I grab a cab, and I give him the address of Doktor's house. He's an African-American cab driver, and he says, "Are you sure you want to go here?" I say, "Yeah." We get to the house. I barely shut the door and gave him money and he was out of there. He knew Doktor's house; he knew the Black House, and he knew what LaVey was up to. That was kind of funny. I got out, and I'm just standing there. I couldn't figure out how to get into the house, but Doktor's domo came out and greeted me and brought me into the house.

There I met Blanche and sat in the little anteroom for a while and absorbed everything. I was just floored. After a while Doktor came out, very charming, larger than life, looked at me, and said, "Robert Johnson . . . I like that name; one of my best friends was named Robert Johnson." We just hit it off right off the bat, and we started chatting about everything under the sun, and we were talking way into the wee hours until we decided we wanted to grab something to eat. Sure enough, we went to Olive Garden of all places, which happened to be one of Doktor's favorite haunts.

The charmer that he was, he loved to flirt with the waitresses and do his little tricks and play his little games. He would give them different names. He would say, "Oh, I'm Joe Blow." They would say, "Party of Joe Blow!" And he'd say, "No, we've been waiting here, I'm Gary Green." Then they'd say, "Gary Green?" And he would go, "No, what are you talking about?" This would go on three or four times; it was very funny. So that was the original meeting with Doktor. We discussed literature and music and film and the Church, and he played some music for me. It was a fascinating evening.

What would you say are the greatest contributions from him in terms of impact on your life?

He validated the idea that a religion can be fun; a religion can be uplifting and without guilt, and celebratory without penance. That's an amazing thing, to say, "Yes, my religion is Satanism, and it's because I love life, and I live every minute of life, and this is where it is, and we only get one time around." For all of those with whom the dark side, the dark inertia, resonates, that was wonderful, because our tribe can relate to all the gothic horror, and the mystery, and the occult—although not in the occultnik sense—but the occult itself, the hidden. I think all of us at some time were interested in religion, and mystery schools, and things like that. As a matter of fact, I think occult interest is the flip side of religion. It really is. I mean standard religion is supernatural, and the occult is also supernatural. It's just the flip side of that; it depends on how you perceive it. Doktor really gave the world this new way of thinking, without the shame and guilt.

Is there any idea or concept that's still very special or relevant for you in your life?

Having been a Satanist and been involved with Satanism for so many years now, the culmination of that—the pinnacle, if you will—was my being able to write *The Satanic Warlock,* which is now part of the canon. Even in my wildest dreams I never thought that would happen, but it did. As a matter of fact, when I did meet with Doktor LaVey that time, I said to him, "Why is there not a counterpart to *The Compleat Witch*?" or *The Satanic Witch,* as it became later. He replied, "Well, no one has decided to write it. Why don't you write it?" In 2016, around the time of the Church of Satan fiftieth anniversary, I said to Magus Gilmore and Magistra Nadramia, "I'm thinking I might . . . somebody should write *The Satanic Warlock;* what do you think?" They said, "Yeah, you!" That sealed the deal. I said, "Okay, this is my calling, this is my raison d'être, this is what I'm supposed to be doing now." I sat down, and I did it. It is a primer, and it's by no means all-encompassing. It's not what Doktor LaVey did, but it is an extension of what he did, as *The Compleat Witch* was, as *The Satanic Rituals* was, as Magus Gilmore's book *The Satanic Scriptures* is; they're all extensions of *The Satanic Bible.*

If you think back to that moment that you just told me about, do you see it as just a kind of nice gesture on his part, or could you see it as some kind of seed sowing on a conscious level from his side?

That's an interesting question. Maybe. You know, I don't want to be so brash as to say, "Well, Doktor saw something in me that said I should write the book," but I hope so. Maybe that magic was there, you know, and it just took some years to build; to really understand and study. To study the human animal as he did, and know it so well. My speaking with many, many male members of the Church of Satan, and listening to their problems and their successes and their relationships, and how they walk in the world, and so on and so on and so on, had given me the stuff: the background. I had subconsciously, unconsciously, absorbed all of those things, to be able to sit down and write the book in a relatively short time. I think it took me about a year; it just started to flow.

A lot of women contributed to this, in their visions of men, and what they think of warlocks and how warlocks should be, and what makes a warlock attractive, and all of that stuff; they were just as important to this. All of that input, combined with what I already knew—my philosophies—I pulled together.

What do you think were the greatest changes that he brought for America?
He challenged Christianity. That is the biggest of all. He gave a home to all of the alien elite who felt that they had no home. I don't just say the broken toys of the world. Those, too, but he also gave a nod to everyone who didn't quite feel as though they fit, and that's still true today. Anyone who is out of the norm—their sexual proclivity is different: gay, straight, trans—they're all accepted; no one really cares. If you're a Satanist, indulge in your pleasure! It's about pleasure. He gave America the right to pleasure, and I think that's very important. The S-word scares the hell out of people. To this day, people will not touch it. I have had many business dealings gone bad because of it, but so be it. They don't get it; we do get it. And more importantly, the religion allows everyone to be independent, and yet be part of something. We could all go our own ways, and think our own ways, and do our own ways. But that common thread of Satanic thought is there all the way through: that black thread, that black flame . . . however you want to describe it.

What do you think was the key to his controversy? Was it merely the S-word or was it something else?

It was that in 1966, and before that, of course, anyone who embraced Satan and built a church around Satan was blasphemous to the max. I mean, how could you possibly do that? "Those are baby killers . . ." It was that nonsense of the Black Mass and baby boiling and the nonsense that was built around Christian myth. At the time, though, his timing was perfect. It was a time in society where the rebel was heralded. Even Hugh Hefner, the founder, publisher, and editor of *Playboy* magazine, where I worked for a number of years, had written his own version of the beatitudes at one time. One of them was, "Blessed is the rebel, for without him there'd be no progress." Anton LaVey was the quintessential rebel, and the timing couldn't have been better in a time that loved rebels. Who is the arch rebel? Satan. It all fit.

What do you miss the most about him?

It's his papal presence. Although Magus Gilmore has filled it more than anyone possibly could, or probably will ever, the founding father, the "Black Pope," gave Satanism its beginning. It's a ridiculous analogy, but it was almost like, well, Christ died and Christianity grew. Then Doktor died and Satanism grew, you know. He certainly wasn't a savior in that respect, but he was the progenitor of it. Also, his friendship is missed. I think we could have had a lot of fun. He would have been so proud to see what members are accomplishing now, in all areas of the arts, in music; everywhere you will find a Satanist who's just kicking ass! I think he would be amazed to see some of the parties that we've had, some of the conferences, and the books that have been written, and the movies that have been made. And what you're doing today. I mean, this is all part of LaVey's legacy; this moment would not have happened without him. So even though we miss him and his presence, it's still there.

In my opinion, one of the key things that made LaVey so unique was his active integration of his own life experience into fields that are traditionally established, and that newcomers simply adapt to, such as occultism or philosophy or religion—structured things. I wonder what your thoughts are on why this was. How would you define the character traits that made him such a creative developer?

I had a little bit of discussion with him about this. You know, he was a crime photographer. I related a bit to him with this, because I actually was a crime reporter at one time. I used to work what they called a "cop house," which was a midnight to 8 a.m. shift. You saw all the most gruesome stuff in the world. I believe that kind of experience gave LaVey a different view of the world, and it made him realize what the real nature of man is: that we are animals. I think that probably was the foundation, in addition to his work with the big cats at the circus and doing stuff like that. To see the real gritty side of humanity, and see what real evil is, and what man is capable of doing—knowing his dark side. LaVey was very much a purveyor of darkness. At that point, his understanding the dark side of human nature gave him the basis of his philosophy. I think that was the good grounding of it.

One of his quintessential traits was his active integration of pop culture that had been forgotten or discarded, and that thereby, according to him, contained a force that could be tapped into and used for magical purposes or pleasure. Do you have any memories of songs or films, or similar expressions that he displayed for you as being such magical works?

Oh, absolutely. As I pointed out in *The Satanic Warlock*, LaVey and I really connected on all of the terrific terms for women. You know, *broads* and *skirts,* and we would talk about *gams,* and use words no one had used since the 1930s and 1940s. So they absolutely had magical roots to them. The way you could use them in conversation—especially around people who didn't know what they meant—was just amazing, those things in particular. I enjoy vocabulary and what the words elicit. You know, my favorite word for a woman—and LaVey and I talked about this at a dinner one night—is a *tomato.* How great is that, you know? "Look at that tomato!" It is so descriptive. It wasn't only that a woman was soft and curvy, but she had red, rosy cheeks, and she was flush with sensuality. . . . So those words in particular were great.

And then of course there were the other things: him talking about magic tricks, and the Johnson Smith catalog, with all the whoopee cushion stuff and things like that. He would bring the conversation back to that, and it would spark some idea. That itself, obviously, is lesser magic, because it starts the mind to wander into those forbidden or forgotten realms, which is very powerful. You know, it's almost hypnotic in a way. You stop and say, "Oh yeah, *gams,* that meant a woman's legs. Oh yeah, I remember . . ." And the other one goes, "Oh, I remember those Betty Grable movies. . . . Weren't her legs insured for a million dollars?" And then you're up and running in a great conversation.

When it comes to creativity, I get the impression that LaVey was happiest when he was playing his tunes or telling his stories and writing his essays, meaning, being immersed in his own expressions that he mastered so well. But those things, playing music or writing something, usually also requires a second party, a listener or a reader. Did you ever get the impression that he expressed himself mainly to have that second party experience, or was the expression in itself the most important thing for him?

Without a doubt, it was most important to him. Because as Satanists, we treasure and value our own personal environments and worlds. I think what he did was that he had to please himself first—before he would share it with everyone else. He was the epitome; he was the walking billboard for complete masculinity and confidence, because he really didn't care what anyone thought. One of the major problems with men nowadays, or men in general, is their lack of self-esteem and confidence. They're frightened to do anything, because they have an attachment to outcome. As the Buddha said, "Wanting or hoping is the basis of all misery," something like that. A paraphrase. LaVey didn't have that attachment to outcome.

And frankly, he didn't give a fuck, whether he was composing music or writing or whatever. It was just, "This is the way I see it—might is right—this is the way I see it." That's what exuded confidence. And again, this is what his followers are very attracted to, this sense of all being and knowing. It's a quality that almost all gurus have; not that he was really a guru in that sense. But he created a church, you know? If he was even one iota worried about other people, it would have never happened.

Can you see any similarities between LaVey and other notable creative people of the time? You know, regardless of what they were doing or what they were thinking. Meaning, would you say that there was something zeitgeistish about him?

Yeah, absolutely. I personally know this. It's Hugh Hefner. Hefner emerged in the early 1950s. LaVey was about ten years later. Hefner was a de facto Satanist. The *Playboy* philosophy is built on hedonism and epicureanism, and there is no shunning of race or sexuality. It was all acceptance, and pleasure based. Hefner and LaVey were very much in tune with each other. Not that they were really contemporaries, but in effect they were, because *Playboy* actually did come into its own in the mid-1960s. That was the heyday. In the 1950s it was pumping along nicely, but it really happened in the 1960s; especially with the changes in society in the United States and the world. The free love movement, sexual freedom, all of this stuff. Hugh Hefner was a de facto Satanist.

Inside the Black House, which would you say was your favorite room?

The Den of Iniquity. It was just so much fun. It was just another world, like a Disneyland. And you know, those mannequins . . . it was a little frightening in a way, it was titillating in a way, it was . . . the LaVey sense was palpable. That was a fun room. He set that up deliberately. I mean, he knew that was going to evoke emotion. That is so much a part of the psychodrama that he loved to use, you know. That was absolutely part of it. That was my favorite room.

Were there any quirks or habits that you found odd in LaVey? Meaning, unexpected expressions of moralisms that might have seemed un-Satanic and perhaps stemmed from the times or from the religion that he grew up in, things that you sort of didn't see coming?

The one thing that stands out was his intolerance for assholes. As much as he said the whole philosophy is about "do what thou wilt," to borrow from Crowley, LaVey couldn't suffer real assholes. So there was a bit of a dichotomy there, you know? It's like, yeah, everybody could do their own thing, but if they're doing *that* stupid thing, you have to get rid of them.

I recently thought about that myself. They're calling these people who are deliberately having Covid-19 parties, and licking grocery store shelves and grocery store products, and sneezing on them on purpose, you know . . . they're called "covidiots." And these covidiots are really a contagion that should be eliminated. So as much as I say, sure, do your own thing . . . but no. There's a limit.

In the 1960s it was pretty much, "Yeah, do your thing, man." A hippie kind of freedom. But you couldn't have a society of only pot smokers. It just doesn't work. LaVey knew that. As much as there was freedom in Satanism that way, there is an appreciation of structure, and of how things should work, and, more importantly, manners. LaVey to me was a consummate gentleman in a lot of ways—especially with women. He would seduce them, and he would touch their darkness, but yeah, he was very much a gentleman. He knew the manners of the day; he knew manners of his childhood in the 1930s. Those manners were not prevalent in the 1960s. They were kind of being lost with feminism. Opening doors for women, that is still a problem today, which is ridiculous. But at that time it really was; it was not cool to do that. Anton LaVey was anticool in a very cool way.

Did you ever feel that LaVey sometimes put on a show because it was expected of him, rather than because he was genuinely in the mood himself?

Absolutely. In the early days, when he would appear on TV in his devil garb. I mean he was decked out in capes and horns, you know.

Was it kitschy? Yes. Was it a little corny? Yes. But he did it on purpose. He was a showman, you know; he got that from his carny days.
Even some of his early pictures, when he was looking like a pachuco.
You know, where you'd have the brim hat and the pencil mustache
and the cigarette. He was playing the role. He was playing with all
those roles. That's also what I said in *The Satanic Warlock*: warlocks
kind of gravitate toward an archetype, because that's what's inside.
They want to pull that archetype out and show the world, "This is
who I am."

LaVey absolutely played with those archetypes, and almost always
in a Satanic way, because of the symbolism. No one else was doing it.
It was shocking, it was irreverent, and it was, "Oh my goodness, how
could he?" But he probably didn't feel like dressing up like that all the
time; knowing that when he was in the house, he didn't dress like that.
That's part of the shtick; that's part of the drama. Again, it's part of the
psychodrama, part of the show. He was absolutely a showman that way,
and that made it work.

***Do you think that there was something, or maybe some things, that he
would have done differently in his life if he had had the chance?***

I think that if somehow he were enormously wealthy, he probably would
have pushed more for a huge Satanic community. It was talked about
at times, where there would be cities that were Satanist-built, or towns
at least. Where people who were of like mind would inhabit and have
their own thing—like an adult Disneyland.

Or* Westworld? *That was a film he liked.

Or *Westworld,* for sure. A place where people would live that way. I
think that probably would have been something he would really want
to do. And maybe even have a more coordinated effort for Satanic
thinkers; almost like a Satanic think tank that would have propagated
the idea of Satanism throughout the world. I think that because of how
LaVey grew up, and the years during which he grew up, he was more

analogue than digital, if that makes any sense. He would probably be more inclined to have people do things, rather than have everything done online.

When you worked on your book, The Satanic Warlock, *did you ever think about, "How would Anton deal with this passage or this angle?" Meaning, was he present in some way when you were working on the book?*

Absolutely, he was the inspiration for it. He actually blessed it, for lack of a better term. My ideas started to line up, but always with Doktor's ideas behind them. We had great discussions about what masculinity was, and he was so far ahead of his time on some of that stuff. It was because of *The Satanic Witch*—as far as intersexual and interpersonal dynamics go—that he was way ahead of his time. The omnipresent feeling that I got when writing the book was that he had already said a lot of what I want to say from a woman's perspective, so I can't repeat that. But I can compound, I can add on to it and clarify, and give my own opinions on certain things. Some of the stuff in the *Warlock* is similar to what's in the *Witch*, but maybe improved on or modernized because of society. But his spirit was always there.

Why do you think it is that he decided to start with the Witch and not the Warlock?

Because he knew women have the power. Women are the choosers; men are the chasers. And being that Satanism is the most carnal religion in the world, the basis of it is sexuality and the sexual attraction. It's what makes the world go around. He knew that. So he knew that, "If I write a book about women and show them their power . . . and, by the way, wink, wink, men, you'd better read it, too."

In one fell swoop he gave the women the power to be women, and it exemplified how they can have their power, and what they can do with it. And also told men, "Hey, buddy, take a look at what's going on over here, and then you'll understand." So he did both in one shot.

If he had written a book about men at the time, the women would be saying "Well, you don't know everything." But he revealed the secrets, and they agreed. And then the men kind of got the insight, too. That makes sense.

Are there any subjects or details in The Satanic Warlock *that you think he would have objected to? Are there subjects or details in* The Satanic Witch *that you object to?*

As for *The Satanic Witch,* there's a difference in younger women today, because they grew up with a different perspective on life and society. They became more infected with this feeling of entitlement and "girl power," and that it's bad to be sexy because you're being objectified. In today's world the book is not resonating as much with most women. Also, I think in *The Satanic Witch,* the "clock" can be confusing to a lot of people.* They just don't understand where they fit on the clock. "If I'm a masculine man, but I want to get whipped, how can that be? If I'm a six o'clock and my girl's a three o'clock? Just because I'm a masculine man, does that mean I want a feminine?"

What I don't think he makes clear, and it may be just because I don't remember, is that we all have a degree of masculine and feminine. We all do. It's a sliding scale. Some men are very masculine; they go to one end of the spectrum; and some are not very masculine. But we all kind of float in between there. There's some more masculine and some more feminine. A man can be in his feminine in what he does. He can be an artist, which is being in your feminine, yet sexually he can be in his masculine and like to whip his mate, you know? So I think that could have been more included in *The Witch.* I don't think it was clear enough. But maybe, just at the time, no one was thinking that way.

Everything is subject to the criticism of history; everything is always dated, in a way.

---

*For an explanation of the LaVey Personality Synthesizer, please see note in chapter 5, "Bewitched, Bothered, and Bewildered," page 60.

Right. And in *The Warlock*, he might have objected to my using some of my personal experiences in there. Only because he may have thought people would have thought of them as contrived.

I really like that they're there, because that's a sign of our times, you know? We are our own little reflectors, and by being personal in this sense, people can relate easier.

He gave me some of the ideas that are in my book. If you understand what Satanism is, my book is a manual in the same sense as *The Witch*. Like, for example, the quest for power. I said in the book that power is monumentally important to people, because if you have power, you can control your life. You have the power over your life, and that's so, so important.

When you hung out with LaVey, was he interested in hearing about your experiences from the world of adult entertainment? Was he curious about it?

To an extent. You know, he was familiar with the girly books. Some of the earliest articles about Doktor were in the girly magazines; they loved him. So he was kind of interested. He was more interested in my name, because of the connection with Robert Johnson, the blues guitarist. He would tell the whole mythos about the song "Cross Road Blues," where he goes down to the crossroads and makes a deal with the Devil. He really liked that a lot. More so than that I was in the adult business.

But he knew the magic of the adult business. He knew the power of pornography, particularly with men. So I think that's why he said to me, "Well, why don't you write *Warlock,* because I knew where the women were coming from, and you know where the men are coming from." *Playgirl* was a women's magazine that was part of our company, but it really wasn't a women's magazine—95 percent of the subscribers were gay men. Women just don't have that visual connection; they really don't care about a man's naked body, you know. That's secondary. They care more about the man as a whole.

But I actually did a mock cover of Doktor on the front of *Playgirl* magazine and put some cute little lines to it, and I gave it to him. He enjoyed that. I think he said, "Well, where's the centerfold?" And I replied, "You have to pose for it." And he said, "You don't have pages big enough for that." That was just truly Doktor!

One of the things that has struck me as very, very interesting as a phenomenon in itself, but also because of the Satanic or LaVeyan connection, has been the development of companies like RealDoll, who make these really humanlike sex dolls, basically. They grew from being kind of stiff and mannequin-like, to being like totally Galathean creatures. It has been amazing to see that thing develop over the years. I'm just curious if you have any thought or insight about why you think it is that those things were developed at that specific time? I mean from a sexual point of view, or from an adult entertainment point of view?

Before that, blow-up dolls were around for a long time. Blow-up dolls were around from the 1960s and 1970s. I actually wrote something in *The Warlock* about artificial companions and how they were progressing. And I did mention RealDoll and a couple of other companies, how they're progressing, and how these nonbiological mates will be. I don't know why they merged when they did, but I could speculate.

My speculation is that with the advent of the internet, and the oversaturation of pornography, there is this inherent need for men who saw so much pornography that they wanted to experience it and just couldn't. Maybe they were inept, or they couldn't find girls like that, or they couldn't have the type of sex they wanted. If they were into BDSM and they just couldn't find the girl, for whatever reason, that they wanted to have BDSM sex with, or they had a particular kink or fetish . . . with a doll, with a doll that's humanlike, they can live out their fantasy. And that's a very Satanic thing: to be able to live out your fantasy and live in that world. I can only speculate as to how that happened.

It just could have been a confluence of the porn zeitgeist that was out there on the internet, and the technology that progressed at the time. The skin, the feel of skin, the plastic that felt more like skin. It's getting better every day. So that and, of course, part novelty. Some really rich guys would buy these things just to say, "Look what I got!" So that kind of fueled the fire.

There's also this aspect, when you speak about the strictly Satanic aspects, of it being a sexual trigger. It's a fantasy thing that you can actually indulge in. If I were to speculate, I would say that when that wears off, I think that at least a portion of the people will have another kind of relationship with their dolls. And that's where the LaVeyan concept comes in: that it becomes a companion. It's not merely a blow-up sex doll. I do suspect that some people have developed a more real, intimate relationship with their dolls than just using them and then cleaning them up.

I've had this theory kicking around in my head with this constant talk about gender identification, and, you know, "Who is what and who isn't." When I was working on *High Society* magazine, there were a shit-load of ads for transsexuals and gay men in this totally heterosexual magazine. Now, why? I made it my business to try to figure out why, because so many men were bi-curious at the time, or so many were even more interested in transvestites, or even hermaphrodites. Anyone who can offer both worlds . . . a transvestite could dress up like a woman one day and look like a man the next day. So they have all of their fantasies met in one person, so that kind of fits with what you were saying about the dolls, too. You can adjust it to be whoever you want.

There will always be the prurience, the sexual incentive. But then, when you're over that hurdle, or maybe satiated, then something else comes into play. You either become terrified of it and discard it, or you delve into it and find something possibly quite interesting.

That is so much a male trait. We are just built to be attracted, especially heterosexual men, to be attracted to the female body. And once we have what we want, we want it different. We want more. We want something else, and it has nothing to do with emotion. I often say that some men could approach sex as if they're playing tennis, you know? "Yeah! It's fun! I'm going to have a great time, I'm going to get a workout, and then I'm going to walk away from it." There doesn't have to be an emotional attachment there. That freaks a lot of women out, but that's another story.

LaVey advocated a strong and pretty clear gender division. But can you see any Satanic benefits in our kind of dysphoric culture and identity politics, et cetera, in which this division is inherently questioned?

Yes, because I think that as true Satanists we are very much of the mind of "Live and let live." If people identify with one gender or not, or both, or whatever, that's all fine. LaVey had homosexual friends, he had lesbian friends; they were part of his inner circle at times, and it was all fine. But I think that today, because it's such a sore point—or it's just in your face constantly—that we have to understand it. It's tantamount to what was going on back then, too. Satan is not going to tell you, "Oh, you're weird," because you think you're a guy but you're really a woman, in a woman's body. Nature is a mad scientist. We know that. So, whatever floats your boat. Anyone who is typically or strongly against accepting that is really just dealing with their own fears; their own fear of maybe wanting that or wanting to do that, because it's different. Well, by virtue of being a Satanist you are different, okay? Understand, you are different. You are the rebel. Again, that's a track back to Hefner and his being a de facto Satanist. "Blessed is the rebel, for without him there'd be no progress."

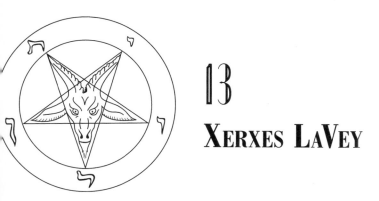

13

Xerxes LaVey

"I appreciate that people feel that I have a unique perspective."

Xerxes LaVey is the son of Anton LaVey and Blanche Barton. He is an anthropologist.

I'm curious about whether you have concrete memories of your father, and also of the Black House?

I do have some memories of my father and the Black House. You've got to remember that even though I was very young, this was a very impactful time. With him falling ill and us moving it made a pretty big dent in my memory. But with a lot of early childhood memories you're looking at things that are very dreamlike; very clipped and surreal, but still I remember him doing little drawings for me. I remember a lot of the Black House; maybe even more than I remember my father. As a child, when both your parents are working and milling around the house, you have a lot of time to explore. I remember the bright purple living room. I remember the eclectic mishmash of furniture from different styles and eras—all of it vintage. You had stuff from the Victorian times, and you had these sort of recreation Renaissance pieces, and you had these sort of early mid-century Art Nouveau pieces. I have faint memories of the "front ritual chamber" my father created. I remember

215

it had an old organ and a fake Egyptian sarcophagus. But moreover, it's general moods and feelings.

For all its attempts at spookiness and intimidation, I remember the Black House as a very sort of cozy but cluttered museum-like environment. It was a dense artist's house, you know; honestly not that dissimilar from your own. I see a lot of books and ephemera there. It was the same with things my father had collected throughout his life and appreciated. It's crazy to think of what an icon that house has become. To me, it was home. I remember things that would break through the façade. As the classical Japanese saying goes, "A fish in a well doesn't understand the ocean." So you don't know. Everything is normal to you as a baby. But . . . there were things such as people shooting at the house, right? Or people coming by and gawking, or yelling at the house or something. That's very surreal to me. There were secret passages. I saw them when we were getting ready to move. My dad did not take me up through them when I was very little because they were tight. And you know, there were nails sticking out, and lots of cobwebs. It wasn't a place you'd want to take a kid. A lot of these weren't necessarily secret passages like the ones one would imagine in a Dracula film. Anyone familiar with Victorian construction will know there are a lot of false walls, to facilitate maintenance at the time and also to act as insulation—air gaps to keep heated air in when it gets cold—and it certainly got cold in San Francisco. I've heard that it was a bootlegger's house before he owned it. I don't know the verifiable truth about that.

Did you have a particular favorite cubby, or some room or place that you loved the most?

In all honesty I cannot think of a distinct place in the Black House that I would have called "my favorite." I was such a young child that I basically figured wherever my parents set me was the place to be. I do recall very fond memories with my maternal grandfather, who lived with us. He was such an understanding and open man, which I would expect would be necessary from someone whose daughter chose the life-style my mother did. He lived in the converted garage and storage area beneath the Black House. He had a fully fledged studio apartment and I have fond memories from when I was an older toddler of his teaching me to use a Macintosh Plus and Sega. He was always an early adopter of new technology and insisted my parents step into the present and have a computer. I believe I spent the majority of my last couple of years at the house with him. So I would say his apartment and the stoop out front of the house where he taught me about the world and told me stories about his life would be my most favorite parts of that house, and those are certainly my most cherished memories of my time there.

Were you proud of your father as you grew up?

I think it's worth delving into a bit of specifics about the process of his passing and leaving us. As a child, I remember him as being a very car-ing and loving father. I cannot remember an instance of him yelling at me or anything like that. I am quite certain there would have been some butting of heads as I grew older, though. But when I was that young, he always made an effort to be his best self. He was always joyful with me. And that must not have been easy because his health was not great at that time. And I know he was in a lot of physical pain. As a young child, I really had this idolization of him as a father; not what he repre-sented as "Doktor Anton Szandor LaVey," but as my dad, and I missed him. I missed having a father who would draw me pictures and point out ducks on a lake or show me cool movies.

His death, and also his legacy, were traumatic to me as a child. I was born during the "Satanic Panic" and growing up in that environment, and knowing there was this sort of innate hostility that I perceived as being towards my family . . . it was hard. It was hard to feel secure. I found myself very worried about people knowing about my father's identity, and either being offended and alienating me, or being out-right hostile. As a young kid I would see letters from delusional fans or Christian extremists and that sort of thing. I remember communicating my background to friends I made, or friends' parents. My mother was very protective of me around strangers.

That was juxtaposed with the fact that my mother took me nearly everywhere, and I spent my childhood with a vast number of sort of Satanic "aunts and uncles." After my father died, until my late tweens, I was always included as much as I could be in get-togethers with Church of Satan members. They would take me to museums and zoos, talk with me and listen. And I suppose I assumed that was normal and expected.

Did you ever experience that there was almost an exaggerated respect in a way that you couldn't understand at the time, but that you can see now?

Absolutely. And I appreciate your bringing that up. I started to understand in my teen years that I was benefiting from a place of very significant social privilege. A lot of these people viewed me—and I understand the feeling behind this—as an extension of my father. I was viewed symbolically. So they were very fascinated in knowing me to know insights about my father. I know there were also those that genuinely felt concern for me as a young child without his father as well. And I am grateful for that.

Conversely, I was always raised by my grandparents to be very modest about my accomplishments. Not to brag and not to be bigheaded. So it's this weird contrast. I certainly think having so many people supportive of me as a child acted as a counterbalance to the trauma of my father's passing. But it was strange living in two worlds; one where I was embarrassed by my past and one where I was put on a pedestal for it.

As I have gotten older I have taken ownership of my personal history, and I do not particularly mind people knowing my background. As I grew older I realized no one actually blames a child for who their parents are, unless they are profoundly broken themselves. Any interest I have in the occult and my father's impact is largely academic, but I do not mind joking with friends about it, or discussing it. But it is odd to meet people who expect me to be this brooding Gothic caricature, or a "devout Satanist" who constantly name-drops my father only to be met with an outdoorsy yet bookish young Jewish man. I once had someone thank me for "not being a dick"; that stuck with me and really did make me feel proud.

The interesting thing is that you have obviously done a great job of individuating into yourself. There's no precedent, either for you or for the others around you who get to know that this is who you are. You don't have a manual saying, "In situations like this, I should act like this." It's all organic and intuitive. And the same thing for the people around you. If you look at it from the point of view of general American culture, I'd say that to have some kind of celebrity heritage, that's something that you're supposed to exploit. I think Americans get confused when people don't do that, when instead they are humble about it. And who, for various reasons—including safety—say that, "I'm proud of who I am, but it's not my career." I think that is more confusing to people in America than the fact that you're actively guarding your safety. The benefit of being a celebrity is looked upon almost like it's some kind of divine grace.

Regarding celebrity; I cannot imagine how I would be seen as a celebrity simply based on my family tree. My paternal grandparents are not considered celebrities, at least I don't think they are! But I am very well aware of the privileges that I have as somebody whose parents were socially well connected, and I present as white and well educated on top of that. Financially, though, after my father passed, we were not well off. Remember, I came from a family of Bohemians, and there weren't deep wells there, financially. At least to my knowledge. Once the inheritance ran out we survived primarily on assistance, and I was raised in large part by my grandparents. I suppose I've had this sort of hyper American experience of simultaneous "celebrity," anonymity, and poverty. That is what taught me to become my own person.

People do seem to be very surprised that I don't emphasize the sort of completely unearned celebrity status. Because that is not what

Americans born of famous people do. Americans love to instead commodify everything, even existence. But I've never wanted to ride on his coattails. I should add that growing up, I didn't think of my father as a celebrity at all. I thought of him as this relatively unknown figure, which he certainly wasn't—even at the time. And he's only grown in celebrity status since then. By the time he passed, he was a known alternative figure. And now he's just a celebrity.

That ties in to the mainstreaming of Satanism and Occultism. As a social scientist I feel strangely lucky to see that cultural shift from such an intimate perspective. Occultism as a whole was absolutely massive in the 1970s, with this sort of "witchy vibe." And there's a resurgence of it now. I think we're in a new golden era of mainstream occultism in America. We're seeing such films as *The Witch* or *Midsommar,* that are just straight out of the 1970s aesthetic playbook. And you've got witchy things being sold as fast fashion now. It's become popcorn.

I specifically want to address my father's appearance in *American Horror Story*. It was a surreal wake-up call to see that his work is that well known. I don't have a lot of justification to complain about him appearing in the pop-culture pantheon. I can certainly criticize individual portrayals. But . . . he's a public figure.

In a sense you can always look at it through really Satanic goggles and go down the Jayne Mansfield and Mae West route: all publicity is good publicity. So although it's a validation at the same time, it must have been so weird for you because it's not only that they've made him look like that, but they actually say his name, too. That makes it even weirder. I was cringing. I couldn't keep watching.

What I picture is some witchy girl living with her parents in Wisconsin. I picture her sitting there with her heavy eyeliner and her witchy jewelry that she got at the local Forever 21, or a pentagram shirt from Etsy. And maybe an astrological print tapestry that she got from Amazon hanging up behind her. And she's watching that show. She probably loves *American Horror Story*. And it may look like this is a surface-level affectation. But I want to be very clear when I say; that person represents a level of understanding and inherent tolerance that her parents probably don't have. Even though at this moment occultism might seem like a fad, or this might appear as cultural appropriation—in some cases, it definitely is—it is a very good thing that people like this exist who are "transparently mainstream" occult. They pick up *The Satanic Bible,* and they read the "rules of the earth," or the "Satanic Sins," and then they have a better understanding of what Satanism actually is than your average person off the street did ten years ago. Or if not that, then they read up on spiritual occultism, Wicca, paganism. That is a gateway to being more open minded and understanding of difference. And they're voting.

There was mention of The Satanic Bible *already in* The X-Files, *and also in* Californication, *and I'm sure many other places and shows, too. It's been around for a long time, so of course someone intelligent enough will sneak it in there. Now it's almost like your father's face is the iconic thing, not the book itself. It's become a logo.*

I've seen enamel pins with a sort of simplified version of his face, where it's just black and white. I've seen patches and T-shirts with just his face on it. He's a symbol now. There are times where it's shallow and just using occult imagery because, "This looks cool or spicy. Yeah, this will spice things up." I definitely cringe when I see people with a very sort of surface-level misappropriation of occultism, or T-shirts with occult imagery that some people find sacred and religious being sold as "fast fashion." But then I have met plenty of actual practicing Satanists that will buy anything with a pentagram on it. In any case I am happy that people are saying, "this is cool" rather than, "this is evil and worthy of hate." If Satanism can be accepted as mainstream, then anything can.

Can you see things in videos and photos of him that you can see in yourself?

People have told me that we speak in a similar way. I do not know if I agree with that, but he was one of the first people to teach me the

English language, so it stands to reason that I would pick up some habits. There are also certain interests that overlap. For example, we both like film noir movies, we both like cars, and he was very interested in firearms, while I am interested in military history and sport shooting. I also have found myself independently drawn to similar views to my father's on individualism as they relate to advocating for personal freedom and autonomy. We have some significantly different views aesthetically and philosophically, though.

I don't think my father would have wanted it any other way. He walked his own path separately from what was expected. I haven't followed in his footsteps, but in not doing that, I have. I think we also have a similar foundational belief that people should be allowed to live as they please without being told to conform to some "official standard," so long as they do not harm anyone else in doing so. I think we came to those same conclusions for very similar reasons. I have tried to learn more about my father's true history and family. I really pushed my mother to do genealogy research when I was younger. And I have tried to verify aspects of his life to really understand who this guy was.

You present yourself as an anthropologist. When I think back on your father's early life story, all of these colorful experiences that he had in different environments with different kinds of people, it was basically fodder for his own anthropological evaluation that eventually crystallized itself in his philosophy. He often made references to when he worked at the carnival and the girlie shows; that they taught him about people and how they function for real—not how they claim to function, but how they actually function. So that's a deep, deep anthropological study that was going on. I don't think it was strategic from the beginning. But when it was time to go from the Magic Circle to the Church of Satan, he had all of this wealth of firsthand data.

It's sort of Gonzo anthropology. But if I am being honest, it is not anthropology as a science. He was not conducting a study, and he certainly did not try to leave out internal or external biases, but he was certainly conscious of them, and that is more than I can say of many journalists. I think what he did is far closer to journalism; he created a massive archive of experiences that he had. He had a very stable upbringing with a middle-class family, but as a Slavic Jew he was an outsider among his peers, so he latched onto weird tales and pulp fiction and old horror stories and music to become who he was.

I too grew up as an outsider because of my background, but I think it did me a lot of good. I am glad that I did not grow up in a culturally homogenous environment as I would have, either with my father or with a stereotypical American family. By constantly having to work through my own upbringing and biases and view both Satanism and broader American culture from the outside, I have been able to be more open minded.

Keep in mind that most people never get to that point of self-realization; of being aware of the fact that you're aware. You can then say that "life is really not that bad because I can see all these facets and also appreciate them, and I can say no to the ones I don't like." Most people are just accepting what they've been dealt.

Especially in American culture, but it's global. We see materialism supplant genuine connection; we see the surface level, a sort of symbolic idea of who people are. I have never cared about the surface-level bullshit interaction. I'm really interested in knowing people. You get a much richer experience of the world when you know people. Most people are only highlighting these surface-level things when they could be presenting what they really think philosophically. When you do that, you start finding connections; you start finding things that you have in common with strangers, and you start relating to them more.

I think the dividing line is simply that you and I, we are aware of it. We are aware that there are many benefits in the potential in this wonderful creativity and technology and progress in material things. But it becomes a problem when that takes hold of the focus that essentially should lie elsewhere; it should lie on interhuman communication, and not on representation.

Exactly. It's so easy to get caught up in this idea of consumption without meaning; this habit of just going about your life in a pattern of work, shop, sleep, work, shop, sleep, and not questioning it. You have to create breaks in that cycle. I will give my father credit for that; he did create breaks in that cycle for a lot of people. He also idolized these forgotten objects and places. A sort of materialism without consumption; for example, he had a fascination with Sutro Baths, the destroyed amusement park on San Francisco's shoreline. I can relate to that feeling. For me it mostly comes from art and architecture.

And let's not forget cars and mechanical objects. He showed me his collection of guns and knives. I told him that I have a fetish for old fountain pens and beautiful pens in general, and he showed me some of his collection, too. He certainly had an appreciation of what humans are actually capable of. Architecture is very much in the same vein.

Yeah, exactly. For him, it was more mechanical things. He saw the beauty in these utilitarian objects and saw the design touches and appreciated them in a deep, innate way that I think a lot of people wouldn't.

Or maybe they're just not conscious. Because people certainly choose between different cars, but the aesthetic choices are very few, such as, "Do I want this color or that color?" They buy the cars that the dealers offer to them, basically. I think it ties in a lot with the philosophy. What has power? The things that were discarded by the herd or the masses, and that weren't commercial successes. Of course, there were then fewer left in pristine shape. And then they become almost like totem figures or art objects because they're so weird. Your father explained the magic of objects: they cannot be mass marketed. Things need to be unique.

He definitely loved out-of-the-way things. He liked objects created by somebody whose personal passion lay in what they made. The people who say, "I'm going to make this, I'm going to do this—even if it's only a 'spruce goose' that doesn't take off all the way." I don't know what my father thought of Howard Hughes. I feel that they were kindred spirits in that regard. He just adored these niche things such as hand-painted silk neckties; again, a sort of small-scale fetish object; this alternative art thing that was popular for a while. I suppose he was a protohipster in a sense. The original.

He had this concept that I am not sure he came up with: "total environments." It's a created space and passion project. A film set or diorama—like Disneyland. The Black House was a total environment for him. One specific thing was this artificial speakeasy bar he had created in the basement. There was a jukebox, and he had these mannequins set up as if they were patrons. That place started to bleed out and away from the Black House through people's stories. It started touching other people, and they became privy to that world he had created. I see a serious parallel with Disney there. He created this bubble that touched other people. It's crazy for me to see just how widespread it's become.

Absolutely. This sort of connects with the original premise I had for the film: this thing where people came in during the last decade of his life, and they had quite similar experiences. My theory is that he wanted to secure not just a legacy—the books were already out there and people would always be talking about him—but also specific things that he cared for very much, as pieces of a puzzle that was part of a greater joint puzzle. He curated the interest. It was disseminated in parts so that it could create a total environment on some kind of weird magical level.

I can see that. Yeah, he really did curate his own legacy in a sense and left the guidebook behind for how he did it. All the content and history that influenced him. It's interesting to see how Satanism appeals to so many different people. There are Satanists in every walk of life; a lot of them have common interests, though. And it makes me wonder if it's a chicken or the egg thing. Would a twenty-year-old who really likes

Sammy Davis Jr. then discover Satanism, or vice versa? I think that's kind of the point. He's set this thing up where artists or movies, or all these things, would become sort of associated. I think on the front end it was very intentional to arrange these curated lists. And then, on the back end, it was just a matter of knowing a lot of people from all walks of life. My father was an incredible marketer.

If you only have a metal band screaming "Satan, Satan," that will only appeal to simpletons. But if you have a bouquet of mysterious things and say, "What the hell does this little flower have to do with Satan?" then the coin will drop. You will realize it and can call it an inclusion of various things that all become generators in your own bouquet. I think what he did was not so much a strict formulation; he actually set an example. That, I think, is what makes Satanism so vital. Many people can write occult books, or philosophical books, and call it this or that, but he had Satan—a very "ballsy" thing to use. He walked the talk. You simply can't buy that. That is why people in every generation find him so reliable and inspiring. Of course, he went against the grain. But he was even more "protocreative," encouraging people to indulge in the most maximum sense in what you liked. And of course, everybody wants to do that. I think some people get lost in the maze, or in the forest, and they only see LaVey; they only see his things and his preferences. But when you have your own bouquet, and you have your own eclectic tastes, then it becomes a truly beautiful thing.

I cannot tell you how many times I've been put off by encountering someone who tried to emulate Anton LaVey to a tee. He was an advocate for authenticity and individualism if nothing else, so it is profoundly ironic. But he had a very cultivated image of himself, right down to insisting his book be called *The Satanic Bible* against his publisher's wishes. He curated his coverage, his appearances on television; he would guide the interview and ensure that he was framed how he wanted to be, even if this interviewer was incredibly antagonistic. But he was certainly playing a character in a sense.

Your father had a complicated relationship with his daughters. I'm just curious: have you had any contact with them over the years?

I have had next to no contact with my half-siblings my whole life. In fact, I was raised as an only child, and I only have faint memories of them. They grew up in an incredibly unusual and, I imagine at many times uncomfortable environment, so I cannot blame them for having conflicting feelings about our father or his legacy, as do I. I do not know if they have any interest in talking to me, or if they communicate with each other. I have not made an effort to contact them because I would not want to make them uncomfortable.

Your father was an only child. Are there other relatives on your father's side that you have been in touch with?

I would like to know the Leveys better. I am sure they are wonderful people, but so much time has passed and I am so far removed from that side of my family that I would be a stranger. I would not want to breach any sort of comfort that they have.

We have talked about your being interested in genealogy, and that your mother had also been involved in that. It's an endlessly fascinating subject, isn't it?

It is, and I would love to know more about the Leveys. All I know is that my father's immediate ancestry was from Ukraine and Russia on his mother's side, and his father was Jewish, with his family having come from France. Supposedly, I have family from Romania or Georgia, but I am not sure of the authenticity of that information since I have yet to find corroborating documents.

How would you define yourself in terms of philosophy or even religion?

I appreciate your asking. I identify as a secular humanist, nonpracticing Jew, and not particularly devout Buddhist. Much of my practical philosophy is political in nature or based on scientific data. In

America my views are seen as quite clearly left wing, but in the vast majority of the world I would be seen as center left. I have long held a Left-Libertarian streak.

There is certainly a lot that I could agree with my father on as far as not having a herd mentality or ensuring that oneself is capable of self-reliance, but I don't consider myself a Satanist or occultist as such.

Is there any particular text or book or essay or chapter of all of your father's writings that you love the most, and that has meant something special for you?

In particular? I imagine it may come as a surprise, but you will find far more knowledge of his writings from someone who has carefully studied them as a practitioner. In fact, I only read *The Satanic Bible* out of sequence. I think that is certainly the work with the broadest appeal by design, and I believe my father formulated a very good mirror that people can hold up to themselves and see a Satanic archetype within them.

But if you want to know who Anton LaVey truly was, you will find it in his array of essays and papers. *The Satanic Bible* and *Satanic Witch* have been well documented as collections of influences and writings that my father reformulated and added to. They are certainly still greater than the sum of their parts and clear treatises on his philosophy, but the truth of who he was is in his writings where he opens up about his views and ideals in a less structured way.

He left reference lists in various books; name-dropping people who had been inspiring to him. Have you actively sought all of these out? Has that been an ambitious plan on your side to see who the hell these people were?

Honestly, not really. At least not as a significant effort. I certainly have no plans to watch, read, listen to, and examine everything that influenced him. But I have taken some time lately to familiarize myself with his influences to better understand him.

People who met him during his last decade often describe him as a father figure. I think I did, too. Mainly because of the age difference, but there was something else, too, that had to do with almost like a guru or a teacher kind of vibe—although he never expressed it like that at all. What I'm curious about is your take on whether he took that on consciously in his handling of people during the '80s and '90s? Perhaps simply because of the fact that he was aware he was getting older, and he had this incredible collection of memories, insights, philosophy, and stuff that he needed to make sure it ended up in good hands; in good soil.

I think there was a conscious effort by him to develop the persona of a wise man: a hermetic persona. A lot of it came naturally, but a lot of it was intentional; it was him saying, "Okay, this is how people see me. I'll lean into this; this is the sort of image I evoke. I won't push it away." Because, going back to the roots of the Church, he saw himself as a teacher. I think he knew his health was failing, but he didn't know how much time he had left, so he tried to formulate his legacy as best he could.

He was as human as we all are, in the sense that we are not only what we define ourselves to be, but also to a great extent what other people project on us. He took on that role even during the Magic Circle, and possibly before that, where was he was the disseminator in a way. He had had those projections for a long, long time.

He certainly was seen as a teacher by many, and I think he enjoyed that image. He seems to have loved the limelight and enjoyed sharing what he found interesting.

Have you ever come across some things that you feel that he left for you to bloom?

That's an interesting question. I think I certainly learned to appreciate his work as I got older, and while I do not agree with all Satanic viewpoints on human behavior, I agree with the desire for individuation and self-determination. I could imagine he would want that from his child.

The last time I was at the Black House was in the summer of 1993. I actually had my hand on your mother's belly when you were in there. Your father was so incredibly proud. And I remember the exact words that he used—a beautiful Americanism: "See, Carl, I can still cut the mustard!" Do you think that he decided on fatherhood in defiance of old age?

I think that played a part in it. But also I think my mother made him feel young again. Their relationship had a significant age difference and certainly had an unusual dynamic. My mother has always shown herself to be exceptionally devoted to my father and his identity, so I think it was an emphatic act of love and devotion on her part. I have no first-hand resources to glean his perspective from, but I think he at times forgot his age and had quite genuine feelings for her as well.

Do you find things in yourself where you sort of realize: "Oh, boy, my dad would not have liked this . . ."

I do not see how he could have reasonably objected to major decisions I have made. I have a very concrete sense of ethics. Maybe he would have told me to loosen up. He may have objected to my listening to music that he didn't understand, or my enjoying aspects of culture he did not appreciate.

How do you see his legacy evolving? Do you think that he'd be happy with the story so far?

I think he would have really mixed feelings. He wanted Satanism to be exclusive. He wanted it to be this closed ecosystem of cultural outsiders whom he saw as intellectually exceptional, culturally refined, and worth being around for him. He had a general distaste for pop culture as a whole, which is ironic, because many of the things he was obsessed with and loved were pop cultural artifacts. I think he would be a bit disappointed that Satanism is seen as less toothy by normies.

But I think at the same time he would take a lot of pleasure in how he's become a cultural figurehead. Nobody cares about the televangelists or Satanic metal music corrupting children's minds. Dad won that culture war, and I think he would take a lot of pride in that. Even though he might not like the commercialization of some of the imagery he adopted, he'd be happy that it still pushes some buttons for "the olds."

That was his dream though: to become an icon. And he did.

You mentioned this potential scenario of your butting heads with him about certain issues. What do you think those issues would have been?

I think we would have disagreed significantly on matters of sociopolitics. He saw himself as apolitical, but philosophically, I see that as impossible. He might not have voted, but he certainly had beliefs. I am much further to the left on many issues than it seems he was. I'm an ardent egalitarian and not a Social Darwinist, even if I think weightlifting and knowing how to rely on yourself in the wild is important. And I can't imagine my father would see much value in collective action or economic leftism.

He certainly had some questionable sources as well, and I do not see why he felt so influenced by a work like *Might Is Right,* given how incredibly anti-Semitic, sexist, and racist it was. Nor do I understand Satanists' fascination with the incorporation of fascistic imagery such as the Wolfsangel. At least that was around before the Nazis. The Sonnenrad on the other hand, which I've seen used by Satanists from multiple groups, was commissioned by Himmler himself. I suppose the goal is to be as shocking as possible, but it is quite bizarre given my family's heritage. I know it is not just the CoS that has "fashy" folks interested in it; the problem springs up in all sorts of occult and pagan groups. I suppose that it's due to their anti-Abrahamic nature coupled with the fact that they're seen as so edgy, so they attract people from the political fringes. Ironic, considering it's a philosophy that espouses equal rights and sexual liberation. Perhaps the Church should make more efforts to call out bad actors, but I get the feeling they don't care too much about how the general public views them and would rather handle such matters internally. It is worth recognizing these things.

That all being said, I have certainly met bigots from other philosophies as well, and the majority of Satanists I've met are good-natured and tolerant people.

The Church of Satan was accepting of trans people and other people from the queer community long before most other groups were. Not only that: it boasted members from numerous racial and ethnic backgrounds at a time when desegregation had barely been passed as judicial law, much less as practice. Now, both the CoS and Satanic Temple have publicly advocated for LGBTQ rights, and the CoS endorsed Black Lives Matter. So I am sure my father and I would have found common ground on shared interests and more general cultural liberalism.

Is there something that you would like to add to this interview?

I didn't really know my father as long as some people did. That said, I appreciate that people feel that I have a unique perspective. I see two men in Anton LaVey—the historical figure and my father. More than anything else I think that humanizes him for me. You can offer a fair critique of someone's views and actions while still respecting them. I may not agree with everything he said or did, and I may not understand all of it. But I still admire my father's ambition and ability to carve his own path. Satanism isn't anti-science, and people take out of it what they look for going in. I can safely say it has done more good than harm. I do not think Anton LaVey should be vilified or venerated; he was a complex man worthy of complex analysis. Maybe he was a self-help guru in a cape, maybe he was a prophet of the culture yet to come. If nothing else I am proud of the legacy he built and the positive influence he has had on so many people. I have had people tell me that his work made them feel like they weren't alone for the first time—that it kept them going or motivated them to get their life in order. If the cost of American culture's becoming less judgmental, more liberated, more tolerant, and more open to outsider perspectives is an unauthorized Baphomet T-shirt at Zumiez . . . then maybe that's a fair price to pay.

14

JIM MORTON

Jim Morton, San Francisco, 2019.
Photo by Carl Abrahamsson.

"I really admired him and his love of movies."

Jim Morton is a film historian and writer, currently specializing in East German cinema. In 1985 Morton edited the book *Incredibly Strange Films* (1980), together with Boyd Rice for RE/Search Publications.

How did you first hear about Anton LaVey?

I probably first heard about Anton LaVey just like almost everybody else, which is when *The Satanic Bible* came out. I was a teenager in Tucson at the time, and I picked up a copy of it. Because I was very much into anything weird and witchcrafty, I enjoyed the book. It wasn't what I expected, but it was a fun book. I could kind of see where he was going in terms of some kind of logical, hedonistic approach to life, mixed with a little bit of carny mumbo jumbo. I dug it, because I enjoy that kind of thing.

How did you first come into contact with him?

I came into contact with LaVey many, many years later. I'd lived here in San Francisco awhile. I had moved here back in 1978, but I didn't meet him until about 1984 or 1985. I believe I met Anton's daughter, Karla, before I met him, because we had mutual friends. I got along quite well with Karla. Boyd Rice, I think, was the first one who had gone to meet him, and then I went out and met him. Then at various times I would go to meet him, and Boyd spent a lot of time there. Jack Stevenson went out a few times. We watched old movies with LaVey, because that was really the thing that he and I had in common.

I didn't really have much interest in Satanism—I still don't—but I do love old movies, and he loved old movies. If you could just show the films from 1947 all the time he would be a happy man. I knew a lot about those old films from the 1940s, so he and I could talk about things that I couldn't really talk to other people about. Like the films of Märta Torén or Allison Hayes, or these sort of second-level starlets that never became well known to the average person. That's pretty much how he and I got along; that's what we would talk about. We never talked about Satanism, never talked about the Devil, never talked about witchcraft. But we did talk about our favorite directors, our favorite movies, and the books that those movies were based on. Like, of course, *Nightmare Alley*, which probably everybody by now knows is one of his very favorite books and movies.

How would you say that those meetings and those film screenings impacted your life?

When I met Anton I had already put out the *Incredibly Strange Films* book, and that's probably why he was even interested in meeting me at all. As for whether there was really any impact on my life, I don't know, except that I really admired him and his love of movies. It's kind of sad that most people only really know Anton as this sort of goateed, shaved-head, Devil-worshipping guy with a knife and naked woman on an altar; it's just such a little tiny part of him. He knew carnies, he knew magicians, he played the organ regularly at the Philosopher's Club, he was at one point the only registered theremin player in the musician's union in San Francisco. . . . He was a really interesting guy who had lots of interests and lots of passions, and he just sort of got pigeonholed into

"Mr. Satan," Church of Satan, boom, that's it, and everything else kind of doesn't get talked about. That, to me, is the most fascinating thing about him. I've always been fascinated with the stuff nobody else is, so it might just be me.

But still, that original thing, the original imprint, was his own creation. When you met him, did you ever feel that it had almost become like a burden to him?

When the whole Church of Satan thing started I wasn't around, but it seemed like LaVey was really enjoying getting a great deal of celebrity. He had Jayne Mansfield and Sammy Davis Jr., all kinds of really fascinating people. Eddie Albert would come over and play guitar and sing, and he really seemed to enjoy it. But at a certain point I think it just became kind of a procrustean bed, where any attempts to explore things outside of that field would be hampered by that image. I guess that's probably true of all of us to a certain extent, but I'd say more so for LaVey than most. And then, by the 1980s when I met him, it was just these young acolytes who would shave their heads, grow goatees, show up at his house, and say, "Oh, I want to be an individualist just like you." I don't know whether it drove him crazy; it drove me nuts.

What would you say has been LaVey's greatest contribution to your life?

To be honest, it's probably my friendship with Karla, because I became much closer friends with Karla after meeting Anton. I don't see her as much as I'd like to anymore. I think maybe the thing that I've most taken away from meeting Anton was to not follow his example, strangely; to not stay in one place, to keep a moving target. Which is why I went into the East German cinema instead of continuing to just write about exploitation films forever. At some point I'll stop writing about East German films and I'll write about, I don't know what, Disney films, or something so outside of anything I've done before that I will lose all of my fans—that's my goal!

What would you say are the greatest changes that he brought for America in general?

I do think that the Church of Satan did bring some changes, but they're subtle changes; I don't think there were big changes. It's hard to tell sometimes, because the media will always take any new philosophy, and mold it into the story they want to tell. That is partly why I started writing about East German films, because I realized that what I knew about East German films was based on Western media telling me what East Germany was about—which turned out to be a lot of horseshit. So it does get tainted by that to a great deal, and that's where it gets hard to separate the wheat from the chaff.

He had a very specific sort of concept of Satanism as being an examination of how all of the things that people do enjoy have, by religion, been made "Satanic." His perspective was that, "If everything I like to do is Satanic then, damn it, I'll be a Satanist!" I can relate to that completely, and I think that more and more people appreciate that aspect of it. You're going to have the guys who wear black clothing on days when it's 120 degrees outside and listen to music they don't even like; there's going to be that, so there's always good and bad. I think there's definitely some bad aspects to what he presented to the world, but I think that if people can just think about stuff for themselves, there's a lot of good in there, too.

What do you think is the main key to his controversy? Is it just the word Satan, or was there something else?

Most of the controversy surrounding Anton I think does come from the word *Satan*, because it's such a powerful word. There are certain words that it's really dangerous to tread around. I've had friends who have tread around even more dangerous concepts and ended up falling into the abyss. He was talking about it in a really interesting way, but there's this knee-jerk reaction that's going to happen. It's like when you say "Hitler" or "Jesus"—which is not to conflate the two. There are just certain words that have so much built-in meaning that, when you try to talk about them in any truly objective way, you really can't, because all the oxygen has already been taken out of the room.

I think that's kind of true with Satan, too. So when he said Satanism, of course the media immediately went, "Satan! Satan! Satan!"—to quote the Butthole Surfers. I could see what he was doing, but it's just that the media is always going to win. This is kind of what it comes down to. They control enough to where you can steer them away from the nonsense a little bit, but it's a never-ending battle. You're constantly pushing against that nonsense, and I think that will always be true. It's just the nature of media—especially American media—because it wants to find quick, simple, easy answers to everything. Some things are complicated, and when you encounter a complicated issue and you throw this facile response out, you're squandering this wonderful opportunity to examine things. *Satan* is a dangerous word.

What was it like when you watched movies? I remember that it was either him or Blanche bringing out VHS cassettes from another room. But I know Jack Stevenson also screened 16mm films. . . .

To be honest, the only films I ever watched at Anton's place were on 16mm. We never watched VHS tapes, and that was partly because usually when we got around to watching films it was together with Jack Stevenson. He would usually bring a 16mm film, and Anton had a few himself. I'm not sure I could tell who had what anymore, I know we watched *Confessions of an Opium Eater*. There was one film that Anton had that unfortunately he couldn't find but that we were going to watch; I had to watch it later. It's a fantastic film; it's called *Yanco*. It's a Mexican film about this kid and a violin, and it's very moody and strange. So sometimes he would actually explain some film that I hadn't seen, or a film I had seen but hadn't seen in a while. I'd go back and watch them later, so it was really like a little master class in films at his place.

How did the actual screenings come about? He of course knew about Incredibly Strange Films, *and Jack was around at the time. Was it like a carefully planned, social thing or did it happen in an improvised way?*

The film screenings were definitely not improvised. I know that the times I did go with Jack, he brought a 16mm reel. Anton actually had the front room set up with a projector behind a wall; he had it set up like a little movie theater. It was really nice; you could sit and watch the movies and not have to listen to the whirring of the machine, either, because it was in the next room.

Do you have any memories of any specific film memorabilia around?

I don't remember much in the way of film memorabilia, except, of course, he did have a poster of *Nightmare Alley*. I mean, it always comes back to *Nightmare Alley*. Frankly, judging from the films that we talked about that were some of his favorites, it does seem that if you really want to get some idea of Anton's aesthetic, just go to 1947 and watch all of the movies on the list. There were some great ones back then, of course: *Nightmare Alley, Out of the Past, Brute Force*. Those were all from 1947 as well, and I'm sure there were a lot more.

Another film that he really loved was The Gangster. *It had the same kind of philosophical quality as* Nightmare Alley. *The gangster is an unwilling gangster, just like the guy in* Nightmare Alley. *He does what he does because he has no other place to go.*

I do think Anton enjoyed film noir particularly, and partly for the reason that they weren't black and white. . . . Well, they were *in* black and white, but they didn't present black-and-white solutions to things. The hero could be the bad guy, you know, as in *This Gun for Hire*. He's a killer, but he's also the protagonist. I think that appealed to Anton a lot, because I think he recognized that you can't look at the world in this really simple, cut-and-dried approach that is still foisted on us a lot: "This is good, this is bad." I still see it today; nothing's much changed, except the films are in color now.

What would you say that you miss most about him?

I just miss going over there and chatting about films with him. I really

love the movies of the 1940s. By that I don't mean only the film noirs—
I have friends I can talk about film noir with until the cows come home.
But just all that other old stuff: the comedies, the romantic comedies,
the romances, the fantasies, the war films, and the cowboy films . . . I
love cowboy films, and I can't talk to anybody about that kind of stuff.
But I could talk to Anton about it, and I do miss that.

*Did you ever feel, when you were there and talking to him about these
things, that he tried to influence you in some way, to carry things onward?*

I can't speak for everybody, but I never felt that Anton was trying to
groom me or get me to follow a specific agenda. That may be true for
other people, but I never, ever got even one iota of his trying to influence how I thought, or trying to promote some viewpoint. We'd talk
about films, and we'd talk about magic—because I do magic, too—and
that was about it, you know. I didn't get over there as often as I would
have liked.

But we'd go out and eat dinner and talk about god knows what.
It was always very casual and very little about anything to do with
the Church of Satan. Sometimes he'd be griping about what assholes
people could be. One time we were leaving his place, and this gang
of rowdy jocks came driving by, and some guy stuck his head out the
door and said, "Hey, is this where that devil dude lives?" Anton just
went back inside. Blanche and I went down, confronted them, and
they drove. When we came back later somebody had sprayed some
kind of powder all over the front step; it looked like a fire extin-
guisher or something. Just stupid stuff that he would have to put up
with on a daily basis.

*In my opinion, one of the key things that made LaVey unique was his active
integration of his own life experience into fields that are traditionally
"established" and that newcomers simply adapt to (occultism, philosophy,
religion, etc.). What are your thoughts on why this was? How would you
define the character traits that made him such a creative developer?*

First and foremost, it was because he never took anything at face value. This is a trait he has in common with other creative artists. While there is no profit in reinventing the wheel, too often people take the things they are given at face value because others say this is how things are. Anton was never afraid to ask, "Why?" When you do that, sometimes you'll find that things people take for granted are all wrong, from the ground up. A lot of his Satanist philosophy seems to be based on this fact.

On the same topic: one of the quintessential traits was his active integration of pop culture that had been forgotten or discarded, and thereby contained a force that could be tapped into and used. Do you have any memories of songs, films, et cetera, that he displayed for you as being such magical works? Have you woven in similar explorations and practices in your own life?

I don't know about "magical." Remember that Anton came from a carny background. Magic in that sense is a bit different. Both Anton and I were fans of carny magic and understood the lady in the blindfold who could not only tell you what was in your purse but give you a rundown of your entire life's experience. Magic is a secret and a trick. It's best that most people don't realize this, though. There's a reason it's called arcane knowledge.

When it comes to creativity, I get the impression that LaVey was happiest when playing his tunes, telling his stories, and writing his essays; that is, being immersed in his own expressions that he mastered so well. But these usually also require a second party: a listener, a reader. Did you ever get the impression that he expressed himself mainly to have that second party, or was the expression in itself, for himself, the most important aspect?

Anton was comfortable in his own skin. I always got the impression that he would have been happy enough playing his organ and watching old movies. I don't know that these things really require a second party to enjoy. He did like turning on people to things they weren't familiar with, but he also liked discussing these things with people who knew about them already.

Can you see any similarities between LaVey and other notable creative people at the time (regardless of their particular expressions or views)? Meaning, would you say there was something distinctly zeitgeistish about him?

Perhaps. As individualistic as we like to act and think we are, we are still rooted in the time in which we live. Anton was no different. I do think there was something of the zeitgest in *The Satanic Bible,* but I'm sure he was aware of that and understood its importance to the time.

Inside the Black House, which was your favorite room, and why?

I never took a tour of the entire place. Besides the den and the kitchen, we usually ended up in the front room watching movies. Other than that, we'd go out to eat. I never did get to see the bar downstairs. It sounded pretty amazing, but as soon as I got there, we would usually end up in discussions of films, followed by a screening of something that either he had or Jack Stevenson brought over.

Were there any quirks or habits that you found odd in LaVey? Meaning, unexpected expressions of moralisms that might have seemed un-Satanic and perhaps stemmed from the times or the religion he grew up in? Things you sort of didn't quite see coming?

His most quirky characteristic was his rather rigid—some might even say procrustean—vision of what constituted beauty. He outlined that in *The Satanic Witch.* Beyond that, his loathing for honeydew melon was the only quirky characteristic I noticed.

In the LaVeyan encouragement of fetishizing objects and environments (working with ECI, creating total environments, for instance), it's not that far-fetched to talk about an ensouling of these objects (or spaces) that one has an intimate relationship with. Did he ever give the impression that he felt that way about human beings? Meaning, that he could feel OK with using the word soul *or* ensouled *or* spirit *or* spirited *when talking about humans? I guess the extension of this question is whether you ever saw signs of his not being a 100 percent strict materialist?*

None of us are strict materialists, not even Ayn Rand, as much as she'd like to think so. We all have our quirks. I can't really say how he felt about the soul, but I do think he recognized that man is a unique animal. I honestly don't think he ever expected or wanted his philosophy to become the mainstream norm. It is an elitist philosophy that requires the hoi polloi to continue life as usual. It is a philosophy that comes with great responsibility. Unfortunately, too many of the people attracted to it should not be given the keys to the kingdom, but that's me talking. I never heard him say anything on the subject.

Did you ever feel that LaVey put on a show at times because he felt it was expected of him rather than because he was genuinely in the mood himself?

Not with me. If he didn't feel good, we'd just choose another time to meet up. Blanche was pretty good at taking care of him in this regard.

Did you perceive him as being sensitive to what others thought or felt about him?

Sometimes. It could be a real pain in the neck when some yahoos would show up in front of the house. I don't think he cared what they thought, but I do think he cared that their asininity could interfere with his life.

Were there any films that he showed you that you felt were unexpected or anachronistic? If so, why?

The most unexpected one for me was the one I told you about: *Yanco,* which is the story of a young boy who can't stand the sounds of the city and becomes obsessed with a violin. It's shot in black and white and is as beautiful and tender a movie as you'll ever see. Other than *Yanco,* he also turned me on to *The Doll,* which you might be more familiar with, since it came from your country. It's about a night watchman who becomes obsessed with a mannequin and takes it home. Definitely worth checking out!

Is there anything you would like to add, a special memory or something that you're thinking about now?

There is one kind of little memory that I'm not proud of, but I think I'll add it anyway. Anton of course loved music, and because he was Anton, I think a lot of times people would assume he would know about something when he didn't know about it. I've experienced that, too: "Hey, Jim, were you at that screening of *Faster, Pussycat, Kill! Kill!* when Tura Satana showed up?" No, because I didn't know about it . . . "Well, I just assumed you knew about it."

I did that once with Anton, where I assumed he knew that Leon Theremin was going to be at Mills College, so I, my girlfriend Michelle, my friend Monte Cazazza, and his girlfriend Michelle, we all went to Mills College, and we got to listen to Theremin talk, and we got to shake hands and say hello to Theremin—which to me is like meeting Tesla or something! And then his granddaughter played this amazing piece; she was like Clara Rockmore quality on the theremin. I mentioned this to LaVey later, and he got so angry: "Nobody told me about it! I would have been there in a heartbeat!" I felt bad about that. I've been there and done that myself, so I know exactly how it felt at the time. That's probably the most unusual memory I have to share.

15

MICHAEL MOYNIHAN

Michael Moynihan, Vermont, 2018.
Photo by Carl Abrahamsson.

"He was a very talented artist in numerous ways, and a unique philosopher."

Michael Moynihan is a writer, editor, and musician. He is the author of the books *Lords of Chaos* (with Didrik Søderlind, 1998) and *The Secret King* (with Stephen Flowers, 2007), and the editor of *American Grotesque* (2014) and *The Command to Look* (2014).

How did you first hear about Anton LaVey?

I first heard about Anton LaVey through *The Satanic Bible*. I heard about the book before I heard about him in his own right, and I believe I was about thirteen years old. I had started to become increasingly rebellious and started to get into music that was not the normal music on the radio: punk rock and then more esoteric things such as Throbbing Gristle. This was in the early 1980s; Throbbing Gristle had just broken up. Through punk rock and the Sex Pistols and things like that, I started to get interested in Dadaism and Surrealism, and I also developed very critical, caustic attitudes toward organized religion. I started to get interested in the occult, also through the Surrealists.

I was investigating all these things on my own, and I was reading a lot. I'd always read a lot; my father always encouraged my sister and me to read. At that time there were a lot of independent bookstores around where we lived, so I would go and comb through the shelves. I started looking in the occult section, and I came across *The Satanic Bible* and bought it, as a paperback; that was my first exposure. Around that time, I'd really gone off on my own tangent. I was doing things that were totally different from my friends and the people my same age.

I moved into my own world, with my own interests and my own contacts. I started writing to people, I started going to music concerts by myself, and I was also watching lots of movies. I actually used to stay up late at night. I had a room in the basement of the house, and I would sneak up into my parents' bedroom. All we had was a black-and-white TV that was barely worth watching—which was kind of a good thing—and you had to change the channels with a pair of pliers. I had realized my parents were really sound sleepers, so I would actually creep up into their room, open the door, take the black-and-white TV, unplug it, and carry it downstairs to my room in the basement. I'd sit under the covers and watch midnight movies on this independent television station: the only one that would screen old films. Every night there were different ones. One night it was *Rosemary's Baby*. I saw that and was totally fascinated by it, and by the Satanic figures in that movie, who are very charming and erudite; they're sort of the antiheroes of the film. So that was fascinating.

Then I read *The Satanic Bible*, and that's how I came to LaVey. Oddly enough, it was kind of underwhelming, because I already agreed with most everything that was in there. I was impressed on the one hand; it was like a voice expressing things that I, maybe, hadn't formulated, but that I basically was in complete agreement with. At that time I was so into conflict, and opposing opinions, and going against them, that it was almost . . . I just thought, "Well that's great, but I kind of already feel that way." I didn't pay a huge amount of attention to it, but it definitely registered.

And how did you first come into contact with him?

By the end of the 1980s, I was living in Belgium. I'd started doing electronic music myself, and I had a project called Coup de Grâce. I was invited by these artists over in Antwerp, Belgium, who called themselves Club Moral, to come over there, first to play concerts when I was sixteen or seventeen, and then I ended up living there. They lived in an old factory building, so I made a room in the building and lived there. I stayed there for a few years, illegally. It wasn't a squat, but it was not a place that was legal for habitation, and I didn't have a visa or anything like that. I would go back and forth to the States every three months, and then go back.

I'd been listening to Throbbing Gristle and Boyd Rice and SPK and all that kind of stuff, and I got in touch with Boyd Rice. I was at a flea market in Belgium, and I found a Peggy March single. I bought it, and I sent it to him. He wrote back and was really excited, and then when I moved back to the States shortly after that, we started speaking on the phone, and we had a really great rapport. We'd speak almost every day and discuss all kinds of ideas, and he eventually asked if I wanted to collaborate with him on a NON concert—to come and perform as NON.

We did three concerts in Japan. He was living in San Francisco, so I flew to San Francisco first and stayed for a few days, and we worked out the details of what the performance was going to be. At that time he was visiting Anton LaVey regularly, and he said, "You've got to meet Anton; you'll hit it off, and he'll really enjoy meeting you." I said sure, and we went over there one night, and it was the usual thing: you arrive there in the evening and you leave in the morning. It was fantastic. Then I believe I went one more time after we got back from Japan—we went over again and saw him then. We immediately hit it off and had a phenomenal, very special time there, and that was the beginning of the contact.

How would you say that those first meetings impacted your life?

I was already somebody who had a kind of a clandestine world of my own—one that I had pretty much created outside of any expectations, or contrary to any expectations from parents, school, society. I had dropped out of school the day I turned sixteen and had just gone my own way and done my own things that I was interested in—the rest of the world be damned. I think meeting Anton was really inspiring in the sense that you went into his world. When you went to visit him, you went into his universe, and it was like a parallel universe where he had done that for his whole life and created his own reality. That was really inspiring to know that there was this sort of secret, shadow, nighttime world, and that there were people living in it, and sort of simultaneously doing their own thing. It was inspiring and encouraging to know that they were out there, and to meet more of them.

Did that change after he died in 1997?

The feeling that there's a secret cabal of like-minded spirits hasn't changed. Once you meet a few of them, then you know that they're out there. That just stays with you, and in some sense, those types of spirits and people are immortal. If they're doing things in the world and affecting culture in any way, then they will be immortal—if they're doing the right things and they're true to themselves. In that sense his death, while it was unfortunate and came too soon and too suddenly, doesn't change his influence. In a certain way he's undead; he's still alive, like any great spirit or soul.

Is there any idea or concept that's still particularly relevant for you?

In many ways, LaVey's Satanism and the Church of Satan overshadowed a lot of the subtleties and nuances of his philosophy. I think it'll take a lot of time for that to get its proper due and to be seen in a balanced way. People still react really viscerally to his existence and what he was doing, and they're not interested in the subtleties. There were all kinds of ideas that he put forth in his essays and when you'd speak to him that are absolutely relevant, more relevant than ever. One concept that I think is like that is the good guy badge, which is an interesting phenomenon. The more you have a secular society, you see it more and more. It used to be that the religious figures were sort of wearing the overt good guy badges—whether it's the collar or the robe or whatever. But now it's more of a sociopolitical thing. I think you see that affecting America, absolutely, and much of Europe as well.

It's probably going to keep spreading with people who have a one-way opinion of what's correct and proper thought behavior. It's always cloaked in a kind of moral garb—that's what the good guy badge is. And of course these good guys are rarely good guys in their private lives, and I think we're seeing that now. They are often behaving in exactly the ways that they claim they're fighting against. I think he was very perceptive about those kinds of foibles of human behavior and human psychology—feeling better than, and superior to, the next guy, and all that. Those kinds of thought, which Nietzsche also expressed, are very timely, now more than ever.

What do you think are the greatest changes that he actually brought into a general American mind frame?

I don't know that LaVey changed the American mind frame. I think it was maybe more that he was very much in touch with a certain aspect of the zeitgeist; he was in tune with the times. Quite often contrary to the overt, prevailing, most obvious things, but he was in tune with other currents that were underneath the surface and going parallel. You might have overt currents like the hippie phenomenon, which he was not a part of and very much against in many ways, but there was also an undercurrent of other esoteric, countercultural people who were not just part of that, who didn't fit into easy categories, and weren't members of movements. I think he understood that.

In many ways his philosophy, and Satanism as a way of looking at the world, is a completely postmodern thing, which, regardless of your opinion about postmodern theory or things like that, there's absolutely something to it, in the sense that we live now in a time where we can see so much of the past, and we no longer live in traditional societies; basically, the rules have been broken, for better or worse. You can actively pick and choose and create your own reality based on the things that resonate with you.

LaVey was completely in touch with that, and aware of that, and advocated that. I think he was very perceptive in that regard. As far as occultism, I think in many ways he was against the grain there, as he was in other areas. But he was sort of a precursor to such things as chaos magic; that couldn't have happened without LaVey's approach, and the more postmodern approaches to the history of magic and occultism, where you can use the things that work and ignore the things that don't, and get rid of the dross and the sort of musty old robes and all that. He's an interesting combination of somebody who was very modern on the one hand, but he's also, I think, an antimodernist in many ways as well. He has his foot in both worlds.

If we stick with the big American picture, do you feel that he has been misrepresented in America, and if so, how?

It depends who's representing him, of course. I think he's been misrepresented by the people who oppose him, who don't understand him. But then again, how could you expect them to? By adopting the mantle of Satanism, he, I'm sure knowingly, was treading those waters and was going to get those kind of reactions. Those people aren't interested in subtleties or looking beneath the surface and seeing what he's actually saying. As soon as they hear that word, or think about that imagery, it's colored by their own views and attitudes, and usually colored by a Christian background—often with medieval fantasies and quasipornographic images that are of course lurid and titillating to them at the same time as they're horrified by them.

He must have been well aware that he was going to stir that hornet's nest, and he did it consciously and deliberately; otherwise, he wouldn't have chosen that mantle. So yes, those people don't understand him, but they don't understand a lot of things, and they're not interested in the gray areas. By definition it's either good or evil, and never the twain shall meet.

Whereas LaVey was somebody who was much more in tune with the reality of human nature and the gray areas of existence, which is really where everything happens. He knew that. The real secret, I think, to his philosophy, is that it's a *Lebensphilosophie,* like Nietzsche talked about, which can actually be lived by human beings because it's not contrary to human nature. Whereas most of these big religions have set something up that is almost impossible to fulfill. It's contrary to human nature in many ways. LaVey was good at eviscerating the kind of hypocrisy that is going to be the result of that sort of situation, where you have an impossible belief system. There's no way you can follow it, really.

Do you think that his impact on that philosophical level would have been different had the S-word not been there?

Satanism is inherently problematic in certain ways, and that was one reason, when I first heard about it, I wasn't that attracted to that side of it. I strongly disliked Christianity. I wasn't opposed to blasphemy per se, but it also seemed that there was no reason to joust against it—it was better to just ignore it and try to have it not influence your life. Whereas LaVey was deliberately provoking a lot of reaction by taking that term on.

On the other hand, if he had said he was some kind of super individualist or egoist, I don't think it would have had the same impact. It wouldn't have attracted people's attention; it would have been much smaller; he wouldn't have been written about in the press; he would be sort of a footnote to the counterculture. I think he's more than a footnote because he had the guts to just use his instincts and, even knowing that he was probably going to have to be explaining himself until the day he died, he went ahead and did that. Because you have to get people's attention somehow, and then you can try to get your ideas across. If nobody's even listening, you're not going to get any message out there.

On a personal level, what do you miss most about him?

I guess I miss knowing that there's a colorful character like that— they're so few and far between. It's very rare that you meet somebody who really has a magical persona—that it's not just ideology, or talk, or perhaps they've done a few interesting things. When you met LaVey in person you knew you'd met somebody unique, who had created his own reality. That's an incredibly rare thing, actually, and the older you get you realize just how rare it is. Those kinds of people are so few and far between; it's so special that when you do happen to encounter one and spend any amount of time with them—even just minutes—it sort of changes your perspective on things and, I would say, actually renews your faith in humanity a little bit.

LaVey was very much a misanthrope who didn't have much use for the vast majority of humanity, but the best parts of humanity come through in someone like him, and in that against-the-grain persona that was just him. It wasn't an act and it wasn't a show, despite what his detractors might say; but they don't know because they never actually spoke with the man or met him. I think that's it. There's just so few of those people that one meets in a lifetime. It's nice to know that they're out there in the world.

What about his legacy? What do you think will happen to it?

I think he will be better understood over time. Some people have to die first before there can be a balanced assessment of them. I think that his ideas will be taken more seriously; that he wasn't just a sensationalist or a publicity hound. He really wasn't. Somebody who is a publicity hound wouldn't become a recluse for decades and decades like he did, for the latter part of his life. I hope there will be a more balanced assessment of what he really represented in the bigger picture, in the cultural picture, and in the artistic picture. He was a very talented artist in numerous ways, and a unique philosopher. There are obviously people that follow his work that are aware of that, but they're the minority, for sure. A character like that, who is such an iconoclast, has to pass away, I think, before other people are going to dare to get close to what he was actually saying, and think about it in a rational, intelligent way.

Is there anything you'd like to add?

There's the question about what impact did he have on my life . . . I would say one tangible thing that he did was to leave a lot of clues for people. He was actually a voracious reader and a voracious follower of obscure cultural trends, artifacts, personalities; he was really a sort of historian of the underworld. He would leave little clues in such things as the dedication lists in *The Satanic Bible;* or in his essays he'd mention obscure people; or in *The Satanic Witch*—the bibliography is like a geological mine that you can go into and find all kinds of previously unknown gems and bring them back up to the light, really obscure things.

In the dedication list of *The Satanic Bible,* he mentioned the photographer William Mortensen, and he talked about Mortensen's book *The Command to Look.* Mortensen stuck in my head, and I started to find some of his books. I didn't find *The Command to Look* until much later, but I found a bunch of his regular manuals, like *Outdoor Portraiture* or *Pictorial Lighting*—different things that on the surface look like these very boring, old, outdated photo books that would no longer be relevant in the age of digital cameras and all that, but when you actually open these things up and start to read them, beyond the text, he would have his own photographs. And those are truly strange and weird in the best sense of the word. They're disconcerting, and they are disconcerting in the context of this sort of almost sterile manual. I started collecting those when I would find them, and I got a big group of them.

Adam Parfrey from Feral House was visiting us here in Vermont. I had an old photographer friend who was over for dinner with us that night, and after the dinner I just said, "Adam, have you looked at these Mortensen books lately? They're incredible; the banal sounding ones are actually filled with weird stuff." Adam said, "Oh, I think I know what you mean, yeah, I've got some of those." I pulled out the stack of them I had, and we all started looking at them and were amazed by them. I said, "Adam, Feral House really should do a Mortensen book," and he said, "Oh, I've always wanted to, but I've never been able to pull it together, but it's always been an idea, and I've talked to a few people about it before." I said, "Well, look at this stuff; it's begging to happen." Adam said, "Well, do you want to do it? Do you want to work with me on it? If you want to do that, I'll do it; we'll do it." We decided to do it that night.

We got in touch with Larry Lytle, who is a Mortensen expert and who's been researching Mortensen's life in minute detail for decades. Adam had spoken to him before, but they'd never been able to really connect on a project. But we basically talked to Larry and said that "we're going to do these things, we're going to do a coffee table book; either you're with us or you're not."

At first Larry was a little skeptical and worried about the reputation of Feral House, and about my reputation. But we all went out to the archive in Arizona, where Mortensen's material is all held. Larry knew that place like the back of his hand, and he got to meet Adam and me. He said, "All right, I'm with you on this; let's do it."

And so we did the coffee table book *American Grotesque,* and we did a new edition of *The Command to Look,* for which I wrote a whole essay about the LaVeyan connection to Mortensen, investigating that in about as much detail as you possibly can; that's an afterword to the book; it's quite lengthy. So that's now part of my life. And Mortensen's having a renaissance in the wake of those projects. It's only sad that Anton wasn't around to see them, because they definitely bear his stamp. He was one of the first people to pick up on the importance of Mortensen in the scheme of things.

Mortensen is another trailblazer: an iconoclastic person who's both modern and antimodern at the same time; against the grain, yet sort of capturing some really important current. Now you can see his influence in all sorts of ways. Lots of things that he imagined have come to pass, just like LaVey imagined things that came to pass later. Photoshop and all sorts of modern things of manipulation like that are things that Mortensen dreamed up in his own head.

16

PEGGY NADRAMIA

Peggy Nadramia, Poughkeepsie, New York, 2018.
Photo by Carl Abrahamsson.

"Without Satan, he probably could have been the mayor of San Francisco."

Peggy Nadramia is a writer and editor. She is the high priestess of the Church of Satan and is married to its high priest, Peter Gilmore.

How did you first hear about Anton LaVey?

I saw him on television. I believe it was around 1970; it was a news broadcast, and it was probably something that came out in response to the release of *The Satanic Bible,* and also the release of *Satanis.* I think they came out roughly around the same time. There was footage from *Satanis* on the evening news, and I was at a friend's house, and it was around Halloween, so they had to have this scary ritual footage. I remember him in the horns and saying, "Hail Satan!" I guess I was about twelve years old. That was the first time I ever saw him or knew anything about him. I was introduced to *The Satanic Bible,* and the whole idea of a Church of Satan, by Peter when we were in high school together.

But it was really kind of interesting, because right around the same time that I met Peter, and I was learning about Satanism—I hadn't even read *The Satanic Bible* yet—my aunt dropped off a shopping bag of used books. We used to do that in our family—trade a lot of paperbacks—and in that pile of paperbacks was *The Devil's Avenger,* the little paperback by Burton Wolfe that was the biography of Anton LaVey. I actually read that before I read *The Satanic Bible.*

It just opened up this whole world to me: that people could be whatever they wanted to be, they could be a weird kooky couple like the Addams Family and live in a black house. I was brought up Irish-Catholic, and it was a very insular kind of family clannish thing. You usually married somebody that you knew from the neighborhood. Suddenly, it was like you didn't have to worry about any of that any-more; you could be whatever you wanted to be, and have a lion in your house; real adults did this, and adults could do playful, fun things, too; they didn't have to just go to work every day and be boring. So, that actually meant almost as much to me as *The Satanic Bible*—it just opened up a vista of possibility.

How did your first meeting with LaVey impact your life?

Meeting Anton LaVey, talking to him, exchanging ideas with him, hearing what he had to say about my ideas, and his reflection to me of his opinions about things—it just gave me so much courage and so much determination to go forward. It gave you that kind of feeling that I guess every parental relationship should really give you: that you can do it, that you're on the right track, and that you should just keep going in that direction. I can't overemphasize how great that was, and how formative that was.

One of the times we were visiting—it was always kind of a sad moment when we'd be leaving the house for the last time; we knew we'd be hitting the airport soon—he gave me a hug, and he pulled me in really close, and he put his mouth near my ear, and he said, "You do everything right." Who doesn't want to hear that from a parental fig-ure? Whenever I have my down moments, or question what I'm doing and where things are going, I just try to remember and hear his voice in my ear: "You do everything right."

You met several times during the course of your becoming more and more involved with the Church of Satan. Did you feel that you got to know him closer the longer it went?

Sometimes we'd be there for a whole week, so we got to see him on a daily basis and got to see the guy he really was. He wasn't always putting up; it wasn't like a state occasion every time we saw him. I feel like we did get closer. He certainly wasn't a perfect person. He had his moments; he had his little outbursts and things that would annoy him and bug him and tire him out. Certainly, as we know, all our friends have their moments when you see the good and bad in them, and the things that they work to overcome.

This kind of appreciation and resonance that you felt with him, did that change when he died in 1997?

I don't really know how to answer that. I have very strong memories of him, of talking to him and watching him and hearing him. I can't say that my perspective on any of that has changed. What I've learned by reading a lot of our archival materials, and early versions of things and letters he wrote, is that he never changed that perspective on Satanism. He always had a very strong idea of it. He formed it along the way; he tweaked it and nuanced it, but it was always very much in the direction that it wound up in in *The Satanic Bible* and is further elucidated in his essays. I can't say that there's been any revelation.

What would you say has been LaVey's greatest contribution to your life, on a personal level?

He gave me so much courage and so much confidence that my viewpoint on things was the right one: it was on track, it was the right one for me, that I shouldn't back down on any of it, that I should never feel like I need to take a back seat to anything. That I really just have to stick with my individual expression of Satanism and not worry about what other people think it should be, or hope it should be.

Is there any particular idea or concept that you got from him that's still extra relevant today?

He said to me once that the animals should be our gurus. What he meant by that was that we should observe them when we want to know what our real priorities should be. Animals have their priorities. It's oft quoted that they don't lie awake at night and weep for their sins. I think he felt very strongly that when we're worried about whether a thing is important, well, would an animal think that was important? Would an animal make that choice? Of course not.

He really strongly felt that we have this feral nature in us, and we have the intellectual capacity to be incredibly vicious. But we can also use that capacity to refine our impulses in a direction that is helpful for us and will help keep our species alive and our planet alive. Animals don't do these self-destructive things; they don't destroy their environments. We really need to keep that in mind.

What do you think were the greatest contributions that he presented to America?

I think he felt strongly that church and state need to be separate; that we can't keep going with a country that's founded on these kinds of loosely based biblical proclamations. We need to understand that everybody's got a different religious bent, and that's exactly why it needs to be kept completely separate from our laws and our legal procedures. There's no reason for so many of these silly laws. If you go back and look at them, they're completely based on some presuggested biblical proclamation, and I think that, for America, that would definitely be his strongest admonition.

In what ways do you feel that LaVey has been misrepresented by general culture or specific individuals; what do they usually pick on that you know are misrepresentations?

Specifically about LaVey himself, the man, you always hear this, "He was a carny showman; he was just in it for the money." These things are just so patently untrue. He was a carny showman, but his philosophy is a sincere one and is, anyway, not even inconsistent with the idea of being a carny showman. A carny showman could very well follow this philosophy, so I don't see how that somehow turns into an insult—or how people think that somehow overturns his philosophy or his accomplishments with that philosophy.

He was a carnival person at a time when it wasn't cool to be a carnival person; there wasn't a culture of people who love tattoos and geek shows. Of course they have to overturn that for him, you know, "Oh he wasn't really that." Well, he was, and he talked about it at a time when it wasn't cool to talk about it. Somehow that seems to be bound up in the idea that his philosophy was not a sincere one. That, I think, is the biggest misconception or piece of misinformation, or disinformation, about Anton LaVey that goes around. They like to just throw that out—it's like a convenient sound byte—but it actually has no bearing on his philosophy or the way he lived.

What do you think was the main key to his controversial status? Was it mainly the S-word or was it his person, or his presence?

I think it was definitely Satan; that he represented Satan; that he was often depicted by writers and journalists as the "personification of Satan on Earth." That is definitely the thing that got him all the negative publicity. In actuality, he was an incredibly charming person. He had dozens and dozens and dozens of friends; he had friends that remained loyal to him to their deaths, even when he was kind of retreating from the world a bit, and not really answering phone messages or mail. These people would keep writing to him. I've seen their messages to him: "Tony, can we have lunch? Tony, how are you doing out there? Tony, there was a big earthquake; how are you and the family?"

He inspired a lot of friendship and devotion and loyalty, and he was charming. Without Satan, he probably could have been the mayor of San Francisco, for all I know. Enough people liked him, and he was humorous, he remembered things about people. I don't think he ever would have lacked for a lot of positive publicity if it weren't for that *S*-word thing.

On a personal level, what do you miss most about him?

I miss his humor. I miss that there's so many times when things come up, and I've said, "Oh my god, would Doktor have laughed his butt off at this," or, "Oh boy, just this guy's name would have made him crack up." He loved that thing where a person has a name that totally suits the silly thing that they're doing, or their crazy position in life. He loved things like that; he loved corny jokes; he would have loved the irony of so much of what's going on in the world today. It makes me sad when I realize that I can't tell him about that anymore.

How do you see his legacy now and in the future?

I hope that his work continues to stay in print and continues to give people the freedom that he wanted them to have. He truly felt that his philosophy was one that freed people; it made them free, and it made them happy, because it allowed them to be who they really were. I hope that going forward, his legacy is that he was the man who unfettered a lot of people of their religious backgrounds, their guilt, their lack of confidence in who they were. I hope he's seen as that: the man that unfettered them.

In my opinion, one of the key things that made LaVey unique was his active integration of his own life experience into fields that are traditionally "established" and that newcomers simply adapt to (occultism, philosophy, religion, etc.). What are your thoughts on why this was? How would you define the character traits that made him such a creative developer?

What comes through most strongly when you review LaVey's writing from the early days of the Church of Satan and his coining of the Satanic philosophy is the urgency he felt in getting his message out there. He was well read but directed by his own tastes and preferences, which allowed him to absorb the writings of other philosophers on a completely unfiltered level. He drew what he wanted from them and knew immediately what he didn't need. His mission was to speak directly to readers who he felt would find his philosophy liberating and his ideas directly accessible.

This came, I feel, from a deeply ingrained sense of being right about human nature, a constant checking and rechecking of his observations against what hundreds of years of academia was teaching us about people. He knew he had something and he had to get it out there. He was confident, and he was driven. He had self-doubts, as his correspondence shows, but only about how his work would fit into a professional realm such as publishing—never about his message or his ability to deliver it. Today we might just say that he was Fired Up!

On the same topic: one of the quintessential traits was his active integration of pop culture that had been forgotten or discarded, and thereby contained a force that could be tapped into and used. Do you have any memories of songs, films, et cetera, that he displayed for you as being such magical works?

There was a point in the later years when he'd acquired a bookshelf audio system with two cassette decks and multiple inputs for microphones. Several of his visitors from this time remember recording songs in the kitchen with him, and he would usually assign you a song to learn before you came over. The songs he recommended for me included "Ten Cents a Dance," "Moanin' Low" from the film *Key Largo,* and "No More Love" from the film *Roman Scandals.*

He was mainly focused on the atmosphere around these songs and the contexts in which they were presented: the tired, overlooked, worn-out woman delivering a gentle condemnation to the world and the situations that created her downfall. When I'd completed the last take of "No More Love," he looked at me and said, "No one else in the entire world has sung that song tonight, or any other night, for years. Now we've created something and sent it out into the ethers—watch Diamanda Galas start singing it now."

He firmly believed that viewing and performing neglected works was an act of magic; I can only speculate about his goals, but I think he was trying to keep his own visions and aesthetics alive in the universe somehow. It was certainly a magical feeling to share this with him.

Have you woven in similar explorations and practices in your own life?

My indulgence in the re-creation of Tiki, Polynesian Pop, and Exotica spaces and experiences have made use of his principles, both the magic of forgotten lore and the idea of Erotic Crystallization Inertia. Our Victorian home has also been the location for some magic from the past; we've played old records on our old Victrola, had live musicians in and out of the house playing macabre music from long ago as part of our Halloween celebrations, and a ukulele strumming away at an afternoon tea.

When it comes to creativity, I get the impression that LaVey was happiest when playing his tunes, telling his stories, and writing his essays; that is, being immersed in his own expressions that he mastered so well. But these usually also require a second party: a listener, a reader. Did you ever get the impression that he expressed himself mainly to have that second party, or was the expression in itself, for himself, the most important aspect?

I don't think there's any question that it was the act itself that fulfilled him. He was truly a Phibesian wizard at those keyboards, playing long into the night whether he had listeners or not. He was moving sound waves and other waves with those sounds, and that was his aim.

It should always be remembered that he was a visual artist as well, and he never stopped drawing and doodling—I've seen the evidence of this in the archives, where his doodles often accompany his notes about a future project, which he'd describe not only textually but visually. He was a highly visual person; he loved looking at things and creating and manipulating imagery. He was delighted with Photoshop and CAD but could also never pass up a nice little piece of white paper that needed a sketch of a nearby person or animal, a car or a boat he'd been imagining.

Can you see any similarities between LaVey and other notable creative people at the time (regardless of their particular expressions or views)? Meaning, would you say there was something distinctly zeitgeistish about him?

I see a pretty strong parallel between LaVey and Hugh Hefner. Hefner was a champion of personal freedom, sexual and otherwise. He was deeply opposed to religious oppression and saw it as unhealthy and poisonous, as did LaVey. Despite what has been labeled the exploitation of women in his magazine and elsewhere, Hefner was a strong supporter of the ERA, reproductive rights, and autonomy for women, as well as LGBTQ+ rights.

Apart from Hef, I think LaVey was unique. Even as he espoused individual freedom of expression and advised his readers to throw off the chains of their accepted view of God and the Devil, he was also lashing out at the mushy relativism of the androgynous, flower-power culture, the hypocritical white witches, and advocating responsibility to the responsible. He wasn't just criticizing the old, organized religions—he was kicking out at all the phony spirituality of the new ones, too. "When all religious faith in lies has waned, it is because man has become closer to himself . . . he no longer can view himself in two parts, the carnal and the spiritual, but sees them merge as one, and then to his abysmal horror, discovers they are only the carnal—AND ALWAYS WERE!"*

Inside the Black House, which was your favorite room, and why?

It's very difficult to pick a favorite room in that house, because each one evokes memories that are different in nature but all so precious. We spent so much time in the Purple Parlor, the reception room where we also watched movies. The first time we visited, there was the most beautiful

---

*LaVey, *The Satanic Bible* (New York: Avon Books, 1969), 45.

mermaid stretched out and holding up the glass for the coffee table. In later years, the tombstone replaced her. The mummified armadillo, the infinity mirror, all the books, would welcome us back on each visit.

The kitchen was where the concerts took place, where magic was created, and also where we could enjoy the cats, and watch the snake, and gaze at those crazy murals on the walls while we completely lost touch with what time or what day it was. Off the kitchen was the bathroom, an experience in itself, with more murals, signage, and the World's Largest Cobweb wafting gently overhead.

I would have been happy to spend the rest of my life in the Den of Iniquity. 'Nuff said.

I guess the room I feel most privileged to have entered, and spent time with him in, would be the front ritual chamber. The history in that room, the resonance from the walls and objects, was palpable. Even after his death, sitting in there was like being in an old theater, alone, as total silence falls but you feel the space expanding around you, awaiting the next pin drop of sound. It truly felt like time-out-of-time in there.

Were there any quirks or habits that you found odd in LaVey? Meaning, unexpected expressions of moralisms that might have seemed un-Satanic and perhaps stemmed from the times or the religion he grew up in? Things you sort of didn't quite see coming?

Considering that he was about the same age as my dad, LaVey was remarkably open minded about sexual orientation, gender, racial equality, and alternative lifestyles—in fact, I think he was in favor of the pursuit of alternative lifestyles of every and any kind because he thought people were often too repressed and downtrodden by archaic religious beliefs to really live the lives they wanted. He was very pro-woman and always thought they were his best allies and often the power behind many thrones.

That's why it always brought me up short that he was antiabortion. He was very concerned for the rights of the fetus; a woman in this position had brought herself there and should take responsibility for the consequences. He was big on responsibility. However, he never pushed this conviction on others to the extent of issuing any edict or rule about abortion being somehow anti-Satanic. I think he correctly perceived how personal a choice this was for every individual, and individual freedom was central to his philosophy.

In the LaVeyan encouragement of fetishizing objects and environments (working with ECI, creating total environments, for instance), it's not that far-fetched to talk about an ensouling of these objects (or spaces) that one has an intimate relationship with. Did he ever give the impression that he felt that way about human beings? Meaning, that he could feel OK with using the word soul *or* ensouled *or* spirit *or* spirited *when talking about humans? I guess the extension of this question is whether you ever saw signs of his not being a 100 percent strict materialist?*

What I sensed in him was a deep regret that he would eventually die, and not be around to see his son grow up, to watch his own influence in the world expand and take shape, or to continue to experience the good things in life. He was too much of a realist, though, to make immortality of the soul or personality more than a passing fancy. He said that we live on in the brains and sinews of those whose respect we've gained, and he didn't go on the record to change that position.

His references to an afterlife, a continuation of a strong ego in the material world, seemed wistful to me, not displaying a whole lot of conviction. That said, I'd never call him a 100 percent strict materialist. He believed in magic; he defined magic, but he also knew it could manifest in an infinite number of ways. I see his magic continuing to unfold, as I see the magic of other friends who are no longer "here." And I know you do, too.

Did you ever feel that LaVey put on a show at times because he felt it was expected of him rather than because he was genuinely in the mood himself?

By the time we got to know Anton LaVey in the late '80s, I think he was well past putting on a show for anyone. It was truly a case of been there, done that. He'd already decisively ceased his "stuffed rats and tombstones" media cooperation; what he was in the mood for was the exchange of ideas. When he put together an evening's entertainment for a guest, it was mainly to elicit a response and to hear what that person would say.

Did you perceive him as being sensitive to what others thought or felt about him?

I don't think he ever cared what people thought or felt about him, as long as he wasn't being judged unfairly. He seemed very indignant when lies were spread about him, or when people accused him of making up stories about his past. He rankled at certain persons who had taken on the role of his "Boswell," and he'd say that word in the most disparaging of tones.

Do you think there was something or some things that he would have done differently in his life, had he had the chance?

My short answer is no. I've read through a great deal of his personal writings, formal and informal, and put together a lot of his life's story by conjecture and what I'd call circumstantial evidence. He may not have achieved the heights of wealth and independence he'd hoped for, but as he said himself, he had what he wanted, and who he wanted, within reach, and nobody was his boss.

He was adept at looking at what others might characterize as stumbling blocks and pitfalls along the way, and seeing how they needed to happen and how doors were thereby opened for good things to manifest later. We all do that to some extent, but he was always able to perceive that a regrettable relationship could also be the conduit for another, more positive person to come into his life. And all that said, I'm pretty sure there were some people he wished he'd never met. "How do I buy back my introduction?" was a favorite line of his.

During the '90s, you and Peter weren't only publishing The Black Flame **but also** Grue **and anthologies such as** Narcopolis **through Hell's**

Kitchen Productions. Did LaVey usually [provide] feedback on things you sent him?

He read *The Black Flame* pretty carefully and would usually comment on most of the articles. He prized a good visual presentation of Satanic material, and as the magazine represented the Church of Satan, he wanted it to look sharp and professional, and I think we came through for him.

Grue was a journal of modern horror fiction, and I don't know that the stories were always to his particular taste, as he'd grown up with *Weird Tales* and noir paperbacks; our stories sometimes strayed pretty far from the norm—Karl Edward Wagner called what we were doing, "the raw edge of horror." But he'd often say something about the illustrations and was always proud of the attention and awards the magazine was earning.

Was it important for you that he should like Hell's Kitchen material like that? Was there something he suggested to you, publishing-wise, that never came to fruition?

Well, it was very important that he approve and enjoy the material we produced that was involved with Satanism, and that was definitely the case, or he wouldn't have allowed us to call *The Black Flame* the official publication of the Church of Satan, nor would he have directed Magistra Barton to send her manuscript for the history to us, instead of elsewhere. He didn't preapprove our material, but he did let us know where he thought we could make improvements or push some elements. As far as suggesting projects for publishing, he just wanted more. More real Satanism in the marketplace could only be a good thing, a great thing.

Toward the end of LaVey's life, the internet quickly established itself. Did you talk to him about it, and the need for an online CoS presence? Did he seem interested in the possibilities of the web?

His ideas about the internet were mixed at first, as all of ours were, because none of us had any idea where it was going or how it would look. Initially, he thought the Church of Satan shouldn't have a website because that would put us squarely on the line of conforming to mass appeal. "Everybody's doing it." But he quickly keyed in to the idea that the Web made narrowcasting possible to a degree that was unprecedented in human history—he saw that not unlike the zine revolution that immediately preceded it, websites and message boards could cater to the most specific of interests and fetishes; aficionados of the obscure could find each other and create and share new material with a target audience. He was very enthused about that.

He saw that the Church could now be found by far-flung adherents of the philosophy, and our essential tenets shared quickly and accurately, in ever-increasing numbers. Peter discussed ideas with him for what the site would look like and what it could contain. Doktor LaVey was particularly interested in the idea that he could work on recordings, writings, or drawings and upload them immediately without the need for intermediaries, publishers, or record companies. Think of how much we've missed—imagine a world with him in it, doing all that!

Becoming involved in CoS and eventually leading the organization is a big responsibility, and a visible one. How did your family react along the way?

My mother was concerned when I brought home *The Satanic Bible*. Strangely enough, I'd already read *The Devil's Avenger*, because it had appeared in a shopping bag full of books from my aunt (her sister), so she couldn't exactly complain about bad influences. While I was at school one day, Mom picked up *The Satanic Bible* and read it for herself; she told me later she was relieved that it didn't require any blood sacrifices or sex—her main concern. My dad wasn't really aware of my Satanic interests and just saw it all as part of my being a creepy young girl who liked monsters.

The first time Peter was scheduled to appear on national television, I was very apprehensive. I had visions of angry crowds waiting for us on the street, or of opening our mailbox to find it full of hateful threats. There was very little of that; he did get recognized in an airport immediately afterward, which was weird, and hate mail is just part of the job around here. What he got a lot more of were excited greetings from neighbors, waitstaff, postal workers, and, yes, family members who would exclaim delightedly, "Hey! I saw you on TV!"

TV, we discovered, trumps Satan. TV is the real god, and when you've bathed in its benedictions, You Are of the Body. People in our neighborhood started calling him Padre; we received extra fortune cookies.

My family has never been anything less than accepting of this strange detour my life has taken away from the path of normalcy. They're genuinely happy when they see Peter appear for the thousandth time on the History Channel, or when his picture rolls up in some silly clickbait article. They know who we really are.

Is there anything you'd like to add?

In the beginning, Anton LaVey fervently believed in the liberating power of his philosophy. He was certain that when people, all kinds of people, read his words, they'd happily drop the shackles of their former religion's dogma and oppression and declare themselves fulfilled Satanists at last. Some people did, but some people were so charmed by him, so amused by the delightful wickedness of shouting, "Hail Satan!" that they joined up for the hell of it. Anyone who smiled on him, who told him his little black book made sense, during his days as a very public celebrity, might be gifted with an issue of the *Cloven Hoof,* or a poster, or even an honorary red card. These people drifted away.

The years went by, and LaVey continued to observe humanity and those who stepped up to align themselves with his philosophy, along with individuals who simply demonstrated a form of de facto Satanism via their creative works or books or other output. He realized what a minority Satanists really are. One observes a decided sea change in his writing and attitude toward the last decades of his life that points to his conviction that true Satanists were born that way. He saw his work as it functioned for this small alien elite—people who found Satanism as a mirror of their true perspective, not just a rebellious position for fun and games. We were his monster kids, instantly comprehending this amalgam of rationality and fantasy he'd created for what it was, a strategy we'd employed since childhood, working everyday magic into a clear-eyed vision of what was real. And I think he was satisfied with that.

17
JACK STEVENSON

Jack Stevenson, Copenhagen, 2018.
Photo by Carl Abrahamsson.

"His memories were alive, and his stories were alive."

Jack Stevenson is an American writer and film historian/collector, who runs the cinema Husets Biograf in Copenhagen, Denmark. His books include *Fleshpot: Cinema's Sexual Myth Makers & Taboo Breakers* (2000), *Land of a Thousand Balconies: Discoveries and Confessions of a B-Movie Archaeologist* (2003), and *Scandinavian Blue: The Erotic Cinema of Sweden and Denmark in the 1960s and 1970s* (2010).

How did you first hear about Anton LaVey?

I first heard about Anton LaVey when I moved to San Francisco. I had probably heard about him before that, but in 1990 I moved to San Francisco. The people that I was hanging out with knew him, and eventually we were invited over to the famous Black House. There was a girl called Becky Wilson, and she was a real mover and shaker on the scene; she knew a lot of people. She introduced me to Terry Zwigoff, and we went over to his house one night. She also knew Anton LaVey. Anton played the organ in his home, and at that point he had amassed a lot of music and was thinking about putting it out in some form. Becky was friends with Gregg Turkington, who had a record label. So Gregg met him, and they got along great. Gregg put out LaVey's "Honolulu Baby" 7-inch single.

There was also talk about movies, and I was invited over along with Jim Morton, a friend of mine and the editor of the *RE/Search* issue called *Incredibly Strange Films*. We started to go over and hang out once in a while—maybe one night every three weeks or something— and I would bring my projector and show 16mm films. It was always on 16mm, and LaVey had a lot of 16mm hanging around. I remember one night after the movie we all got in his van and drove to an all-night diner in the Sunset District; that was hilarious and great. It was a great experience, being up at three o'clock in the morning, with him driving through the deserted streets.

Kenneth Anger stayed at his place for quite a while, too. I had never met him before that. We talked about a lot of film obscuria. Blanche also turned me on to some of the people who had been involved with screening the movie *Freaks* in the film society circuit. I interviewed these people, and that's the basis of my article on the movie *Freaks* that has appeared in several forms.

Once I went over by myself. I brought my projector over and we screened his 16mm print of *Rasputin*. These were delightful evenings. Just being in the Black House was a very atmospheric experience. The first few times we went in he would be playing the organ, and then one time he emerged from the hidden fireplace—there was a staircase that he could access and that went down into unimaginable treasures down there. It wasn't a huge mansion. I mean, it was a fairly large house, but it just had all kinds of secret alcoves, and a whole mystery and aura about it. It was, of course, a shock when it ceased to exist.

Can you remember what he had on 16mm?

He had *Witchcraft '70*—it's like a mondo film. He had the spool that he was in. He had some real jewels in the 16mm department. I think they had a print of *Freaks,* too. They also at one point showed me about a hundred original stills from *Freaks*. They had a massive collection of incredibly valuable movie memorabilia from these kinds of darker films. At that point he wasn't actively collecting anymore, I think.

How did these meetings impact your life? Did it change your life in some way?

It was definitely a highlight of my time in San Francisco. It was a great, great connection to other people as well. I can't remember when it ended or how, but we fell out of touch. He was there, alive and well, long after I left San Francisco. I would say that, yeah, it definitely impacted my life, just to get to know him and his vast knowledge, and also his very friendly nature, and having these great evenings over there. It all became many cherished memories.

Is there any idea or concept that you associate with him, or from the specific film focus, that's been especially vital or relevant in your life?

I always liked his stories about playing the organ at these grind houses, and this mixture of live music and movies, and striptease, and sort of . . . it's this very dark aspect of movies, what movies were all about at that time: B movies, exploitation movies, in this very "grind house" vein. Which of course now is completely gone; that lower end of movies is completely gone.

Now people are watching movies on YouTube, and they don't get the experience, which is sometimes the best thing you can get out of it. So he harkened back to that; he was a living relic of that. Not a relic, but very much alive, and his memories were alive, and his stories were alive. He was the last link. He played in the 1940s and 1950s in these kinds of theaters. He gave me more of an appreciation for that as well. That's basically how I knew him, through the prism of movies. Of course, the movies branched out into everything else.

A topic that was like a common denominator could bloom into something completely different through his encyclopedic mind. He had so many stories about different things and forgotten people.

Precisely, forgotten people: that whole level that has not been written about or not been celebrated, basically. I'm not sure if any books ever came out that focused on this aspect; it would have been great, had I stayed there, to focus more on that and perhaps do some kind of publication about it. But I have the memories of these evenings.

If you look at him as a kind of a cultural phenomenon, and not just on your personal level, what were the greatest things that he brought into the American mind frame?

He is considered one of the leading "Satanists," with quotation marks around it. When you talk to other Satanists, they have very strong views about each other, and there's some who take it more seriously, and some less seriously. What he did was necessary; he popularized it, basically.

If we stick to this general American level, do you think that he has been misunderstood or misrepresented in any way?

He's been used as fodder by the right wing, and by Christians. He was a publicity seeker, in a good way, but you have to listen to his own words, and not the words of those who would seek to misrepresent him, from the right wing or from conservative media and so forth. I think for a long time he was kind of a punching bag for them. It got him publicity, and it gave him a chance and a platform to get his own philosophies out. His own philosophies made sense, but he did exist in opposition to the Christian hypocrisy and dogmas.

What do you think was the key to his controversy: was it merely the word Satan, *or was there something else?*

Satan, and the fact that he surrounded himself with sexy women. He came from a background of show business, so he knew how to get under people's skins. He knew that most people were suckers, and he basically also knew how to give people what they wanted, but also to put his own philosophies through: to form his own philosophies and publicize them, and form this movement that he had.

Let's talk about the Incredibly Strange Films *book. . . . Boyd Rice was a good friend of LaVey's at the time, and he was putting material into the book. Do you think that LaVey found stuff for Jim Morton, for instance, or for Boyd and then on to Jim; films that would otherwise not have been mentioned even in that spectacular book?*

Oh yes, there's no doubt that he formed their appreciation of obscure cinema, and Anton was coming from a different perspective. Not so much from what we call trash cinema or 1960s teen cinema; he was coming from an earlier perspective, a darker sort of carnival cinema; films that had darker themes about death and horror. He was a great connoisseur of horror cinema and definitely made an impact; they could have interviewed him for a whole chapter of that book. In fact, there could have and should have been an article exclusively on his love of film.

What would you say that you miss most about him?

When you take away all the hype and everything, he was just great company; a friendly, interesting, and fascinating guy—somewhat against his public persona. It was great to be in the house; it was great to have contact with somebody who recognized and appreciated the mysticism of places, and old movie theaters as well, in the many stories he told.

It's a tragedy that he passed away. I mean, everybody does, but he did take a bit of lore with him. He was at that stage not so accessible. In the early 1990s his ex-wife had a lawsuit against him or something. I also think *Rolling Stone* magazine did a hatchet job on him at one point. But he was really a great American mythic figure, and I'm happy that I got to see him—albeit at the end of his career.

At some point, it became fashionable to attack him, or to disbelieve him, or to not really grasp what he was about, basically. Also, from other Satanist groups, they considered him a charlatan in some way, because he was a man of show business. We did something here at the cinema with a Satanist group, and I mentioned LaVey. They just dismissed him, so there was a competitive idea there, or some infighting, I think.

What do you think will happen to his legacy in terms of the work, the writings, and the way people remember him?

I think his legacy will grow. It's too bad that there wasn't more done before he passed away, to kind of cement that legacy. Particularly, as I said, with film; what he knew about film, and his experiences from that world as well.

Is there anything that you would like to add, in terms of this kind of personal relationship, or some special memory?

I became friends with him, but I only knew him through these seances when we went over to his house. I have some very precious memories of him: always at midnight or 1 or 2 a.m. We always went over when it was very late and very dark out and left his house when it was still dark out. He was a man of darkness. I cherish that memory of him.

In my opinion, one of the key things that made LaVey unique was his active integration of his own life experience into fields that are traditionally "established" and that newcomers simply adapt to (occultism, philosophy, religion, etc.). What are your thoughts on why this was? How would you define the character traits that made him such a creative developer?

I think that because he was not from the academic or scientific or religious world—he was from a world of his own creation—he was in possession of an open mindedness and spoke to and built on his own experiences, as you say. It is also why he is difficult to categorize. He doesn't fit neatly into any box.

One of the quintessential traits was his active integration of pop culture that had been forgotten or discarded and thereby contained a force that could be tapped into and used. Do you have any memories of songs, films, et cetera, that he displayed for you as being such magical elements? Have you woven in similar explorations and practices in your own life?

I think it was his love for and understanding of pop culture, and his ability to draw on it and refer to it, that makes him unique. When I visited his house, we did not discuss momentous philosophical concepts but rather just watched movies on a 16mm projector or watched him play the organ. I also think his understanding of the central role of pop culture marks him as quintessentially American.

When it comes to creativity, I get the impression that LaVey was happiest when playing his tunes, telling his stories, and writing his essays; that is, being immersed in his own expressions that he mastered so well. But these usually also require a second party: a listener, a reader. Did you ever get the impression that he expressed himself mainly to have that second party, or was the expression in itself, for himself, the most important aspect?

I think his joy and need to be around people went back to his carny background, where one always played to the audience. Without the audience there was nothing. He was not one to contemplate sterile concepts in private; the essence of everything he was all about was flesh and blood. He was no stilted theoretician debating sterile philosophies in an ivory tower. He was the guy playing organ at a grind house movie theater and taming a lion.

Can you see any similarities between LaVey and other notable creative people at the time (regardless of their particular expressions or views)? Meaning, would you say there was something distinctly zeitgeistish about him?

I don't know; I never met anyone quite like him. I found him utterly devoid of any pretension or elitism, but he was in his own class; like a visitor from the shadow world of the '30s or '40s. I could not imagine today, if he were alive, sitting around with him and watching a movie digitally on a big-screen TV. He knew the hypnotic power of analog machines.

In the LaVeyan encouragement of fetishizing objects and environments (working with ECI, creating total environments, for instance), it's not that far-fetched to talk about an ensouling of these objects (or spaces) that one has an intimate relationship with. Did he ever give the impression that he felt that way about human beings? Meaning, that he could feel OK with using the word soul *or* ensouled *or* spirit *or* spirited *when talking about humans? I guess the extension of this question is whether you ever saw signs of his not being a 100 percent strict materialist?*

The Black House itself was a total environment. Physical spaces were always key in everything he did, and I was entranced by his descriptions of old raggedy movie theaters and circus environments. There certainly is a spiritual element to old environments. I think in his own way he was a spiritualist. I certainly got spirit vibes in his house. But spiritualism and denial of the flesh, et cetera, have been such key components of organized religions that have wreaked havoc on the world that it might be understandable that he would disavow that.

Did you ever feel that LaVey put on a show at times because he felt it was expected of him, rather than because he was genuinely in the mood himself?

Never. When he played the organ it was because he was 1000 percent into it himself, maybe even too much so! When we talked or watched movies or drove out in his van to an all-night diner, or anything, I never got the impression he was doing anything out of a sense of obligation.

18

RUTH WAYTZ

Ruth Waytz, Los Angeles, 2019.
Photo by Carl Abrahamsson.

"Anton LaVey's legacy is everywhere forever."

Ruth Waytz is a writer and editor based in Los Angeles.

How did you first hear about Anton LaVey?

He's been a part of the culture my entire life. I happened in 1960, and he was happening in the mid-1960s. He turned up in a lot of things and places in the world. He seemed interesting to me, and even before I knew much about him, he was just sort of a part of the culture.

How did you first come into actual contact with him?

I was fortunate enough to be introduced to LaVey in person through a couple of different sets of circumstances. I had first been working as the research director at *Hustler* magazine, and we did an interview with him. As the research director I was responsible for the accuracy of all printed material in every Larry Flynt publication. I had staff, but I wasn't going to hand this one over to anybody, because I had known who he was for so long. I ended up speaking with Blanche Barton, who became a very good friend. And then, through another set of circumstances with another friend, I kept hearing, "Oh boy, LaVey would really love you." Eventually it got set up, and it was delightful. We were instantly fast friends, and it was just wonderful.

How would you say that the first meeting, or those meetings that you had later on, impacted your life?

I don't know that I can differentiate one from another. I spent a lot of time up there. At one point I was up there probably once a month. At first, I would spend the night in hotels. There was a particular hotel or motel—I think it was the Seal Rock Inn—that was close to there, and it was just delightfully dumpy. But as we became closer friends I would stay at the Black House. There was a room upstairs that I believe had been Karla's room, and I would stay up there. It became not only a part of my life; it became one of the best parts of my life. It was something to look forward to. During the time in between the visits, I would amass little trinkets, books, things, and junk that he would like. The electric fart machine: huge hit. Probably one of the best presents I think I ever got to give him—certainly hours' worth of amusement from that.

I was either just back from there or planning to go there; it was a lovely thing, and I knew that it was always something to look forward to. When you go out to a restaurant with people and somebody jumps out of the kitchen and yells "Diablo!" at you, it's kind of a memorable thing; you remember that. He had a certain aesthetic, and I share that aesthetic: the stockings, the garter belts, the high heels, the seams, and the pencil skirts. I really indulged him.

Being there, did you feel an increasing sense of resonance with the philosophy?

I had not read *The Satanic Bible*. I certainly knew what it was, and I knew who he was as a result. But my philosophy and his philosophy . . . we just agreed with each other. I didn't need to read a book to know that I agreed with him. Eventually, I did read *The Satanic Bible,* and on a subsequent visit I mentioned, "Hey, you know, I read a book!" And he was like, "Oh, really? Which book did you read?" "It's this thing called

The Satanic Bible." He asked me what I thought of it. I said, "Oh, I don't know, I probably could have written it myself. I kind of liked it."

He loved that. I know people like to bash on him and say that he was an egomaniac, or that he didn't have room for other people's ideas. But at that moment, if he had been a jerk, he would have been angry; he would have been resentful, and he would have wanted to keep a distance between him and me, and we would have these roles: that he's the teacher, and I'm the pupil. I never felt like that. We were always equal, and he was tickled pink that I could have written that myself. We were just on the same page about so many things: kindred spirits. To ask me where I was in the philosophy, or to want to know how knowing him personally enhanced my philosophy . . . I don't know that it did or it didn't. I just am. We like to say that Satanists are born, not made. It's always been a part of me.

What would you say has been LaVey's greatest contribution to your life?
It's difficult to say what any one single contribution is to anyone's life. I don't know . . . I miss him. Maybe he just really brought out my bullshit detector, which I'm grateful for.

Just by being himself, he had this uncanny capacity of bringing things out in, I think, all of the people who came there. While I've been making this film, I've gradually developed this theory that he actually consciously concocted a legacy by sowing little seeds in the people who were there.
I absolutely agree that he knew what he was doing. He picked all of us, and then we all came together and made the big thing.

Good, so I'm not alone in thinking that.
No, not at all! It's one thing to say, "Oh, all the world's a stage, and we are merely players." But I met a lot of really interesting people through him, and I've met a lot of interesting people after him; just talking about this, and being interviewed, and being on NPR and talking about this . . . I've given lectures at universities, and I've really met a lot of very

interesting people. That's a terrific legacy: that you make people wake up and think, and that they know it's okay to wake up and think about stuff. That's really important.

Was there any moment, or moments, where you felt that he had sort of picked something out to show you, specifically?

Well, there was always something going on with him. Since I did get up there so often, and I was concocting little care packages for him, there would be things where either he would say, or Blanche would say, "Oh, next time you come we need to do this, we have to do this." We would go to his favorite restaurants, and he would do little things that were just . . . I don't know if it was just for my benefit, but it certainly felt like it was for my benefit only—and I really enjoyed that. Or if he came across a book that he would recommend, or a film that he would recommend, or something that he wanted to definitely make sure that we talked about. I know that there was always an agenda.

Among all these things—the philosophy and your personal memories— is there any idea or concept, magically, that's still very relevant and vital for you?

People ask me how magic fits into my life all the time. There's prestidigitation magic, "Hey, I can pull a rabbit out of my hat," and there's parking space magic, there's all kinds of different magic. Largely, I like to say I lead a charmed life. Magic permeates every bit of my life, and as we have the concept of greater magic and lesser magic, I would say pretty much my whole life is lesser magic. I get whatever I want whenever I want it, and whenever I need it. I never question that because it's always been that way.

What do you think were the greatest changes that LaVey brought for America?

I think that in America, he did bring an end to a kind of prudishness. He brought forth the idea of indulgence over abstinence, which is our first principle: that Satan represents indulgence, not abstinence; it's just about embracing life and taking life and wringing out every last bit of whatever you want. He didn't care much for hippies, and I can see why. Because hippies were about unconditional love, and Satanists are about purely conditional love. I don't love you because I have to; I love you because I want to, because you have inspired that in me. I think that's really, really important. People are drawn to me because I have that no-bullshit attitude. If I love you, I'm not faking it; I'm not lying about it. I do believe that we are all human beings; we are all the same organism, and as such, we have a lot of similarities. But to not call a spade a spade; to not say that someone's behavior is abhorrent . . . I'll never accept that.

He had a lot of competition: Hugh Hefner, the bomb, the moon landings, but I do think that we have been able to shoehorn ourselves in now. I am open and out as a Satanist, as are many, many of our members. Some of them are not, and that's totally fine, too, but I think that we are able to move forward and do our thing a lot more freely than we were. I can't imagine living in the 1950s. I don't think I could make my living doing what I do, being who I am, if I were born in the 1940s or 1950s. I think that he really just broke the doors down, and we all went rushing through.

So you're saying that he brought, through his writings and his presence in media, a different kind of awareness to pickiness, in a way? A stratification awareness?

Yeah. Through his writings, he brought us the encouragement to make our choices known, and to make our preferences known: to say it's okay to be a snob, and that I'm going to wear nice clothes, and I don't like it when people wear toddler clothes. All my friends know better than to wear shorts around me, because, you know, grown-ups should wear long pants. The idea of this divine right to be comfortable . . . first of all, I'm not comfortable when I look like shit, and I'm not comfortable when everyone I have to look at looks like shit. I long for the days when people got dressed up to do things. I get dressed up to do things. If I have to leave the house, then I'm in some sort of costume; it should be a pleasant costume. I get better treatment in the world than somebody who's in some tracksuit somewhere, because I demand that with my presence.

Do you feel that LaVey has been misrepresented? And if so, why?

I think any dead person has the opportunity to be misrepresented. There's a pendulum in everything: there's the political correctness, and there's the political incorrectness. LaVey, as a dead person, and as someone who's been dead for more than ten years, is easy to misinterpret. "Oh, he was all about Might is Right, and he's a Nazi, and he's a fascist, and he's blah, blah, blah, blah, blah." People are lazy, and they believe what they read, and things that other people write, and those people don't always have the dead person's best interest at heart. They have their own agendas, and they will lie or twist or misrepresent whatever they need to get their own point across.

I get bothered by that with LaVey, because a) he's not here to defend himself, and b) a lot of that is just crap. Anton LaVey was a very forward-thinking, open-minded person. I think that he is often misinterpreted. His lack of tolerance for bullshit is misinterpreted as fascism. But I will reiterate that the Church of Satan was always, and it still is, completely open to all persons of all persuasions and all inclinations, as long as we are like-minded individuals. If we share a philosophy, we can share a sandwich.

I don't think that it's fair that he's being misrepresented as some sort of fascist or Nazi because he thought that the aesthetic was beautiful. As a Jewish person, I can sit here and say that those Nazi uniforms, they certainly did their jobs. They were inspiring, and that was a success; that was a successful brand campaign. But for me to say that that was a successful brand campaign, that doesn't mean I'm a Nazi sympathizer—because I'm not.

Anton LaVey's writing is a joy to read; he's funny, he's clever. Sure, he borrows a little bit from here and there, but, you know, that's literature, that's writing; that's life, and he never backed away from that idea. He never said, "Oh, I've never read Ayn Rand; I've never read Ragnar Redbeard." Because everybody knows he did, but so what? It's how you say it, and that you say it, that's what's important. It has to come from you. His writing is freaking delightful, absolutely delightful. He just writes about what's on his mind. So even if you don't like *The Satanic Bible,* if you think that's all ripped off—which it's not—why not read *Satan Speaks!?* Read the essays; read him just generally riffing about bullshit. It's a pleasure, and I miss that from him the most, I think.

If we pick a slogan from the LaVey corpus, such as "responsibility to the responsible," that's almost the most heretical thing you can say today, when everybody tries so hard to evade and elope and cover up their own responsibility. Or lack of it. It's a career in itself.

The whole thing with inclusion and diversity and all of this . . . I mean those are really good ideas—those are essential ideas—that our differences are what make us strong and great. But forcing that is totally wrong. That's a thing that LaVey pointed out: forcing that is bullshit. It's still unpopular to comment on it; it's probably more unpopular now because there's such a push to make sure that everything is equal. But just as in George Orwell's *Animal Farm,* everything isn't equal. It's a malicious lie to suggest and insist that it is. All men are not created equal. Some people are really good at some things, and some people are really good at something else. But to force me into a job where I have to do something where I don't have any idea what to do, because I'm a woman or a Jew or whatever, just because you need one of those. It's just wrong, and no one benefits. The whole point of it is that everyone should benefit, and the end result of it is that no one benefits.

It's the very essence of cynicism, because, as Orwell wrote, "Some people are more equal than others." Do you think that the impact that LaVey had would have been different had the word Satan not been included?

I know that everything Anton LaVey did, he did deliberately. If he chose the word *Satan,* and the word *Satanism* for his religion, then he knew exactly what effect that would have. He was there, and he was involved with all of those people; he had his Magic Circle, and he had access to every possible word and every possible name to describe what it was that he was building. He was completely in control and a keen observer of what he wanted to do. He knew what he wanted to do. And so, if he chose the word *Satanism* for this religion, it was specifically because he knew that that was the best possible word to describe what we were doing. It still gets the reaction!

When we drift into these territories, which are basically Satanic Witch **territories, what did you feel when you read that book for the first time?**
I loved reading *The Satanic Witch* because it was new stuff, but not new stuff. It was nothing new, but it was new to me to read it expressed in so many words. It was very helpful to me, as well. That book is a little bit outdated; it's basically just a card catalogue of his fetishes, which is fine, but there's also sound philosophy in it. At one point I brought him a copy to have it signed, and he said, "Oh, the book about you!" Which I thought was very, very charming, but also true! It really is true, and when I was reading it, that was exactly what I thought, "Oh yeah, yeah, I knew that, yeah, I knew that. Oh, interesting, I never really thought of it that way. . . ." So, it was very thought provoking for me. Not that it was news, but I think that it's still a very valuable book today. Even the weird shit in that book about all the crazy smells. I mean, human beings respond to the olfactory stimulus more than almost anything else. So he's not wrong. Even if it isn't in line with your sensibilities, it's still true.

I just found a really amazing book called *Pull Yourself Together, Baby,* by "Sylvia of Hollywood," copyright 1936 from Photoplay Press, and it's pretty much *The Satanic Witch.* I mean, it's not *The Satanic Witch,* but . . . I told Peggy that I would bet her twenty dollars that going through LaVey's library there was at least one copy of

Pull Yourself Together, Baby. And that's great; it's part of the collective consciousness; we all have ideas in a big pool. It has an introduction and chapters on "Personality Diet," "The Personality Figure," "Forget Thy Neighbor," "Glamour Is Glandular," "From the Neck Up," "The Personality Wardrobe," "How Are Your Company Manners," "Poise Under Pressure," "The Art of Being a Good Sport," "This Thing Called Love," and "Take a Chance." This is definitely the same attitude conveyed in *The Satanic Witch.* She's telling you, but from a woman's point of view, "Darling, you're fat. Eat celery, drink black coffee, and shut up." It's hilariously refreshing. I love this book. And it's from the 1940s, so I know LaVey saw this book.

I would wear things for those visits to LaVey's house that I knew he would appreciate. He had a certain sensibility that people don't have now. He was a lingerie enthusiast, but he wasn't a Victoria's Secret kind of lingerie enthusiast; he liked frumpy, dumpy, dirty, stained, "grossinating" lingerie. There's a catalogue called the Vermont Country Store, and they had old-fashioned lingerie. I was sitting there—and this is garters and stockings; this is no pantyhose business—in the Purple Parlor, and we were talking, and I didn't realize the quality, or lack thereof, of these garments. I crossed my legs at one point, and the garter broke, and snapped, and I was just . . . I was stunned. Normally, just like Anton LaVey, I like to orchestrate my performances, so I was pretty sure I knew that he was going to like that. You have that skirt that's just a little too short; it's accidentally showing a little too much, so I played into whatever I knew exactly what he wanted. But when that thing snapped, it shocked me, and it shocked him. I thought he was going to fall out of his chair. It was hilarious, and it was an outstanding moment in our entire friendship. I don't know that anyone had ever done anything nicer for him.

Do you think that The Satanic Witch *has any relevance today? Has it aged well?*

The Satanic Witch was written as a kind of response to the whole unification: that we're all the same, that there's no difference between the sexes. . . . Of course there's a difference between the sexes! And the book was written to celebrate that. Women and power has always been a very delicate equation, and that book was written to not only remind women that they have all the power, but to show them how to use it. It was very generous of Doktor LaVey to spell out so clearly how women can basically manipulate men into getting whatever they want.

Now, there's a good manipulation and there's a bad manipulation, and these principles don't age out. In the cave days there was still a dynamic between men and women, and now that it's hundreds and thousands and whatever years later, there's still a dynamic between men and women. It's different, but it's the same, because, as I like to say . . . because human beings are involved.

I love when people say that: "Oh, we're evolving." We're not evolving! I still have my pinkie toe and my appendix, so we're not evolving. I like to think that we're maturing, which is something completely different. And along those lines, I support books like *The Satanic Witch* and *The Satanic Warlock,* and other books about empowerment and taking responsibility for your own life. You do need to take responsibility for your own life. I need to be responsible for my actions as a human being: not as a woman, not as a Satanist, not as a Californian, not as a blonde. I need to be responsible for my actions as a human being. This is one of the most basic of the Satanic principles: the idea of responsibility to the responsible. I don't need the Bible to tell me what's right and what's wrong. I need my heart to tell me what's right and what's wrong, and I need my brain to tell me what's right and what's wrong.

In terms of memories from the Black House, is it possible to single out a special one?

We spent a lot of time in the kitchen, with him just playing. All of those memories just blur together, and it was fabulous; it was delightful and wonderful. I was very insistent, because I wanted to see the Den of

Iniquity, and there was always an excuse. "Oh no, there are too many spiders; oh no, it's dirty. . . ." There was always an excuse. "Oh, there are no light bulbs . . . ," so I brought light bulbs, because I can be a little persistent, too. And I'm so glad now, in retrospect, that I did kind of insist, because we did get down there one night. We were all down there, and it was just magical; it was delightful. And I didn't see a single spider, just so you know.

How do you see his legacy now, and in the future?

Anton LaVey's legacy is everywhere forever. You can't unring a bell, you know. There are people who, whether or not they realize it, are taking advantage of the road that he paved, of the path that he made—the left-hand path, or whatever. There's so much more freedom now. We're free to do what we want to do and say what we want to say. Satanism is a recognized religion, which I think is important; but it's also completely irrelevant, because it's about personal and individual freedom. Just the idea that you're free to have these thoughts and have this personal philosophy and develop all of these ideas and live your life on your own terms, that's all Satanism. You can call it whatever, but everyone owes a great debt to Anton LaVey for stepping up and saying, "This is what I like, this is what I'm going to do, and these things are all possible." The only thing stopping you is you. So if you get out of your own way, and you decide that "this is what I want to do, and this is how I want to live, and this is what I want to say, and this is how I want to dress," just go ahead and do it. It's all because of him.

In my opinion, one of the key things that made LaVey unique was his active integration of his own life experience into fields that are traditionally "established" and that newcomers simply adapt to (occultism, philosophy, religion, etc.). What are your thoughts on why this was? How would you define the character traits that made him such a creative developer?

LaVey always had his own interests, and he pursued those interests regardless of whether anyone else was on board. I only knew him at the end of his life, sadly, so I missed out on all the early stuff, but what I did see was a man of many passions, imbued with the skill and discipline to explore them and the time to do so. He removed himself from everything except his interests, sending him as deep down any rabbit hole as he liked.

Also, while so many in his field were snobbish, LaVey really got a kick out of embracing what would otherwise be derided as low or common—the Johnson Smith catalog comes to mind.* He never stopped loving the whoopie cushion—and neither should we. So many occultists are one-dimensional. Beyond whatever line they're selling, there's nothing. To me, that makes them boring. After a few hours you know everything you're going to know about that person or philosophy. LaVey was the opposite—our evenings were filled with talk about film noir, cars, art, music, fashion, literature. . . . I never knew what we'd talk about, but I always knew I would enjoy it.

When it comes to creativity, I get the impression that LaVey was happiest when playing his tunes, telling his stories, and writing his essays; that is, being immersed in his own expressions that he mastered so well. But these usually also require a second party: a listener, a reader. Did you ever get the impression that he expressed himself mainly to have that second party, or was the expression in itself, for himself, the most important aspect?

You might say by choosing the life of a recluse, LaVey relinquished his right to an audience. I know he enjoyed having me there, but I also got the strong impression that he spent many hours alone at the keyboards for his own amusement. Yes, he liked having his music and writing acknowledged, but he certainly never grilled me about what I had or had not read. He also spent countless hours fiddling about in Photoshop and writing a newsletter for a fictional town—*The Plotzville*

---

*The Johnson Smith mail-order catalog was filled with novelties and gadgets such as X-ray goggles, whoopee cushions, fake vomit, and joy buzzers. It was LaVey's own "Necronomicon," and he allegedly always had a copy by his bed.

Times—which I believe had an audience of maybe five people; so I'm going to say not everything he did required validation.

Can you see any similarities between LaVey and other notable creative people at the time (regardless of their particular expressions or views)? Meaning, would you say there was something distinctly zeitgeistish about him?

I knew him in the 1990s, and I'd say at that point he pretty much stuck out like a sore thumb. He refused to change course and go along with what anyone else was doing. He had all but left the public eye, choosing to live life on his own terms, in the total environment he created around him. If anything, he was anti-zeitgeist, sticking with his own thing.

Inside the Black House, which was your favorite room, and why?

The downstairs bathroom. From the dumb decorations to the rotten old corncob on a string, that room just summed it all up for me. Plus, I could feel the energy from the red bedroom that was just on the other side of that door. In fact, on what I knew would be my last visit—this was after his death—I made a specific trip into that bathroom. I very deliberately placed the palm of my left hand on the black beadboard wall, thoroughly taking it in and creating a sense memory. I knew I would miss the house, and I wanted to be able to summon not just a visual memory of being there. It worked. All I have to do is hold up my hand, and I'm back there right now. The wall itself has been gone a long time. And yet my hand is right there.

Were there any quirks or habits that you found odd in LaVey? Meaning, unexpected expressions of moralisms that might have seemed un-Satanic and perhaps stemmed from the times or the religion he grew up in? Things you sort of didn't quite see coming?

He had a lot of weird habits, but I wouldn't call any of them un-Satanic or moralistic. I think they came more from being an oddball with a lot of freedom, and his time living with other weirdos. He drank wine from a wine glass, but he slurped it noisily, even in restaurants. Being a bit of a Miss Manners, I asked him about that. He said it was a habit he picked up when he ate and drank with the big cats. He may have just been fucking with me, but I enjoyed the idea and never challenged him on it. If anything, his proclivities were anything *but* morally based.

In the LaVeyan encouragement of fetishizing objects and environments (working with ECI, creating total environments, for instance), it's not that far-fetched to talk about an ensouling of these objects (or spaces) that one has an intimate relationship with. Did he ever give the impression that he felt that way about human beings? Meaning, that he could feel OK with using the word soul *or* ensouled *or* spirit *or* spirited *when talking about humans? I guess the extension of this question is whether you ever saw signs of him not being a 100 percent strict materialist?*

I think he deeply loved things, maybe more than he loved people. Things are at least consistent—a car is always a car. He saw energy, magic, and power in things, but I don't think I ever heard him use the word *soul* to describe anything. We often talked about people he admired or hated, but again I don't remember him using that word.

Did you ever feel that LaVey put on a show at times because he felt it was expected of him rather than because he was genuinely in the mood himself?

Absolutely . . . and not at all. Early in his life I know he often felt like a performing seal, pressured to do his thing on command. Every artist feels this; in fact, that's a big part of the gig. He wanted to be a celebrity. He wanted to create scandal and uproar, and he got both. But it got boring—I remember him saying he would still grant interviews but, "no more questions about the tombstone coffee table." He wanted people interested in his real message, not just the theatrics.

By the end of his life he was exhausted, so he backed out of the limelight. He curated his visitors and was always able to opt out if he wasn't feeling it. Many nights I sat upstairs in the house, waiting for Blanche's call to come join them in the Purple Parlor . . . and more than a few times that call never came. He loved that: keeping even good friends waiting, and we all went along with it because we loved him and seeing him was always worth the wait. Always. And when he did spend time with you, he was really with you—talking about all kinds of topics, but always with you, not at you. I always had his full attention, something both rare and thrilling.

Did you perceive him as being sensitive to what others thought or felt about him?

Like any human being—and creatives in particular—his success depended on getting his message seen. To that end, I guess he cared what people thought of him. But toward the end, no. He had nothing to prove, and he was ready to be judged on his work, which has lost none of its relevance.

Do you think there was something or some things that he would have done differently in his life, had he had the chance?

I'd really like to ask him that one! We may well have discussed something like this; we definitely talked a lot about choices. Maintaining his image may have kept him from publicly admitting "mistakes," but who hasn't wondered how things would have turned out had one pursued other options? Overall, I saw LaVey satisfied with his life. He changed the world. I do think he wanted to be judged fairly and remembered for his work, not the endless petty squabbles that naturally befell anyone who would choose to found an iconoclast religion and live a life true to his own principles. That's bound to ruffle some feathers. That was the point. People should read his essay on "sand fleas" to get his take on the endless parade of useless detractors. LaVey's place in history is secure, which I know mattered to him. His final years were lived entirely by his rules. He was completely delighted by Blanche and Xerxes. He did what he wanted, ate what he wanted, saw who he wanted to see, and answered to no one. I've taken that example to heart, and you know what? It works great!

Larry Wessel, Los Angeles, 2019.
Photo by Carl Abrahamsson.

19
LARRY WESSEL

"The first thing Anton said to me was, 'I just want to thank you for sticking your neck out for Satan.'"

American documentary filmmaker Larry Wessel's work includes films such as *Taurobolium* (1994), *Sex, Death & The Hollywood Mystique* (1999), *Iconoclast* (2010), *Love* (2014), and *Larry Wessel's Palace of Wonders* (2021).

How did you first hear about Anton LaVey?

I think my introduction was through *The Satanic Bible*. When I was in high school, once a year they had book fairs, and they would bring in books from all over the place. That must have been 1973, '74. *The Satanic Bible* was for sale at my high school book fair, and I was intrigued by it. Prior to that I remember Anton LaVey on the cover of *Look* magazine and reading the article about the Church of Satan. I also remember being at the grocery store when I was a kid, looking at the magazines, and I remember seeing an issue of *Time* magazine that asked "Is God Dead?" And I think there was another issue of *Time* magazine about witchcraft.

I also picked up a magazine called *Man, Myth & Magic* at my local liquor store, and it had articles about Satan and modern Satanism, and it mentioned Anton LaVey. The first time I saw the book was at this book fair in high school, and I purchased it. I think it was only three dollars. It was very affordable, and it had a great, dramatic photograph of him on the back. I was intrigued right away. There was a list of his influences in there, and it included W. C. Fields.

I just immediately resonated with this guy and wanted to read his book. I knew that he was someone that I would get along with immediately, and I read it cover to cover in no time at all, and just loved it. As a teenager I wasn't really awkward, but I was kind of on the shy side. I like to consider it my self-help book when I was a teenager.

I had seen *Rosemary's Baby*. My parents are both cinephiles, and our religion, really, is cinema; our church is the movie theater. When I grew up, as a child, I didn't go to church; I went to the movies every weekend with my parents. They're the ones that turned me on to all the great films from the past, too, that we would check out on television, in the days before VHS and DVDs and cable television. We had to wait until these films appeared on television to see them. My folks would always make sure that I sat down and saw films like *The Bad Seed* and *The Treasure of the Sierra Madre,* and all the Alfred Hitchcock movies.

Some of my dad's favorite movies were also Anton LaVey's favorite movies; films like *Nightmare Alley, The Treasure of the Sierra Madre,* which I just mentioned, and a really obscure one that my dad just loved to pieces. It never appeared on television; we always waited for it to show up. It was called *The Bullfighter and the Lady.*

How did it then come about that you got to meet him?

Around 1992 I was in Los Angeles filming the aftermath of the L.A. riots, which took place that year. My friend Adam Parfrey was also living in Los Angeles at the time, and that morning after my shoot I went over to visit. I knocked on Adam's door, and he invited me in; he was eating breakfast. He was talking about a documentary that Nick Bougas was making, and that Adam was shooting sequences for: it's called *Speak of the Devil.* He said that I should be in it because of my love for *The Satanic Bible.* And I said, "Oh, I'd love to be in it! I'll go home, and I have a black suit, and I'll dress up in it, wear a tie. . . ." But Adam wanted me to be just me. I was wearing a red "wife beater"—a sleeveless shirt; I looked pretty awful. But he said, "I just want you to stand on the front lawn, and I'll go out with my camcorder and video-tape you, right now."

I was nervous as hell. But I did the best I could to convey my love for *The Satanic Bible* and how it really helped me when I was a kid. Especially when dealing with my enemies, because of the destruction ritual that LaVey outlines in it. I said I found this particularly good and useful, and I said that I would actually draw effigies of my enemies. I was a good cartoonist, and I'd draw cartoons of these people I couldn't stand, people who irked me. I would destroy those effigies and thus rid myself of all of my feelings and thoughts of hatred. I said it was like a cleansing ritual, and I said it was very, very helpful.

So I rattled all this off to Adam while he was videotaping me, and that was the end of it. I didn't hear anything about it for about a year, until I attended a record release party for a band called Ethyl Meatplow. Warner Brothers was throwing this party for them to release their record. I got invited because I knew members of the band. Warner Brothers was supplying free alcoholic beverages for everybody, so of course the bar was really crowded.

I'm looking around, and this beautiful, beautiful woman made eye contact with me. I looked away, and I looked back at her, and she was just staring at me, and she slowly started gliding toward me. It was like a woman in a wonderful dream, and she came right up to me, and she said, "I know you; you're Larry Wessel. I saw you in the Satan documen-tary." I said, "Really, it's out? Nobody even told me that it was out." She said, "Yes, it screened in San Francisco." She also said, "Anton LaVey wants to meet you. I'm one of Anton LaVey's witches, and right now you can come up and visit me in San Francisco, and I'll set it up so you can visit him; he really wants to meet you. You're his favorite person in the whole documentary."

Well, it just so happened that I had just finished doing a portrait of Anton LaVey. I do collage work, and I did a big collage portrait of him, and I put it in a really fancy baroque or rococo frame, like a museum frame, and it was quite large, too. I had just completed it. I knew he had just had a son, and I thought I would bring this as a gift for his new son when I go up to San Francisco.

Two weeks later I find myself in San Francisco, staying at this beautiful woman's apartment, and she's setting up a meeting with Anton LaVey, and I couldn't believe it; it was like a dream. I thought that I should get him a couple of gifts. So I went to a very old magic shop: a place that sold practical jokes and magic supplies. I went in there, and there was an old man behind the counter. I asked him, "What do I get somebody who has everything, in terms of practical jokes? This guy collects practical jokes, he's an old customer of the Johnson Smith catalog." The old man looked at me, and he said, "I know just what he needs." He reached under the counter, and he pulled out this device. It was a remote-controlled electronic whoopee cushion; it was a high-tech version of the old whoopee cushion. The man said, "I bet he doesn't have this."

I purchased it, and then I went to a record shop that sold old 78-rpm records. I looked for one of my favorite 78 records, that I have several copies of here at home, called "The Darktown Poker Club," by Phil Harris. They actually had a dozen copies of this at this record shop, so I picked that up, too. I went to the Mission District and found a drugstore that sold wrapping paper, and I found some purple and black wrapping paper, and I wrapped it up and put black ribbons on it; I made the packages look really Satanic.

So I had these three gifts to give to Anton Szandor LaVey. The night came when I was to meet him. I showed up at the appointed time; I think it was eight o'clock. I showed up about five minutes early because I didn't want to be late; he had told me to press the buzzer on his gate at eight o'clock sharp. So here I am, in front of the Church of Satan, it's five minutes to eight. The fog's rolling in—it's real cold, and very atmospheric—and I'm checking my watch every minute just to make sure it's eight o'clock, and then I press the buzzer. Just as I press the buzzer, a white van drove up right alongside of me, and the passenger door opened, and it was Anton LaVey. He came right up to me and he said, "Larry," and he stuck out his hand: "At last we meet."

He looked so great, and he said, "I want you to meet somebody." He introduced me to Blanche Barton, he introduced me to his majordomo, Tony, and he introduced me to his new child. He said his child's name is Satan Xerxes Carnacki LaVey. I actually already knew that, because I had inscribed the back of the portrait of him to Satan Xerxes Carnacki LaVey. So here I was with his family, and we entered the Church of Satan.

What happened when you got inside the Black House?

Once inside the house we all sat down. There was Doktor LaVey and Tony and me. Blanche went into the kitchen, and she came out later with coffee and a tray of cookies. The coffee was served in black coffee mugs with a Baphomet symbol on them, which was really great. The first thing Anton said to me was, "Larry, I just want to thank you for sticking your neck out for Satan." I knew he meant being in the documentary and talking about the destruction ritual and all that, but at the same time I didn't realize I was sticking my neck out. He made it so dramatic, like I was really courageous, you know, by saying nice things about him. I told him it was my pleasure, and that his book was really important to me, and it was really easy for me to give accolades to it. He said that I was his favorite participant in that documentary. He said, "You summed up my philosophy better than anyone in the documentary."

I was really beside myself, because of all the praise he was heaping on me. He was so generous that way and really made you feel good. It felt like you were at home and with your favorite uncle; it broke the ice immediately. He said he particularly liked my use of the word *irk*, because I had said that I employed the destruction ritual against those who irked me. He said, "That is a sign of your superior intelligence."

We sat down, and we were munching cookies and drinking coffee, and he pulled a book off his bookshelf and said that he wanted to read something to me. I have a copy of the book that he pulled off the bookshelf; it's called *Star-Spangled Kitsch*. Inside this book there is a poem by Don Blanding called "Vagabond's House." He read to me the entire excerpt from the book. And of course, it was in his dramatic delivery, which I cannot even come close to, but it goes something like this:

> When I have a house . . . as I sometime may . . .
> I'll suit my fancy in every way.
> I'll fill it with things that have caught my eye
> In drifting from Iceland to Molokai.
> It won't be correct or in period style,
> But . . . oh, I've thought for a long, long while
> Of all the corners and all the nooks,
> Of all the bookshelves and all the books,
> The great big table, the deep soft chairs,
> And the Chinese rug at the foot of the stairs
> (It's an old, old rug from far Chow Wan
> That a Chinese princess once walked on).

It's just the most evocative poem you've ever heard, about a person's dream house, and about their travels, and their collection of objects of art that they surround themselves with to remind them of their incredible past. He's reading to me this poem in a room that's his library. It had the famous sign on the bookshelf that said, "If you touch these books your hands will be amputated." So of course, I never wanted to touch any of the books! But it was such an amazing, transporting experience sitting there, having Anton LaVey read to me this poem.

It brought me back to my childhood, when my father would read me poetry. And it made me remember my father reading "The Raven," by Edgar Allan Poe, and "Ozymandias," by Percy Shelley, and on and on and on. It was a very incredible, warm, familiar experience to me, being read to by an elder person, and to have Anton LaVey treat me that way. I felt as if I were his son. It was really, really terrific, and I hung on every word of that poem.

Immediately, when I got back home after that stay in San Francisco, I found that book and purchased it, and that poem has stayed with me all these years. I'm currently making a documentary that's roughly based on the words to that poem: "Vagabond's House." It really made an impact on me.

Then at some point he asked me, "What are you working on, Larry?" I told him I was working on a film about bullfighting, and that I was attending every bullfight in Tijuana; every weekend during the season I would be there in the front row and all over the arena filming the bullfights. LaVey said, "Larry, I want you to know that I'm a very serious aficionado of *tauromachia*—that is, of bullfighting. I attended the bullfights with my parents when I was twelve years old, and the music of the bull ring stayed with me, so much so that when I played the calliope for the big cat acts at the Clyde Beatty circus, I played bull-fight paso dobles. I love the music of the bullring."

I said, "I do, too, you know: I collect all the recordings of it, and when you attend a bullfight, it just moves you and transports you back in time and back into history; back into prehistory." He couldn't agree with me more, and I asked him who his favorite matador was, and he said, "Juan Belmonte." He even had his book in the library, called *Killer of Bulls*. Juan Belmonte was a very rugged, tough guy bullfighter, who had an almost a chiseled face. He was a very, very good icon to resonate with in terms of bullfighting.

LaVey said there used to be a bar in San Francisco called El Matador, and it was run by the great writer Barnaby Conrad. He wrote more books in the English language about bullfighting than anybody in the world. That's actually how I learned about bullfighting, by reading Barnaby Conrad. LaVey said that he had approached Barnaby Conrad and said, "I'd love to play bullfight paso dobles in your bar," because the bar was like a museum of tauromachia, with bullfighting memorabilia everywhere in the bar. He said the one thing that prevented it from being a total environment was the lack of bullfighting music. He said he wanted to provide that on his keyboards, but Barnaby turned him down because he only hired jazz musicians. It was Barnaby's loss, because Anton really knew all of these tunes by heart; he didn't even have to look at sheet music, you know.

So we talked about bullfighting endlessly, and I was really appreciative of his vast knowledge on the subject. I could bring up anything, and he could talk volumes about it. He was very well read, and very well lived; he knew things about just about anything you could throw at him. It really made a big impression on me.

Then it was time for him to open his presents. He unwrapped them very slowly, as if he wanted to save the paper; he was very careful about how he removed the portrait. He took it out, and he looked at it, and he looked at it, he looked at it. Then he looked over at me and said, "Larry, you've captured my very soul." He flipped it over, and I had written an inscription on the back: "to Satan Xerxes Carnacki LaVey." I dated it and signed it, and so it was a gift for his son.

Blanche was next to the little baby boy, and he was in one of those cribs that you carry, like a little carryall crib. On the top of the crib, where you would normally see a little play object or a little mobile, was a black plastic spider hanging down above the baby's face. It was just like a Charles Addams cartoon, and these people were living the life of a Charles Addams creation; it was amazing. My mind was blown.

The subject came back to his playing the calliope, and he said that when he played for the Clyde Beatty circus, he not only played for the big cat acts, but he played for a human cannonball whose name was . . . oh god . . .

Hugo?

Hugo Zacchini! He played for Hugo Zacchini, and he said there was kind of an intermission that would happen at the circus, and right before the intermission Hugo Zacchini's cannon would be wheeled out. It would very slowly come out and point itself toward the audience, and the curtains would close around the cannon so that it looked like a giant steel phallus piercing these curtains, and stay there until the second half of the show. He played the soundtrack for that, and that was one of the happiest memories he had from his circus days.

And then he opened up his second present, which was the remote-controlled electronic whoopee cushion. He couldn't believe it. He had never seen this before, just like the old man in the shop told me: "I bet he hasn't seen this." He was just beside himself, laughing; he was like a kid at Christmas.

He opened up the package and inserted the batteries that came with it, and he started pressing the button. It came in two parts: a speaker that you would hide under the victim's chair and a red button that you would press. It created that sound that's better imagined than described: the loud fart. He made that machine fart over and over, and he was beside himself with laughter. He said, "Oh, I'm going to have a lot of fun with this, Larry. Thank you, thank you, thank you, you know just what to get me."

And then the third gift I gave him was a copy of that 78-rpm recording: "The Darktown Poker Club," by Phil Harris. He said, "I met Phil Harris . . . we were both booked as guests on the Steve Allen Show. I presented Steve Allen with a Church of Satan membership card, and I presented Phil Harris with a Church of Satan membership card. Phil told me 'Anton, I am a born Satanist.'" He said that really delighted him, to hear that from Phil Harris.

So unknowingly, I had given him another perfect gift. That was really tremendous. Then at some point late in the evening we convened in the kitchen where he had his keyboards, and he immediately launched into a medley of bullfight paso dobles. That went on, I would say, for at least forty-five minutes. He went from one to another; many I had never heard before. I recognized the rhythm of it as being a paso doble; these were dramatic bullfight songs.

I was just so impressed: he played everything from memory. Then he launched into the "Ride of the Valkyries" by Wagner—extremely dramatic and wonderful. He played me the theme song from *The Treasure of the Sierra Madre*. He asked, "Did you recognize that? That's the theme from *The Treasure of the Sierra Madre*." I just said, "Ah! That was one of Father's favorite films!" He said, "Mine, too."

He asked me what other films my dad liked, and I said, "Well, *Nightmare Alley,* and I've seen both of those films several times, but I've never seen this third film that he always would mention." LaVey asked, "What film is that?" and I answered, "*The Bullfighter and the Lady.*" He said, "Larry, I have a copy of that. What are your plans for tomorrow? I'd like to invite you back tomorrow. Just show up a little early, and Blanche and I will take you out to Joe's at Westlake. We'll have dinner, and then we'll come back to the Church and watch *The Bullfighter and the Lady.*" Somehow he had taped it off cable television, I believe, because it wasn't available on VHS.

So fast forward to the next night: here I was, sitting there watching *The Bullfighter and the Lady* with Anton LaVey, and we were both just so enamored with it; that brought me to tears. It's such a beautiful film. There's a young woman who's the love interest of Robert Stack in the film, and she's played by an actress named Joy Page. Very little has been written about her; she's not known at all. She's absolutely gorgeous. She was actually the daughter of Jack Warner, and he forbade her to be in movies. She starred in that film against her father's wishes, and he then blacklisted his own daughter and ruined her movie career after this movie came out. It's just horrible to know that, but it makes you love her even more in the film, because she's unique and special. I fell in love with her immediately in this movie.

After the first night at the Church of Satan, LaVey told me, "Larry, I'm nocturnal. I sleep during the day, and I'm awake at night, and when I play these songs in the kitchen, I like to think that they enter the ether and they effect change around the world." It was just so fantastic that he was sharing these thoughts with me.

I remember while we were at Joe's at Westlake on the following evening being very careful to order the proper salad dressing, because I knew that he judged men by what salad dressing they would choose. I chose Thousand Island, which made him very happy, because that's the dressing he had on his salad, too. I asked him what he was having, and he said, "I prefer the petite filet, cooked rare." I ordered the same thing for myself; it was absolutely fantastic.

After we watched *The Bullfighter and the Lady,* we adjourned to the kitchen so he could play his keyboards for me. At the end of playing the keyboards, he said "Larry, I have something I want to give you." Blanche came out and presented me with a Church of Satan membership card and handed me a Baphomet lapel pin. I was now officially a member of the Church of Satan. Many, many months passed after that, and a manila envelope came in the mail from San Francisco. I opened it up, and there was a certificate inside. It was a declaration that I was now a priest in the Church of Satan, and I was empowered to act in that capacity. It was signed Anton Szandor LaVey, and it had his personal symbol on there: an upside-down pentagram with a lightning bolt through it. It was just absolutely terrific. So now I was an honorary priest of the Church of Satan. . . . What could be better, you know?

He was just so supportive and wonderful when it came to my bullfight documentary. He wrote a blurb for it, and it was absolutely fantastic: "Here it is, folks: The World Series, Super Bowl, Indy 500, and World Soccer raised to the highest power. Real people enjoying all the thrills, spills, and chills of good, clean sports. The stars, the spectators, and the hard workers behind the scenes. All this, plus a great musical score. Too bad Larry Wessel wasn't around with his camera in Rome filming the Circus Maximus!" What a great blurb for my documentary!

The second night that I visited him, he handed me a manuscript of a story he had written, and it's all about the remote-controlled, electronic whoopee cushion. It starts with, "My friend Larry Wessel presented me with the most amazing device I have ever seen." It starts that way! "My friend Larry . . ." It was so great! He mentions all these famous battles and wars that could have been won, had they employed this weapon. He told me that he wanted this to be published in a book. He said, "I don't want you to reveal the title to anyone, Larry. . . ." But I think it's safe to tell you now. The title of the book was to be called *The Occult Technology of Power,* and this was going to be a book that he had written. This one was going to be one of the chapters in the book . . . the remote-controlled, electronic whoopee cushion! I was just beside myself; it was as if I had inspired him to write this beautiful piece for this book. I don't think the book has ever seen the light of day, though.

When he had seen my collage, he said, "I love your art, Larry. I've been thinking about putting together an art book with all of the artists I know, including myself, that would depict the various sexual fetishes." He said, "I would like you to illustrate the fetish popularly known as 'battling babes.'" I knew immediately what he was talking about: a catfight. "Your collages would be perfect to depict that. I would love that in my fetish art book." I never got around to doing that for him, and I don't think he ever completed that book. He may have; I don't know if it's still waiting somewhere to be published. But I kind of dropped the ball by not seizing that opportunity and illustrating that fetish for him—I would have loved to have done that. They were always really good and supportive.

A couple of years later—I think it was around 1996—I visited him again, and Peter and Peggy were there. It was great to meet them for the first time. Peter was working on some music with Anton LaVey, and I remember that Peter was reciting a Rudyard Kipling poem that had the words, "trudging, trudging, trudging" in it. I'm not quite sure what poem that is, but LaVey wanted him to read this for a musical score that LaVey was working on. They were working on that, which I thought was really interesting and cool, and I spent another evening with him that lasted all night.

I never saw the Doktor again; I just spent three nights with him in all, but I'll never forget those nights for the rest of my life. I'll never forget him for the rest of my life. I don't think a day goes by that I don't think about him, and that might sound odd about a person that I'd only met three times. But he really influenced me and made a big impact on me.

I like to think that I influenced him, too, because over the years people would complain to me: "Larry, I got my only chance to visit Anton LaVey, and he took two hours of our meeting showing your bullfight documentary." Apparently, he was showing my bullfight documentary to everybody that would come visit him! I just thought that was really great: that he loved my work so much that he wanted to share it with everybody. That really made me feel happy, you know.

Fast forward some twenty-five years and here we are, and you're working on your film: Larry Wessel's Palace of Wonders. *You say specifically that it's inspired by the Don Blanding poem that he read to you. Why do you think that he read that specific poem for you?*

I don't know, but it stayed with me. I realize that I was very interested in the subject matter of this poem, and it meant a lot to me. This idea of the collector has been with me for a long time, and I had wanted for the longest time to make a documentary about collectors and their obsessions, about their objects that they have collected in their world travels and that sort of thing. I've kind of done that with my new documentary; it's a lot like that. It's people sharing their collections of strange, evocative objects. In my little humble studio here, I have a collection of knickknacks and artifacts from my travels, and you'll find things in here that reflect my personality.

I think that I hadn't really worked it out in my mind—like why he chose that particular poem to read to me—but he seemed to know that I would enjoy it, and that I would carry it with me, all these years later; it's amazing to me. Why did my father read to me "The Raven" by Edgar Allan Poe? Why did he read to me "Ozymandias" by Percy Shelley? They stuck with me and formed my aesthetic. I credit my father for that. I've developed a good sense of humor, and a good taste in literature and music and art and filmmaking, all because of my upbringing and my parents, and what they shared with me as a child.

Anton LaVey was sharing with me as an adult; he was continuing that education. A cultural enrichment that an elder, wise man can impart to a younger man. It was like what you read about with tribal elders, you know? I've thought about this a lot: that the knowledge is passed to people through all kinds of forms. It could take the form of a book, it could take the form of a work of art, or a film, or it could take the form of the oral tradition. Anton LaVey was a raconteur extraordinaire, and he could weave a story for you that would just enchant you and bring you in from the very beginning. He was a very, very great storyteller and a great writer. He had that gift, and once he had your attention, and was telling you a story, you did nothing but act like a sponge to soak it up and hope to be able to retain everything that he shared with you, hope to be able to have the capacity to do that. I think I did, because when he unfortunately did pass away, I was just devastated.

I remember it was Halloween when I found out. Somebody had told me that they had heard about it on the Howard Stern show, and they were joking about it, and I thought "Really?" I went home, and I called the Church of Satan immediately when I got home. I was expecting Blanche to pick up the phone, but it was Karla LaVey. I told her how sorry I was, and please express my condolences to Blanche, and I feel really bad about his passing, you know; he meant a lot to me, and she thanked me, and it was very sweet and nice.

Then, I believe it was just a day or two later, Blanche called me and thanked me for calling. She said that she'd like me to write a memorial to Anton LaVey. And I did for the next issue of the *Cloven Hoof.* That was the memorial issue. It was called "The Nicest Man I Ever Met," and a lot of what I've told you about my first meeting at the Church of Satan was written down.

I just wrote it from memory, from my heart, and it just flowed out of me so easily. It's like what you want to happen when you're writing something; you want it just to flow. William Burroughs describes it as basically just writing down what's being transmitted to you, as if it's coming from your muse. Anton LaVey would say that that is deep inside of you, and that's what you're tapping into. You can call that Satan, you can call that the muse, but that's what you hope to be able to have a very intimate relationship with when you're an artist or a creator; you hope that the stuff comes easily to you. I think that with time and age, it does. With me it took a long time, but I'm very comfortable now, creating things, and it comes to me quite easily. It's what I live to do; it's also a passion for me.

It's something that Anton LaVey took very seriously. He told me, "Larry, I love your films. Your films are great; they're like an accounting for your time spent on Earth." He said that at the end of your life, you'll be able to look back and say, I've accomplished all these things, and he said it gives your life meaning when you create. All of the things that he himself had accomplished in his life I'm sure made him very, very fulfilled and happy with himself; he had given his life meaning. That was a great gift that he gave to me, and it was great to be encouraged by someone as great as he was; it was wonderful.

Do you think that it was a conscious decision, to perhaps secure some kind of legacy? Meaning, writers that he loved, ideas that he loved, poems that he loved, movies that he loved, that he sort of disseminated them to people who came there, to secure his own legacy?

Well, that's interesting. I don't think he was selfish in that way about his legacy. I think that he shared these things with people that he liked and trusted because he genuinely felt compatible with them and knew that they would dig what he wanted to share with them. I feel this urge myself when I get with people that I like; I want to share all the things that turn me on, things that I celebrate. Maybe he did have a design in mind, in terms of passing his knowledge on to others. That's very possible, because he was reclusive for so long. Then toward the end, all of a sudden, he opened the door to people. I think that making people members of the Church of Satan and declaring them priests, that probably was by design—because he wanted to do that and extend his influence. But at the same time, I consider it a very generous thing.

I like to think of it in terms of *The Wizard of Oz,* where the main characters are all lacking something. When they finally meet the Wizard of Oz—Anton LaVey—he gives them what they need and what they want, you know. He gave the lion courage, and he gave the tin man a heart, I think, and he gave the straw man whatever; he gave people these gifts that give them great confidence. He certainly did that with me; it was terrific.

I also forgot to tell you about trips to the bathroom, because during a ten-hour stay, you're going to have to go to the bathroom. Well, he had the most wonderful lavatory, and it was decorated in an incredible way: he had a corncob hanging on the wall from a piece of twine, he had a copy of *Jokes for the John* hanging from a chain inside his lavatory; his toilet was an old-fashioned pull-chain toilet that emptied out from a big tank way above you, and then the pièce de résistance was a little sign on the wall that said, "Smile, you're on *Candid Camera.*" And I remember my Satanic witch friend telling me she was always worried, when she was sitting on that toilet peeing, that when she saw that *Candid Camera* sign that maybe Anton had a camera set up in there. She'll never know. I don't think he did, but it was a sign that made you nervous enough to consider that. It was wonderful.

One thing that I'm curious about, on a personal level, is that he gave the impression in interviews, and also in his own writing, about having been involved in what he called the revival of Freaks—**the old movie. I'm just curious if you know anything about how he was involved in that. Was that merely by his talking about it?**

I don't really know how he was involved in that, but I believe him that he was instrumental in reviving *Freaks.* That film was vilified and considered a banned film for many, many years, and it ruined Tod Browning's career. He was a great filmmaker, and *Freaks* is a masterpiece; it's one of my all-time favorite films. It disappeared; it was like a banned movie, it was an unseen movie, and Anton LaVey, with his love of the carnival and circuses, certainly enjoyed that film.

He was really well connected with circus people. These carnies and circus folks were always visiting him, and . . . what do they call it? "Cutting up jackpots" with him—that's their language that they use when they tell stories about their adventures on the carnival midway. I know one of his favorite books he turned me on to was written by William Lindsay Gresham—the guy who wrote *Nightmare Alley*—and it's called *Monster Midway*. What's cool about *Monster Midway*—and *Nightmare Alley*'s the same—is that it reveals a lot of secrets of the carnival: all of the cons and the tricks that are employed to, you know, separate the rubes from their money. *Nightmare Alley* is a masterpiece, and I was aware of that film from very early on.

What do you think his legacy will be? Will it continually be permeated by clichéd things such as the recent American Horror Story, or will he take on a new kind of mythological role that plays a more beneficial part, specifically in American society?

Well, I think his future influence, culturally, will be felt in all of the writings he left behind. I think that *The Satanic Bible* itself is a good starter for anybody interested in his philosophy, and it just continues on from there. And in his other books, such as *The Satanic Rituals, The Satanic Witch,* and also *The Devil's Notebook*. It's a thin volume, but full of really beautiful philosophical observations. In my mind, he should be taught in universities. He should not be just a footnote, but his books should be on the syllabus of any professor in any big university who's interested in the thinkers of the twentieth century. He's one of the great ones at the end of the twentieth century; I put him up there with all the great ones. He'll be taken seriously by anybody who bothers to read him.

I think the people who pay attention to all of the Satanic Panic hysteria and stuff will always be deluded, and getting secondhand information that is just sensational and ridiculous. That's always going to be the case. The general public is not very bright. As LaVey would say, "Their bulbs don't burn very brightly." So they eat up all of this mythology and stories about what Satanism is.

There is a terrible film that came out recently about Anton LaVey and his relationship with Jayne Mansfield; it was a documentary. It was brutally bad, because the people who made it really didn't have a clue about who Anton LaVey was; they just sensationalized this aspect of him having a brief relationship with this beautiful actress, Jayne Mansfield. I watched it with interest because of the subject matter, but the documentary was just absolutely horrible.

I think that's probably going to happen with anybody as legendary as Anton LaVey. It just happens over and over and over: Hollywood makes a so-called biographical film about somebody, and they drop the ball, and they miss the mark. Television does that, movies do that, and they just keep doing it. I guess that's always going to happen.

The Satanic Bible has never gone out of print, and that will always be there for the next kid who comes along and discovers it for himself, and becomes stronger because of it, and becomes influenced by it, and sees W. C. Fields's name listed on the list of Anton LaVey's influences and wonders who that is and checks out the films of W. C. Fields. . . . So he links people up with important things from the past—as every good parent should do, like my parents did for me.

I think LaVey's love of history, and his sharing of it with people, really helped educate people. I think the true legacy of Anton LaVey is best expressed in his own writing, and I don't think you can get anything more direct than that.

He's put himself in front of the camera a few times—certainly that Joe Pyne interview he did was absolutely terrific. He's always so well spoken when he's put on the spot by somebody like Joe Pyne, who's antagonistic to begin with, and who tries to ridicule what he believes. LaVey just fires right back at him so eloquently; he's really good at defending himself. I don't think the flame keepers of legacy are going to be Hollywood or television. I think the actual Church of Satan, as run by Peter and Peggy and Blanche, they keep that fire burning. I'm glad that they're actively keeping his legacy alive. I'm really thrilled that they do that with such gusto and energy.

What would you say makes your films "Satanic?" Or do you define your films as Satanic?

The way I understand Satanism, in its purest form, is that it's the act of creation. Creating something from nothing, to me, is magic. And what is magic, as defined by Anton LaVey? It's black magic. There's only one magic, or magical force, and it's black magic. So, "That old black magic has got me in its spell," is what other people refer to as the muse. It's a source of your creativity as an artist. You bring up thoughts and creative things; they spring from within you, not from outside of you.

If you turn to yourself for inspiration, there's an endless supply of it inside of you, and you just have to call on that. I'm engaging in black magic every time I make a film, every time I write a story, every time I make a piece of art; I tap into that creative energy. That energy is Satanic. I don't think that, looking at what I do, you could say, "Oh, he makes Satanic films." What is a Satanic film? I don't know; it's hard to say. Certainly, *Rosemary's Baby* was one. Roman Polanski really knows how to terrify people, like Hitchcock did; he has powers to scare people. But scaring people, is that necessarily Satanic? I don't think so.

So I don't think of myself as a Satanic filmmaker. But I certainly view creativity that way. I think that Anton LaVey was one of the most creative people I've ever met, and I think that's how he viewed his own creativity. He went so far as to write a bible about it and build a church around it. That's one of the gracious things about Anton LaVey: that he wasn't a con man, and yet people throw this pejorative at him all the time. He never conned anybody; he wasn't a con man. I don't think Anton LaVey ever charged more than three dollars for one of his lectures. I don't know what he charged for Church memberships, but it was some small amount of money. It wasn't a lot, it wasn't like he was trying to bleed people dry, you know, and take their bank accounts like others do. I think of him as a very bright, smart artist who was very generous with people, and he gave way more than he ever took from people.

In my opinion, one of the key things that made LaVey unique was his active integration of his own life experience into fields that are traditionally "established" and that newcomers simply adapt to (occultism, philosophy, religion, etc.). What are your thoughts on why this was? How would you define the character traits that made him such a creative developer?

All of my favorite artists—painters, poets, philosophers, et cetera—are open-minded freethinkers and not only have an unquenchable thirst for knowledge, they also possess a powerful sense of humor. They all integrate their past experiences into their art. This not only personalizes what they create but makes their creations relatable to an audience, giving the audience something grounded in life and something tangible to resonate with. This combined with humor guarantees that what has been absorbed by an audience will be indelible.

As artists grow in age, and gain more experiences, and enrich their own imagination, their creations become more and more profound and multilayered in meaning. That Anton LaVey could integrate his own life experience into such a wide array of established fields makes him quite extraordinary! And how many people do you know that can match his life experiences? He was a cage boy and roustabout, lion tamer and calliope player, fun house blowhole operator and hypnotist, burlesque organist and the first registered theremin player in the city of San Francisco, photographer of "cheesecake" and crime scenes, psychic investigator and ghostbuster, magician and lecturer, founder of the Church of Satan and author of *The Satanic Bible.*

Many years before he formed the Church of Satan and wrote *The Satanic Bible,* Anton LaVey used to give lectures. The lectures were open to the public and dealt with such arcane subjects as lycanthropy, witchcraft, black magic, vampires, ghosts, et cetera. He was an expert in all of these things. The San Francisco police department would call him whenever there were complaints about ghosts. He was San Francisco's official "ghostbuster"!

One night he was called by the SFPD to visit an elderly woman who said that she had a ghost in her attic. Anton climbed up a ladder and entered her attic. Crawling through the cobwebs, he found a small hole in the roof of the attic with an old rusty tin can wedged in it. When the wind blew through the rupture in the ceiling, the can emitted a sort of human moan. Happy with his discovery, he retrieved the moaning tin can and showed it to the elderly woman. "I found your ghost," he said. "Was that all it was? No, you didn't," she replied. "That is not a ghost; that is just a tin can!"

LaVey realized then that this lady's stubborn belief in ghosts and her refusal to learn the truth was identical to the thought processes found in all religious people. This was the linchpin that inspired LaVey to create the antireligion that we now know as the Church of Satan.

When it comes to creativity, I get the impression that LaVey was happiest when playing his tunes, telling his stories, and writing his essays; that is, being immersed in his own expressions that he mastered so well. But these usually also require a second party: a listener, a reader. Did you ever get the impression that he expressed himself mainly to have that second party, or was the expression in itself, for himself, the most important aspect?

I think that what was important to him was the self-satisfaction that came through the immersion into his own creative expressions, and most importantly the sense of accomplishment that came with their creation. I remember him telling me that "creativity gives our lives meaning, and it gives us a way to look back with satisfaction and account for our time spent on Earth."

Can you see any similarities between LaVey and other notable creative people at the time? Meaning, would you say there was something distinctly zeitgeistish about him?

As I see it, the LaVey zeitgeist began on March 30, 1966, with the premiere of avant-garde composer Krzysztof Penderecki's St. Luke Passion, which dramatically explores the death of Jesus Christ. A few days later, on April 8, 1966, two more interesting cultural events took place: *Time* magazine published their "Is God Dead?" cover story, and on this same day the last episode of the popular television series *The Addams Family* was broadcast. A few weeks later, on Walpurgisnacht, April 30, 1966, Anton Szandor LaVey shaved his head and established the Church of Satan. The fires of this "black flame" were further stoked by the publishing of Ira Levin's novel *Rosemary's Baby* in 1967, and then the premiere of Roman Polanski's film version in 1968; 1968 also brings forth Anton LaVey's "Topless Witches' Revue," which leads us to the publication of *The Satanic Bible* in 1969. This black flame has never gone out and still burns brightly today.

Were there any quirks or habits that you found odd in LaVey? Meaning, unexpected expressions of moralisms that might have seemed un-Satanic and perhaps stemmed from the times or the religion he grew up in? Things you sort of didn't quite see coming?

Not really, although I remember mentioning to him once that I used to get up early on Sunday mornings when I was a kid to watch a TV program that was popular in the 1960s and 1970s called, *I Believe in Miracles.* This show was hosted by the charismatic healing minister Kathryn Kuhlman. Anton said that he, too, was a fan of Kathryn Kuhlman's television show, and that he particularly loved the dramatic and frightening way that she would pronounce and elongate the word *God.* Kathryn would always pause before she said it: " . . . Gawwwwwd."

In the LaVeyan encouragement of fetishizing objects and environments (working with ECI, creating total environments, for instance), it's not that far-fetched to talk about an ensouling of these objects or spaces that one has an intimate relationship with. Did he ever give the impression that he felt that way about human beings? Meaning, that he could feel OK with using the word soul *or* ensouled *or* spirit *or* spirited *when talking about humans? I guess the extension of this question is whether you ever saw signs of him not being a 100 percent strict materialist?*

When I presented him with that large collage portrait that I had constructed of him, he studied the collage for quite a while and said, "Thank you, Larry, you've captured my very soul."

Did you ever feel that LaVey put on a show at times because he felt it was expected of him rather than because he was genuinely in the mood himself?

No, I think that LaVey rarely did anything that he did not want to do.

20

INTERVIEW WITH
CARL ABRAHAMSSON
BY VANESSA SINCLAIR

Carl Abrahamsson with Anton LaVey, San Francisco, 1989.
Photo courtesy Blanche Barton.

How did you first hear about Anton LaVey?

I think when I was in my late teens, I was curious and hungry for information—looking for things, in terms of interesting culture, subculture, underground culture, occult culture. In those days there were still occult bookstores, even in tiny Stockholm where I grew up, and they always had copies of Anton LaVey's *The Satanic Bible*. I was fascinated by it; it spoke to me in a way. I bought it and checked it out. It was so easy to grasp. At the same time, I was also checking out Crowley, who was much more technical, and had a much more bombastic language, and was involved in arcane symbols for their own sake, in a way. I found a kind of simplicity in the communication in LaVey that I found was resonating with me. I got *The Satanic Bible,* felt that resonance, and then started checking things out.

There was also a parallel strain, in which I was fascinated by American dark pop culture; you know, the shadow side of American culture: B movies and tragedies, the things that Kenneth Anger wrote about in *Hollywood Babylon,* these personal tragedies and all the dark stuff that was going on beneath the surface of very glitzy, highbrow, wealthy, affluent lifestyles. There was always some kind of tragedy going on. Anton LaVey also existed in that scene, and specifically what fascinated me was his relationship with Jayne Mansfield, who was typically one of these sort of tragic icons. She was great, glamorous, successful, but there was also some kind of tragic undertow in her life. She knew LaVey, and they had had—or maybe they did—a little fling. That kind of stuff interested me a lot. So LaVey also came into my life via Jayne Mansfield.

How did you first come in contact with him?

I was very much a networker, and at this time, when I was in my late teens and early twenties, I always had my own fanzines. I wrote about interesting things, mostly music, but also about movies. I was used to this kind of networking, and I was in touch with Genesis P-Orridge of Throbbing Gristle, Psychic TV, and Thee Temple Ov Psychick Youth. Genesis suggested that I should send the first record that I made with my band, White Stains, to LaVey, because it had a tribute song to both LaVey and Jayne Mansfield; it was called "Sweet Jayne." I thought, maybe that's not such a bad idea. When the record came out, I sent it to LaVey, and—because the lyrics were all about their relationship, I guess—I got a letter back not only acknowledging the receipt, but also expressing gratitude and pleasure. He also, at that time, made me a member of the Church of Satan through that letter. I was of course not only mind blown by it, but also genuinely honored. This was in 1988, and as soon as I could get the money together, I just went over there. We met at the Black House and had dinner, and that was the beginning of some very interesting years in my life.

How did that meeting impact your life?

Well, I was very interested in occultism, but not only from a historical point of view. I also wanted to integrate it into my life—meaning having a magical attitude, a magical approach, trying things out. As with many things that have to do with this kind of self-development, you have to have a set of symbols that speak to you, that you feel a resonance with on a deep level. I found that in LaVey's definition, in his codifying of the "Satanic."

Many of the things that he wrote about and that we talked about, I had already felt a resonance with earlier on: when I was a young teenager and a complete film buff, I always identified with the anti-hero in film noir, for instance, or with the bad guys. Some people just are like that. He had the ability to *not* go down the arcane route, to *not* just be involved in occult symbols from the millennia, but actually pinpoint and say that these are all valid, but Satan is also a symbol of many things in human culture, and in human history. The symbol still has a meaning; it's a kind of timeless, eternal thing. In all of this lingo, or jargon, or symbolism, I could feel a strong resonance—much more so than with other occult symbolisms and systems that I also explored at that time.

Has that changed after his death in 1997?

The times when we hung out, which was almost every year between 1989 and 1993, there was an active infusion of stuff, but also an in-between-the-lines infusion, which was, I guess, some kind of magical thing that he had going on. You know, inviting people over, checking them out, and seeing what they could possibly take on after his demise, in a way. Being in that same time-space situation with him was very influential for me. But I would say that after he died, I reevaluated his work as well as our meetings, in the sense that I think I almost valued them and him even more. That could be an expression of, you know, missing someone or feeling a sense of loss. But the more I've thought about him and his work over the years, or now actually decades, I find that he was such a creative person, both on a cultural level and an "occultural" level, as well as on a magical level for the Church of Satan, but also for me, personally. I think that his actual physical demise has, in a way, made him more alive, more vital, more relevant. But I have to say that hanging out during those years was remarkably inspiring, and I can still feel that inspiration.

What would you say has been LaVey's greatest contribution to your life?

When I started out, I became so infatuated by all the mystical and magical things that I became what I early on called a "magico-anthropologist," being interested in it from a pseudoacademic perspective. But I also wanted to be involved in it very much. I think that what LaVey showed me on a distinctly personal level was that magic is very much a real thing.

You could look at things from a causal perspective, and that's, I guess, what Crowley tried to do in a way, by defining magic as a way to just "cause change to occur in conformity with will." That's beautiful, but there's also, for me, a kind of a supradimension, which is where the actually magical things exist. I would say that for LaVey, that was very much a reality; he was very much what I would call a magician's magician. He was very interested in the arcane lore from psychological perspectives, from the perspectives of manipulation, and also from the perspectives of self-development, but there was nothing really spiritual about it. It was more a hands-on, pragmatic way of learning about life. He started working with that early on, and I think that spilled over very much to me—meaning, that you don't have to stick with the old arcane symbols and systems that were, in a way, pseudoreligious or pseudophilosophical. They always had to do with power structures and mimicking society at large, but in hidden forms. It can fill a function for some people, but I loved LaVey's very creative attitude toward what magic is, you know. It is a causal change, it is manipulation, it is self-development, but you have to weave your own personal stuff into your cauldron, so to speak. You have to make your own dish, your own stew. I did do that, and I think that would have been different if I hadn't met LaVey.

Is there any idea or concept that's still special, relevant, and vital for you?

There were many things that I got firsthand, you know, when you're in a face-to-face situation. You can talk to someone, and it doesn't necessarily have to be an interview where the acolyte sort of asks questions and the master replies. There were so many things going on between the lines all the time. He supplied both signal and also a meta level. The signal was of course him scanning me and saying, "What could this guy be interested in that I'm interested in?"—where you could look for a resonance with someone; definitely in terms of certain types of culture, certain types of authors, certain types of movies, certain types of music. But that's what friends do all the time. That doesn't necessarily have anything to do with magic or, you know, that kind of potential for change. But there was also this thing that I call "between the lines." It was a kind of seed sowing that was distinctly magical, and that's something that he, in a way, taught me; something that I have taken on, and also used on other people. Instead of spilling the beans, or just saying this is how it is—because that's like what a guru does: "Here's the truth, pay me"—but he wasn't like that at all.

There were many times when I felt afterward that something had happened, but not in the moment. In the moment I was just fascinated and sort of goo-goo-eyed at how he could pick out, for instance, a book from the bookshelf. I remember Ben Hecht's *A Guide for the Bedevilled*. He started reading from it while we were having coffee late at night. At the time I enjoyed it immensely as an experience. I couldn't figure out why he did that then, but it was very pleasurable. Later on, I found out that maybe he was actually programming me, in a way, with Ben Hecht, because there were other instances, too, where Ben Hecht popped up. He read from Hecht's *Fantazius Mallare*, too. We watched movies that were written by Ben Hecht, and of course, LaVey had great respect for Ben Hecht. But I think the reason he pulled out those cards with me was to, in a way, program me with that kind of Ben Hechtean energy. I can't define that. Adam Parfrey was another person that LaVey interacted with closely. Look at that influence! Feral House was like a beautiful bouquet of Satanic stuff, essentially. They're not specifically a Satanic publisher, but many of the ideas and people and things and themes and subjects that Parfrey published I would say stemmed from those original inspirations that came from LaVey's mind. In my case, it had to do with movies and literature; I would say Ben Hecht was a key to our transference.

LaVey was such a creative magician, conceptualist, and writer. He wrote about many of these things that he thought about, and that were not part, at that time, of any kind of arcane system of magic. It wasn't part of the Western ceremonial magic canon, it wasn't part of anything; it was just him constructing new ideas. And that was the thing that I liked most about him as a magician: that he could look at his synthesizer park in the kitchen as his main magical tools. And pen and paper: you could write down ideas, turn them into little humorous essays, and they changed the world. That kind of thing, where you looked at cultural expressions as actual magical tools; that was something that was super important for me way back then, and even more so today. So I think that I probably couldn't pick out one singular idea that is still extra special or relevant; it's more like an attitude that he had, which was much more open, creative, free flowing. *Creative* is the best word: he used different things for magical purposes, but mostly those having to do with his own creative mind and his musicianship—just an all-around creativity. And seeing that applied to reality was very inspirational, and I think that's the thing that I've tried to integrate, more or less successfully, in my own life. So I would say it's not a matter of taking one idea or, you know, "Satan," or the provocation of that. . . . It's more of an attitude that says you can use all of your creative skills, whatever they are, for magical purposes.

What do you think were the greatest changes he brought for America?

Well, America is a special place, and there's always a great, almost simplified kind of dualism between "them and us," and "good and evil," and all these things that basically come from a primitive kind of Christian thinking. The time in which LaVey and the Church emerged was very interesting, because you had the very colorful, LSD-induced hippies on one side, protesting the war in Vietnam, protesting the "squares," protesting a kind of a middle-class lifestyle. The hippies were protesting, and then LaVey popped up with the Church of Satan, which was something entirely different. Because he, in a way, also protested, or held up a mirror to the conservative, Christian, rigid, middle-class thinking; saying that people should focus more on being true to themselves, in terms of sexuality, in terms of religious or philosophical interests, and lifestyle, and aesthetics. This was something that was going against the grain of mediocrity and the herd thinking of, essentially, white, middle-class America, which was, and perhaps still is, steeped in Christianity of the very worst kind. Here comes another opposer, another accuser, so maybe they should team up—these two things? But of course, he had as much bile to spew out toward the hippies, because he found them to be mindless, drugged, mind numbed in a way, rather than "opened up," as they claimed to be. Maybe they were, maybe they weren't. But that was his take on it.

So he found and founded something very Satanic: the third position.* He was neither here nor there; he was in the middle, as

---

*See further discussion of the third side, or third position, in chapter 3.

was the Church of Satan: being totally in favor of law and order, and responsibility to the responsible, all these kinds of things that kind of rang a bell with the conservative side of society, but not with the hippies. At the same time, there was this focus on a free, liberating view on individual sexuality, and a nonprejudiced view on race and gender, and all that stuff. It was really about an ultimate kind of individualism. The only thing that mattered was what people did with their lives, and whether or not they were true to themselves. So that rang true for the hippies, too. But I would say that LaVey's third side, that was the truest of all of these things, because he really walked the talk, as did the Church. What was going on at the Black House at that time wasn't free love; it was real experimentation in order to get to know oneself, possibly under a dark light, but a very revealing dark light. Much more so than just dropping acid and having sex with strangers at a love-in. On the other hand, you can say that law and order is a great thing; it doesn't necessarily equate with police brutality or any of the things that we can see going on today that are unnecessarily draconian. That's not law and order; it's something else: the anarchy of unintelligent bullies. But LaVey and the Church were sort of in between, and I think that's the greatest thing that he brought to America: a different kind of mirror, a different way of looking at oneself, but also at society, saying, "All of these things that I can see from my own, unique perspective are fucked up; they are hypocritical on all sides; it's not valid for me; I'm going to go my own route based on my own self-knowledge." That is, I would say, a very valuable thing that he, through his codification of Satanism, brought for America.

Do you feel that LaVey has been misinterpreted? If so, how?

Absolutely. I think that LaVey has been misinterpreted in many ways, and in some ways it's his own fault or design, because when one uses such a strong symbol as Satan, specifically in a primitive Christian country like the United States, then of course you know what you're getting into. So when you choose a symbol and a symbology like that, and have this very dark aesthetic, then I think that you don't do that haphazardly or randomly. He knew exactly what he was getting into. And the reason for that was, at least that's how he explained it later on, was that it was a kind of bullshit detector. If someone constantly asks you, "Why Satan? Why Satan? Why use a symbol like this?" then he could, in a way, discard those people, and go straight to the people who ask real, substantial, philosophical questions, without having to have the basic, shock-value angle explained to them. Why waste time? Because if things had been called something else, there would have been the risk of its completely disappearing in a morass of other self-help things, or self-development philosophies, because there were so many things going on, I would say specifically during the 1970s in America.

LaVey found his niche, and the niche was Satan and Satanism. So by using that strong a symbol, he attracted a lot of people. It happened because he used that symbol and called his codification, or his system, Satanism. But at the same time, I think later, maybe he got fed up with it—got fed up with the attention and threats, and things like that. That's not hard to realize, how you get fed up with that. That kind of strength that lies in the accuser, and you taking on the role of the enemy . . . there's a lot of power in that, that he maintained for the rest of his life. But at the same time, it could have been almost like a cross to bear in a way. He might have had other things he wanted to convey, different kinds of concepts that could have been better presented in different contexts. But by then it was too late.

What was the key to his controversy: merely the S-word or something else?
I would say that the key to his controversy was in part the *S*-word, because, as I said, it's a strong symbol, specifically in a primitive Christian country like America. So that's one thing. But the controversy was probably more that the group, or that he, actually walked the talk. It was not just a philosophy packaged in an alluring, attractive package with a provocative symbol or a logotype of evil or whatever that would attract kids—that's just how kids function—but there was also

something very substantial to it. I was thinking of these active steps to enhance your own life . . . what I call "egotistical altruism." Meaning, that when you're working with and in your own egotism, and living a fulfilled, individuated life, it of course enhances your life. Thereby you send out a kind of energy, and you inspire other people. Thereby it also becomes altruistic. I think that kind of thing was controversial: a lifestyle in which people actually had all kinds of sex within the confines of a religious system, or at least of a magical order. Because most other esoterically inclined people were just looking at cabalistic schema or working with the tarot, but LaVey was going straight for the jugular in terms of getting people to get to know themselves in a better way, and without drugs.

It's just these basic carnal, physical things; sensuality was the key. That's something that people, maybe specifically in America, have been programmed to divest themselves from: to *not* be sensual, to *not* be carnal, to *not* be feral, but rather to go into a state of complacency and programmed so-called comfort. But it's not comfort—it's negative escapism. LaVey wanted to be inspired, and was inspired, by feral animals, and by living like a human animal, because humans are animals, and we have these central, biological needs. It's only through them, and working with them, within or without a magical context, that we can truly get to know ourselves. I think that was maybe a larger key to his controversy than the word *Satan* itself. But of course, those two things put together . . . it's like dynamite.

Would his impact have been different had not the S-word provocation been there?

Yes, I think the impact would have been less had not the *S*-word been there. I think he probably regretted it along the years or decades, simply for reasons that must have been this sense of, "Ugh, why do I have to explain these things again to these morons? I've already codified it. I've already written about it—that should be enough." But I think he got so many threats, and there were so many people who just didn't get it.

He wrote early on that Satanists are born; they're not made. You can't really develop yourself into a Satanist; you're either born one or you're not one. On the other hand, the Church of Satan was a group created as a kind of affinity for individualists. It may sound like an oxymoron or something paradoxical in a way, but that group has successfully existed for more than fifty years now. The people involved don't necessarily feel this need of, you know, clinging to each other and being individualists together. It's more a symbolic kind of affiliation to a dark beacon that represents a very strong individualistic philosophy.

If he hadn't used Satan as a symbol, then the buzz and the success early on wouldn't have been there. As the years passed, the philosophy would have been one among many of these kinds of individuation or self-help philosophies—in his case based very much on Nietzsche and magical lore. I think the use of the word and the symbol of Satan was like the icing on the cake, in a way. It made something happen at a very pivotal and chaotic time in American culture. If it hadn't been there, it would have been a different story. I think he would still have pursued it, but I don't think it would have reached the same kind of pinnacle of provocative power.

What do you miss most about him?

There was a lot of fun. And of course, inspiration when you're with someone who has inspired you before you actually met him, and then just keeps on inspiring. He was very supportive; both LaVey and Blanche Barton were super supportive of all the things that I was doing, in terms of publishing and music, and making books, and my own writing. Any kid wants to hear that. That's a good thing to also carry on, for me, now that I'm in a different position in life. I miss that kind of proximity and dialog, whether it's in the same physical space or at a distance.

There was a lot of magic in the Black House, and that was of course one of his key concepts: to create a total environment that just resonates and generates energy and—I won't hesitate to say it—magical power. Anything that happened there was something you could take away from there and use—to reboot it within yourself and use it for magical purposes. That could have been anything from watching an Eddie Cantor or Marx Brothers movie to listening to him playing old circus songs on his synthesizers in the kitchen. For other people it could have appeared to be just this weird, kitschy kook who lived in an Addams Family–style house. But if you knew where all of these things came from . . . everything had a story. Everything was connected by a dark kind of strain; it all pointed to the same kind of cauldron. That was his specific cauldron: forgotten songs, forgotten movies, forgotten people, all in the stew, all in the cauldron. He was stirring the cauldron, and then tasting it, and then being inspired. Making his magic or whatever he wanted to make, he used his own potion. That's something that I miss now: to take part of that super intelligent and intricate, intuitive, and, in a way, elegant way of working magical spells.

From his perspective, I think he saw in me a strange little guy from Sweden who was unusually knowledgeable about American pop culture. Many of the things that he was interested in, I was also interested in. There was a resonance there, and I think he thought that, "Well, I'll just, you know, pop some seed into this guy, and we'll see where it takes him." I've been very happy how those things have bloomed in my own life.

How do you see his legacy now and in the future?

I think that with film projects like *Into the Devil's Den,* and biographies, and keeping his work in print, he will remain in culture. In the Church of Satan, there are now also new additions to the Satanic canon, meaning that books by others are also integrated in the canon. I think LaVey will increase in stature, if you can say that. I think people will be more respectful, because he has always been a bit detracted, for instance, in the occult community—if there is such a thing—and also within academic environments. LaVey has always been associated with empty concepts such as con man or showman or similar things; I don't even know what they mean. I think that's going to change; I think he's going to be reevaluated. I'm certainly working on doing my part by writing about the brilliance of some of his magical concepts that were new at the time. They were not arcane at all; they were new. Weaving in psychological angles and knowledge of the human mind—there's some brilliant stuff there. I hope that other people will see that, too, and write their own pieces of the puzzle.

Eventually there will be a puzzle in which he is no longer so much of an enigma; he will just be presented as someone who created a change in American culture. I think that was one of his strong points, too: he really understood how culture was the greatest agent of change, whereas other occult groups were just looking at their own belly buttons or each other's butts, and looking deeper into their own systems as a form of negative escapism. LaVey used culture, and that was a very, very smart thing to do. That's how you change things.

ANTON LAVEY IN HIS OWN WORDS: EXCERPTS FROM "HAIL SATAN!"

"I'm an extremely happy man in a compulsively unhappy world."

A1. Anton LaVey, San Francisco, 1991.
Photo by Carl Abrahamsson.

In the late 1980s, after some years of negative exposure under the umbrella of what has been called the Satanic Panic, Anton LaVey decided it would be good to have some new and official information about what Satanism is, and what it isn't. The Church of Satan produced its own infomercial in 1989, the working title of which was "Hail Satan!" Although informative and entertaining, this film was never released. Below are some selected excerpts of what Anton LaVey wanted the world to know.

———

In the words of the once popular song, "It's a Barnum and Bailey world," any accusations that have been leveled at me for being a con artist or a charlatan, I can only say I'm no more and no less than any of the people out there, given the opportunity, would be.

———

The public loves to be fooled. And secondly, they'll pay any price for an identity. If by being fooled they will gain an identity, they would rather be fooled.

———

If it seems I'm a bit morbid about these sorts of things, it's really because I love life very much. It's been said that I can't possibly love life, that I'm a very unhappy man, or must be a very unhappy man. I would say that I'm a very happy man, an extremely happy man, in a compulsively unhappy world.

———

I could never be a humanitarian because I don't really like people. I like persons. . . . I'm really enthused about persons, whereas flocks of people, herds of people, leave me cold.

———

The more people there are, proportionally the more Satanic people there will be, and we're talking about degrees now, too. Some people might be complete Satanists; other people might be 10 percent Satanists, or 40 percent Satanists, but there is that seed or germ or quality, what I would call the chromosome that exists in someone who is born a Satanist.

———

There are so many people who have had great influence in the world, Satanically speaking, that are virtually unknown as Satanists per se. Benjamin Franklin, before he returned to America from England, had met with Sir Francis Dashwood, who was the leader of the infamous Hellfire Club: a group of Satanists in England. . . . Mark Twain, . . . Jack London, Ambrose Bierce, Thomas Jefferson, Thomas Paine, . . . Rasputin in Imperial Russia, . . . and Sir Basil Zaharoff. [T]his mystery man of Europe was instrumental in provoking, if not sustaining, several wars, and he was the inspiration for Daddy Warbucks, Orphan Annie's mentor and protector.

———

The Church of Satan would have nothing to do with something like "breeders," or abductions of children, or stealing of animals, or that sort of thing, because, again, the question: "Why?" Why would someone watching me, listening to me now, want to steal a child's pet? Why would you want to steal a child's pet? Why would you want to enslave someone who only wished to escape from you? That wouldn't be very sound business principles. I would say that it doesn't warrant much discussion except that it certainly isn't very Satanic to want to take anything against its will.

———

I think people in general who conduct themselves admirably should be given special privileges. I don't think people should be rewarded for being malefactors or for being just disturbers. There should be no rewards for malefactors.

———

My idea of a Satanic film is basically a film where the Devil or the Satanists win at the end.

———

The films noir of the 1940s personify the Satanic in films.

———

My idea of Satanic music is music that not only allows a person to feel something, but compels them to feel something . . . music that elicits a gut reaction. Music that sends shivers up somebody's spine. The kind of music that, well, everyone has heard some time in his or her life, that really gets them thinking or feeling about something regardless of who's playing the music or where the music is being played. That's Satanic music.

———

I don't think that we're in a position to talk about justice when there's so much injustice in the world, but until people decide that they want it any different, then I suppose that's the way it's going to be. I have my own code of justice, though. My code of justice says that if a person is out to harm me or anyone that I would care for, they are violating my law; my law being that the territorial imperative, or the boundaries of freedom that I have set for myself or that have been set for me, are being violated.

———

The Church of Satan has been very vehement in its attitude toward church tax exemption. I believe that all churches of all denominations should be taxed to the hilt. If churches were taxed as any other businesses—because that's what they are: simply businesses—the national debt would be wiped out overnight.

———

I don't feel any need for drugs. I never have used or abused drugs. If people want to blow their brains out with drugs, that should be their privilege—not their prerogative, but their privilege. Drugs should be legalized, if people want to use them moderately. But I'm against the use of drugs categorically; I'm emphatically against the use of drugs. I don't feel that it's necessary, and a lot of young people who are Satanists are very much against the use of drugs that would alter their consciousness and allow them to think thoughts that might not be rational or questioning or productive or indulgent, so that they really can enjoy what they're doing. I don't think people who are on drugs really enjoy too much.

———

American writers such as Ben Hecht and Cornell Woolrich are among those that I consider extremely Satanic, insofar as artists that show the raw face of human endeavor, or show life at its most revealing, are very

Satanic. Whether they're photographic artists, such as Weegee or Diane Arbus, or whether they're graphic artists like Reginald Marsh or Ivan Albright or Edward Hopper, these are very Satanic artists. In a roster of Satanic craftsmen, certainly these people have to be mentioned.

———

The idea that Satanism advocates orgies is a convenience that's been used for centuries. I personally don't see any fun in orgies. I've witnessed a few, and they're just not my thing. But I suppose, if people are interested in orgies, that's all right, too. I wouldn't say that it's a prerequisite of Satanism. As a matter of fact, I would say that epicureanism is more a prerequisite of Satanism. Epicurean sex, meaning that you're a little bit fussy about sex partners, that anything or anyone doesn't necessarily serve the purpose. Sex is, and should be, a more personal thing than what it has become.

———

Ritual, or ceremonial magic, to me, is not a lot of ringing of bells and smearing of oils and burning of candles and chanting and that sort of thing. Ritual can be very personalized, *should* be very personalized; it should be meaningful. The greatest and most effective rituals are those that are unique, those that are exclusive, those that are truly occult, those that no one but yourself can understand. These are the things that, because of their exclusivity, stand out like beacons.

———

Now, suddenly, [Satanism has] become a topic of conversation, it's become a household word; I realize that. This is all according to plan. . . . Pandora's box has been opened; 1966 ushered in the Satanic age. The future is ensured, regardless of anything that I may say or do. Satanism is here to stay.

⊰ ⊱

Genesis P-Orridge and Anton LaVey in Conversation

Is it impossible to have no secrets?
Genesis P-Orridge, 1988.

When two iconoclasts meet, there's bound to be interesting things happening. As mentioned in several places in this book, the genesis (pardon the pun!) of my own adventure with Anton LaVey came via Genesis P-Orridge. LaVey acknowledged that, too, for instance in his letter to me from August 18, 1988: "Thanks to magical links like Genesis, more pioneers like yourself are coming forth to shake up the rest of the world." This influential British avant-garde artist had in a similar way merged his own creativity and social, cultural influence with and through a "magical" group—in Genesis's case, Thee Temple Ov Psychick Youth (TOPY). There was a personal friendship between LaVey and P-Orridge present, and also a kinship in the realms of pushing the cultural boundaries by provocation. This particular conversation was recorded at the Black House by Genesis on September 28, 1988, as his band Psychic TV was passing through California (to play on the following evening at the I-Beam club in San Francisco).

Anton LaVey (AL): Yeah, The Mormon Tabernacle Choir . . . it was a group of singers presenting a musical form that, until then, was really unknown in this country. There was the Don Cossack Choir in Russia. But in America there wasn't any kind of mass choral group that sang that kind of very anthemlike, powerful music in a listenable way, until the Mormon Tabernacle Choir came to pass. Through this magical weapon, and through RCA and Columbia and Decca and all the recording companies that, of course, couldn't pass it up, the Mormons were able to establish a certain legitimacy for themselves. It certainly wasn't because of the cannibalism, and it wasn't because of the wives that Joseph Smith had. It wasn't because of the strange behavior, or habits and dress, or anything like that, or initiations. It was because they could come into the homes of Americans and provide music that was inspirational, emotionally moving, and, you know, salable.

That's why I think it's so important as a magical weapon, the music of Satanism, because it can, if it's presented in a different enough form—a form that is palatable or listenable, or in a way that just grabs people—it can run away from the rest of the pack, and it can sort of corner the market. That's what I feel is so important about what I'm doing, or want to do, now. The transition that groups, like your group, are obviously capable of doing—obviously, there are a few others, groups that are malleable or sensitive or chameleon-like in their musical scope—to be able to segue, or slide into something that no one is doing, no one is touching, that has become so neglected that, for all intents and purposes, there's a demand and a totally new market for it. And of course, it will leave the Christians with their Strypers and their Christian rock way in the back, because they'll be picking up where we left off, which they are right now, of course.

It's my idea that the Mormons, in doing that, had such a strong magical lever in mainstream culture, that we could make the same kind of dent in mainstream culture by putting out music the likes of which no one wants to listen to, that the Christians and the mainstream people have neglected and forgotten about, because it's too corny; maybe just they're embarrassed by it. They want to be difficult, you know, on top of things. It's their misfortune. They always become a nickel short and a day late because they're the last to discover what really is going to be in the forefront. And when they finally get around to doing it, it's already passé.

Genesis P-Orridge (GPO): Do you think that's why their instinct is probably accurate in homing in on and trying to discredit music, and hysterically inventing subliminal and backmasking, and all that stuff?

AL: Yeah, yeah.

GPO: They kind of know there's a threat there, but they're not actually locating it; they just know it's somewhere in the music.

AL: They want to maintain a paper tiger; to maintain something that can be jousted like a windmill, like Don Quixote; something that is able to be vanquished with no trouble at all. What would happen, God help them, if their kids started listening to Sibelius or to Bizet or to Liszt or to Rachmaninoff? And I don't mean just as it's played note for note, but I mean interpolations, strong, dynamic interpolations of this stuff, with liberties taken.

GPO: It's the emotional dynamism that's important.

AL: Right. Just in using these things as bases, you know, and not adhering to the conservatory, strict classicism, but in a dynamic, new form without a traditional rock beat, but more as an anthem. Like in a melodic anthem, in a dynamic form with highs, with lows, with orgasms, with detumescence—the whole thing. Bombastic! Bombastically. It's my secret, and this is where I feel people like you, Genesis, and others have the wherewithal, and the talent, and the ability, and the drive to sort of sneak up with these time bombs and plant them. God help them when they do, because their kids are then going to be listening to music, and their parents are going to be saying, "Do you want your children to listen to that?" And of course "that," whatever "that" happens to be, is music that they themselves, their parents or grandparents probably may have listened to in a lukewarm way many years ago.

GPO: They haven't got the imagination.

AL: Right, right, exactly! Bombastic! It was like listening to somebody—an old, scratchy, pre-war recording—doing "The Magic Fire," and then afterward some slick, warmed over, polished, much nicer version that was done maybe two or three years ago, of the same piece. It doesn't sound nearly as bombastic. But the perfectionists and the purists will say it's so much better now than it was then. And I say, is it? Is it really better? Or is it calculated to, perhaps, mask latent emotions in the listener that the old bombast didn't?

Mask them in the listener by its linear control type of delivery by its pure delineation. You can't have a trombone blasting out loud, you can't have a tuba blaring, you can't have a roll on the snare drum, you can't have violins swelling up like wind in a storm. You have to have it lukewarm; you have to have it palatable. It can't lead you to feel something too strong. And of course, when we start giving them that same kind of music, the way it would have been done had there been the technology, perhaps back in 1900 or 1920, then they're going to be in for some real trouble! It can be done, but still, it can be done with a small group, a couple of synthesizers and a good drummer.

GPO: I wish you were coming tomorrow night. I think by your definition it's going to be massively Satanic. We use an Emax sampling keyboard, and the Emax also has drum and bass rhythms on it, but they're almost sort of felt rather than heard. And then there's a real drummer who's really good, too. Paula has six cassette tapes; we're spinning in your speeches and other things, which I don't call "subliminals." I call them "aurals," because you can actually hear them. I'm fed up with subliminals, I don't want them. I want to make sure the people hear the propaganda. I don't want any misconceptions about it, you know. I am here to destroy your status quo daily. No questions. I don't want subliminal; I want blatant.

AL: You don't want them to have to dissect them and pick out and . . .

GPO: I want them to know exactly what we're telling them. No questions. I'm fed up with being subtle.

AL: I'd love to see it; I'd love to hear it. It's being recorded, isn't it?

GPO: Yeah, and videoed. I'll get you a video.

AL: That would be very meaningful.

GPO: We've made a one-hour movie, and it pulses at quarter-second intervals, and it's like a ritual that we've done. But in between is TV snow in ten layers pulsing, so it's interesting. And then there are three red strobes pointing at eye level into the audience that pulse at exactly the same 130 beats per minute all the way through. Relentlessly. There is a fog machine; half the time I'm just appearing and disappearing in smoke, and the rest of the band. We project the film through the smoke, onto the back. We all have torches strapped on everywhere, so like lights go in their eyes and flash. It's wild. Relentless. I said I wanted this show to be relentless; this is the word.

AL: It sounds like it's going to be orchestrated and staged and cohesive. . . .

GPO: There are moments of complete atonal anarchy, and then there's a ballad, and then it's really trance: trance-dance. The idea is to get people into an entranced state. I don't care how many songs there are: five or fifty.

AL: You are quite confident, obviously, when it comes to orchestration, and when it comes to setting up the staging, and knowing what you're going to do before you do it.

GPO: Well, I studied classical music when I was younger. It's also a skill that you can only develop by discipline and doing things for many years. You get this kind of residual building up of that effect. I've never gone away from symphonic structures. I do symphonic, emotional manipulation. I want the effect; I don't care what gets it. I want the effect.

AL: I would imagine that Genesis's performance would be much more highly structured than that one at the Strand Theater,* which was unfortunately not presented to me at all in its format. Well, I could have perhaps provided some advice for cohesiveness, and some kind of helpful direction that it could have taken. Zeena, I think, was a little dismayed, more than anything else, about the lack of organization. And just from an actress's or dancer's or performer's standpoint, the lack of placement and movement coordination on stage. Although obviously the audience didn't seem to mind. It went over very well.

It's not so much how it went over, but how it could have, what could have been. That's what we always think about: what could have been. There was a film called *Man Hunt,* with Walter Pidgeon.† It opens up, and he's in this jacket, sort of a suede deerstalker-type jacket, with a hat, and he's in the woods close to Berchtesgaden. He has a high-powered rifle with a telescopic sight. And Hitler is on the balcony. Hitler's looking out, and he has him in the crosshairs, and he's lying there. And then he sights, he has the rifle right up to his eye, the eye piece of the scope. He smiles, because apparently he eluded all these border guards and all the security around and managed to get that close, and just to that point where if he had wanted to, he could have. And then he just fired that dry firing pin. And then he took the bolt, opened it up, put a shell in, and then chambered the shell, and then he took it out and put it back in his pocket. And at about that time, a couple of guards came through the woods and spotted him. Then the whole film unfolds. He manages to escape and get back to England, because that's where he's from originally.

It's a very fine film, and it's on very magical principles, just the

---

*On August 8, 1988, an event took place at the Strand Theater in San Francisco: a mix between a rally, film screening, and concert, featuring performances by Radio Werewolf (with LaVey's daughter Zeena), NON, Kris Force, and others. The event was filmed for well-known "anti-Satan" demagogue Geraldo Rivera's TV show *Devil Worship: Exposing Satan's Underground.*
†*Man Hunt,* directed by Fritz Lang, 1941.

old concept of knowing that he can. It's like the concept of the Nine Unknown Men*—likening it to a leopard on the bough of a tree, watching all of these small game going back and forth through the jungle; just lying there quietly, knowing that at any time it can pounce, but refraining. That's the magic: knowing that you can, but you don't. It's like keeping a secret, like knowing something and instead of broadcasting it, just holding it in, for no real reason, but just because you know that it's power. That it's something that you know, that they don't know. That accrues a certain degree of power. And it builds like a magnet, like a storage battery. Just the fact that you can, but don't. It's the opposite of overextending oneself, and all that. And it's not masochistic at all. Not at all. It's not self-denial; it's just simply like sex, and allowing yourself to build up and up and up . . . like Sir Basil Zaharoff did.

GPO: How do these people get the power to make that accelerated progress?

AL: Well, I know how Zaharoff got his power.

GPO: Also, like Rasputin: certain characters that . . .

AL: Yeah, you just said it! Rasputin's another one.

GPO: I mean, what is that little price?

AL: They never had to estimate the power of emotion—of a fetish—of the type of person that can be matched up with someone else, and at an opportune time. As I put in the first page of *The Compleat Witch*—this was sort of a dedication or an homage to Basil—he knew the power of a woman, and what being paired up with the right kind of man at the right time could transmit in the way of energy, or sexual energy of any kind, even if it was covert rather than overt: woman to man, man to man, woman to woman. He knew to a fine art these subtleties. So as a match-

---

*A secret society founded in the third century BCE to preserve knowledge that would be dangerous to humanity if it fell into the wrong hands.

maker for intrigues, political and otherwise, no one could ever excel him. But Rasputin was quite close; he was in the same league, I'd say.

GPO: So that, if he worked in bordellos, then he would have picked up, or he would have discovered that skill himself there—in the subtlety in those places and watching the behavior patterns. Just the whole kaleidoscopic intrigue of the bordello, with people coming and going, and keeping your secrets, and role playing, and acting out rituals, basically. So that would be his training to apply to a macrocosm; that's the mastery.

AL: That's right: to a macrocosm. I was about to say that. Not necessarily on a conscious level, but on a knee jerk, or an automatic reflex, a cybernetic level, like a thermostat. Just all the things dropping into place, all the pins in the tumbler of the lock just falling in, instantaneously, like a computer, and getting a readout instantaneously of what is right and correct for the situation. And knowing the time that the readout must be given. The timing, the knowing all of these things. All of his activities were predicated on time, too. Being at the right place at the right time, and in the right guise, too. In France he was a citizen of France; in the Empire he was a Frenchman. In England he was a knight of the realm. In Germany he was with the chancellor, and in Russia he was with the court, or with the revolutionaries, just like Trebitsch-Lincoln.

GPO: It's incredible.

AL: Yeah, yeah, very much so. And metaphorically speaking, there are certain lights that could be shed on the Jack the Ripper case by the modus operandi of people like Zaharoff, which surfaces periodically from one era or chronological period to another—sometimes nascent, sometimes overtly.

GPO: I was thinking about Stephen Ward today. Do you remember the Profumo affair in Britain, perhaps?

AL: Oh, yes.

GPO: When the government war minister had to resign. Christine Keeler and Mandy Rice-Davies—Dr. Stephen Ward was the man who was the scapegoat for the establishment's guilt, basically, because he'd been the same kind of person. He had a fetish for these girls, and he adored being with harlots and prostitutes and *maîtresses*—the underworld. He didn't particularly like to have sex with them. He sometimes liked to watch. He just loved being with them, and he loved high-heeled shoes, and lots of good stuff. He also used to love supplying them to people they were appropriate to. You know what I mean?

AL: In other words, he knew whom to feed the suggestion to.

GPO: And it was perfect! Everyone loved him for it. I recently made a constructive acquaintance of an investigative journalist in England. Apparently, I met him years ago at university briefly. He's been kind enough to start supplying me information he receives that's not normally published, because he's not even working for Fleet Street. They won't have him; he's a bit too radical. Well, he's written a book called *Honeytrap*. I should send it to you; it's very nice; you'd enjoy it. It's on the Profumo case, and he's done a lot of original research on it. He knows who the man in the mask was. It turns out that the CIA and the FBI were involved, because John F. Kennedy also had sex with this girl. So there was a big flap on because there was this Russian diplomat who was also having sex with her. And then there was the war minister in Britain, and then John F. Kennedy while he was over. One or two girls were flown out to America by the CIA, because they were appropriate to certain bigwigs over here. And there was a big hush-hush around Stephen Ward, who apparently committed suicide. Although now there's at least a question mark over that.

AL: Of course. Christine Keeler is not saying much now.

GPO: She is not. Mandy Rice-Davies apparently worked for Mossad.

AL: Yeah, she's in Israel.

GPO: She's in Israel and is rich and had nightclubs. She's very respectable and never talks about it. It kind of fits that scenario on a small scale. It nearly took off to those levels. I mean, it got quite high level, and it got to the point where the Cuba crisis was going on at the same time. People were getting very freaked out. Stephen Ward was being used as a gofer between the British secret service and the Russians and America, in order to pass on secret messages by his little network, you know? And eventually he burned out. He died.

AL: Well, very much like Louis Lepke, who went to the chair back in the days of Murder, Inc.—he never said a word. He held so much that he could have used. A lot of people have done that sort of thing. Ignatius Trebitsch-Lincoln was also last heard from somewhere in China, and just sort of dropped off the face of the Earth. It's all about secrets. How can it be kept by only one person? It's impossible for someone not to spill the beans. And that's such a silly thing to say, because it's very possible that when there are interests at stake, and when there are common goals, or common denominators, when there is a sympathy or some kind of a feeling of affinity . . . there is that secret awareness that by carrying on this secret, you or I are possessed of this power, that if we were to relinquish this secret, we would be stripped of it. But a magician, of course, knows that under certain conditions there would be shared secrets. Let's just say shared secrets. I'd call it shared secrets. And it would behoove the magician to not just let these things out, but as in the Nine Unknown Men concept, allow some leakages, to see them as litmus tests. To see what will be picked up by whom, and how far it will be taken without giving the show away. And that's the true test of not only an investigator, but of a real magician.

GPO: So would that then be a different angle to look at why lots of other people's complaints about magic, the occult, secret societies, groups, networks and so on, are about, "Why does it have to be secret?" The secrecy is always, kind of, one of the things that's mooted on or pointed out. But if we're looking at secrecy as empowerment, then the very act of secrecy, not the secret itself, is actually the magical trick. That secrecy is a process of empowerment for a magician.

AL: That's right. The act of secrecy in itself.

GPO: And that understanding of that is when one is beginning to initiate them.

AL: Precisely. You could tell all kinds of secrets, and they would not be heard; just like the "law of the invisible." If the person is not, let's just say, attuned or empowered or oriented or directed in that manner, toward secrecy, per se, they're not going to pick up much of anything when you just tell the secret—like a stage magician telling the secret of how something was done. Well, usually it's a very simple thing, but let's assume it's not just a case of a hook with an invisible wire holding something up. You don't see the hook, and you don't see the wire, until he takes the hook and the wire and holds a white sheet of paper behind it so everybody can see it. That's giving one kind of secret away. But the way that he maneuvers this, and the way that he presents it, the presentation, and the way that he has had to learn, with incredible effort and practice, how to manipulate this hook and this wire so that it appears to be the way that it is, that is maybe the real secret—the secret of why the trick is effective. It takes perseverance. That's the talent if you wish to call it that: the talent or the art of secrecy, as opposed to just knowing how the trick is done.

GPO: That's a really interesting line of thought.

AL: Once a person knows the importance of secrets, they also know that secrets are candy, and that it is something that can be used as trading material. Like, "I'll tell you a secret if you tell me a secret." Therefore, if you know what kind of secrets are important secrets to other people—they may be bogus or spurious or not even real secrets that matter to you at all—you can, sort of, have throwaway secrecy, giveaway secrecy. But they'll satisfy a person enough so they really think they're getting in on something. It's sort of like the revelations that we get about somebody paying the media off for a particular kind of presentation, on a TV show or something.

GPO: Is it impossible to have no secrets? What state is that, of having no secrets?

AL: That's a good question! You mean more . . .

GPO: I don't know! I don't know what it means; it's just what came to mind.

AL: Is it impossible to have no secrets?

GPO: Zero secrecy, what is zero secrecy?

AL: It's like asking if they're a pinhead. I'm going to quote myself from Dan Mannix's book, *Freaks: We Who Are Not as Others*. Pinheads are the only really happy people in the world, because they never worry, because they don't have anything to worry with. In other words, if you don't have a brain that contains enough thoughts to concern you, you're not going to worry about anything.

There will always be leaders, there will always be puppet masters pulling the strings. The men in black, the MIB, they will always be there. I think that what I mean to say is that we will always be the MIB—one way or another, just I said in *The Satanic Bible*. There will always be those people in the world who are the movers and the shakers: the opinion makers that don't need the legal system, and work around it, and outside it, in so many ways. We're going into a cataclysmic time. The apocalypse is already practically eclipsed; it's pretty much over. Their worst fears are already passed. Now that it hits them, they won't even know it. They won't even be aware, but it is hitting them.

There Is No Such Thing
as Bad Publicity

The following text constitutes my introduction to the book *California Infernal: Anton LaVey and Jayne Mansfield as Portrayed by Walter Fischer* (Trapart Books, 2016).

At around mid-1987, my first band, White Stains, recorded some trashy rock 'n' roll songs in a small suburban studio just outside Stockholm. My mind was filled with American pop culture, especially the noir kind. I was in love with Jayne Mansfield and B movies, and with Kenneth Anger's codification of the personal disasters and perversions of an assortment of celebrities in his *Hollywood Babylon* volumes. I was in love with Anton LaVey's radical reshaping of old, arcane magic, his self-created myth and extravagant lifestyle. No wonder then that these strains merged in my mind as I was writing the lyrics for one of these songs, "Sweet Jayne" (an ode of sorts to the remarkable relationship between Mansfield and LaVey). When the record was released, my friend Genesis P-Orridge suggested I should send a copy to LaVey, which I did. To my surprise I soon received a very friendly letter from the legendary "Black Pope." That became the beginning of a friendship I cherished like few others—and still do.

What I find remarkable is not so much how this entire LaVey-

Mansfield symbiosis and the related photos have been integrated in my life via various unexpected channels, but mainly the insight about the power of the photographic image. For two so publicity-conscious exhibitionists as Jayne Mansfield and Anton LaVey, having someone like Walter Fischer around, almost like a court photographer, must truly have been a blessing. And Mr. Fischer must have been pretty pleased, too. The global market for interesting American movie and other kinds of stars was close to insatiable. The weirder and grander, the better.

The antics and philosophy of LaVey's Church of Satan have been chronicled elsewhere, so we won't delve into those areas here—as has Mansfield's interest in both LaVey and his Church. That story in itself transcends mere mutual reflection and narcissism. The mythological prerequisites for this now (in)famous fable would probably not have been possible without the images shot by Walter Fischer.

Establishing himself as a paparazzo and freelance photographer in the heart of starstruck Hollywood in the late 1950s, Fischer soon had his hands full. Images of movie stars, directors, events, and film premieres were distributed via United Press and other agencies and subsidiaries to photo-craving magazines and newspapers all over the world. I can only assume that Walter Fischer was a successful man, despite the competition that was surely around. One key to this success was of course to strike up as friendly a relationship as possible with the desired star or key person in question. To get to meet a second or third time or, even better, a continuous series of meetings, could mean a lot in terms of image sales. Intimacy makes for better images. This was a mutual aspect, too, of course. If the attention-craving subjects knew that the photographer in question was good, polite, well distributed, et cetera, half of the narcissistic battle was already won.

It's interesting to see how Anton LaVey sent press releases and event information to Fischer, although they were based in different cities. This means that the trust was already there, and both parties knew that a new meeting would be fruitful. LaVey often personalized press releases to Fischer in Los Angeles, to ensure he would show up at

San Francisco's infamous Black House at 6114 California Street, armed with cameras, flashes, and rolls of film. One can only wonder what was going on in Fischer's mind as he was snapping away!

There are a few main sections in this book, if we disregard the strict focus on Jayne Mansfield as a glamour goddess and on LaVey as high priest of a new religion. Fischer shot several times at the Black House (at least one of many lecture evenings, the wedding ceremony for Judith Case and John Raymond, the Satanic baptism of LaVey's daughter Zeena, and possibly more), but they also ventured out together. One wonderful section displays a visit to archivist and film historian Forrest J. Ackerman's dungeon of movie memorabilia, books, items, lobby cards, posters, et cetera. Like LaVey, Ackerman loved the nether and darker side of Hollywood. His own "baby," the highly influential magazine *Famous Monsters of Filmland* (1958–1983), has probably affected more American filmmakers born between the 1940s and 1970s than any other.

Seeing these two jovial gentlemen roaming through "Forry's" archives and collections must have been fascinating for Fischer (as it is for us now). A meeting not only of friendly, like minds and tastes, but also of active history creators hidden from and to the mainstream by their own design.

Jayne Mansfield was enamored with LaVey, and there was surely reciprocal attraction going on. Seeing these two individuals together must have been a pleasure for Walter Fischer, too. Whether out at a restaurant or posing together at Mansfield's Pink Palace in Beverly Hills, sparks were flying whenever they were together—this, undoubtedly, much to the dismay and frustration of Mansfield's partner at the time, Sam Brody. Brody's increasing aggression toward LaVey eventually led to the pair's mythical and actual end. Brody had touched some ritual objects of LaVey's in a spirit of scorn and ridicule, although warned not to. Some weeks later, both Brody and Mansfield died in a car crash.

The images from the late 1960s Black House are amazing on many levels. The house in itself was like a museum of the arcane and weird.

At this time, LaVey lived there with Diane, his second wife, and his daughters Karla and Zeena, and also with various animals—including the lion Togare. But it was also the headquarters for the newly created Church of Satan. LaVey housed his magical classes there, performed private rituals, and also staged semipublic events such as the wedding of Judith Case and John Raymond, as well as the baptism of his second daughter, Zeena (all displayed in this book). When you get to see more than the officially selected (i.e., published) photos, the informality and mirth become very evident. Although a church in honor of Satan was a big and controversial phenomenon in a San Francisco usually permeated by peace, love, and LSD at this time, LaVey always stressed (even in his writings) that a sense of humor was invaluable—especially in an environment as conservative and pompous as the occult. Fischer's images eminently show that being in Satan's lair could actually be quite a fun thing.

The egalitarian zeitgeist's idea of women's liberation didn't find a good home on 6114 California Street. Instead of leveling the sexual differences down to a dull and unisex mush, LaVey wanted to empower women as women. So he placed the most attractive ones on his altar, to be lusted for as generators of sexual energy—not least for the women's own sake. Slightly later, in the 1970s, he wrote an entire book about the subject: *The Compleat Witch,* later on issued as *The Satanic Witch.* His common sense and concrete advice on techniques of manipulation, seduction, self-defense, and many other things caused a stir among the politically correct feminists at the time (and it still does).

Although the images we see in this wonderful book were constructed and adapted to Walter Fischer's needs as a photographer, they also convey what was actually going on. Most of these images were taken in the second year of the Church of Satan's existence. The focus was on getting attention, so LaVey willingly catered to those who wanted to hear about his audacity and what the Satanic message actually was. But he had also been organizing classes and seminars at his home for many years before this new publicity drive. The newsletters and informational posters from the era display a wide range of activities and themes. LaVey's vast knowledge of arcane subjects and people created a veritable dark side university. This is where you could get your imaginary (?) degree in such fascinating subjects as "Semi-authenticated Creatures" (the abominable snowman, bigfoot, Sasquatch, wendigo, etc.), "A Cup of Grue" (man's fascination for the gory and horrible), "The Triumph of Pain" (torture methods and implements, highly inventive sadomasochistic devices and practices, etc.), "Freaks" (the strange world of sword swallowers, fire-eaters, cyclops, geeks, pinheads, Siamese twins, alligator men, midgets, giants, fat ladies [over 400 lbs.], etc.), or why not "ESP and Telepathic Communication" (the production, interpretation, and continuation of dreams, etc.). All of this and more on a weekly basis!

Was Jayne Mansfield a Satanist? That surely depends on how you define the term. She certainly lived by an intensely life-affirming code, in line with the tenets of LaVey's first book, *The Satanic Bible* (1969). But as the book came out after her death, the only information she could have received came straight from LaVey himself—and what better place?

Interestingly, Walter Fischer often sent out little mini-interviews with his photos, suitable for captions or short stories in the international photo journals. According to one such press release/quote collection, LaVey touched on Jayne's interest: "She thinks it's the greatest thing going. She is taking instructions. I made her a priestess and told her the concept of hell and paradise. I give her the usual information: working on ritual and how to cast (spells). She likes to know about witches and love charms. She considers me a High Priest."

In the same press release, Mansfield is quoted, too: "It is very interesting. I know the real basis of his church. I think he is a genius, and I regard him as an interesting person. I am a Catholic and would not believe in his church. I am not a member of the black circle." If these quotes are accurate, then we can perceive a slight discrepancy in the definition of such things as membership or allegiance. However, Fischer was not a journalist eager to find out all-encompassing truths. Drama and discrepancy just added to the power of his images, a phenomenon no doubt encouraged by editors worldwide. On the other hand, both LaVey and Mansfield were PR conscious and both succeeded very well in constructing public personae in line with their psychological needs. As the truth (if there is such a thing) about their complex and ever fascinating relationship will never be fully known, perhaps we should just be content with joyfully taking part in these larger-than-life space-time intersections and the individual legacies of these two true American icons.

ACKNOWLEDGMENTS

Infinite gratitude to all the interviewees and those who contributed to the crowdfunding campaign for the documentary film. Also to Tim O'Neill, Beatrice Eggers, Patricia Behman, Nick Bougas, Adam Rostoker, Jon Graham, Albo Sudekum and the Inner Traditions team, Annabel Moynihan, Miguel Guerrero Sr., Brian Butler, Genesis P-Orridge (for introducing me to Anton LaVey in the first place and for granting me use of the 1988 interview), Peter Gilmore and Peggy Nadramia for their assistance and vast knowledge, Margareta Abrahamsson, Sofia Lindström-Abrahamsson, Mitch Horowitz, the Church of Satan Archive, and most especially to Vanessa Sinclair and Christian Kount, who were of invaluable assistance in the production of this project and book. And not forgetting that old handsome Devil himself: Anton Szandor LaVey.

If you would like to watch the film *Anton LaVey: Into the Devil's Den*, please visit: vimeo.com/ondemand/intothedevilsden (website).

> "I remember an older, grander show. All an old feller like me is good for, anyways, is rememberin'. And my memories are sure more glamorous. I don't want nothin' spoilin' 'em. I'm a circus man and will be until I die. Good night, everybody," he said. And lumbered away, pachydermically, down the darkened Midway, swinging his cane, and faded into the night.[1]

NOTES

CHAPTER 1. STEP RIGHT UP!

1. Anton LaVey, German TV interview, 1974.

CHAPTER 3. ANTON LAVEY,
MAGICAL INNOVATOR

1. Anton LaVey, *The Satanic Bible* (New York: Avon Books, 1969), 155.
2. *Speak of the Devil,* directed by Nick Bougas, 1993.
3. Anton LaVey, *Satan Speaks!* (Venice, Calif.: Feral House, 1998), 8.
4. Anton LaVey, *The Devil's Notebook* (Portland: Feral House, 1992), 138.
5. LaVey, *The Devil's Notebook,* 133.
6. *The Satanic Rituals* (New York: Avon Books, 1972), 11.
7. LaVey, *The Satanic Rituals,* 22.
8. LaVey, *The Devil's Notebook,* 78.
9. LaVey, *The Devil's Notebook,* 80.
10. LaVey, *Satan Speaks!,* 30.
11. LaVey, *Satan Speaks!,* 22.
12. LaVey, *The Devil's Notebook,* 140.

CHAPTER 4.
CANON FODDER

1. Ben Hecht, *Fantazius Mallare: A Mysterious Oath* (Chicago: Covici-McGee, 1922), 86–87.

2. Anton LaVey, "The Metaphysics of Lovecraft," in *The Satanic Rituals* (New York: Avon Books, 1972), 175.

3. Anton LaVey, quoted in Doran Wittelsbach, *Isis and Beyond: The Biography of Cecil Nixon* (Vancouver, Wash.: BUA Productions, 1997), 48.

4. LaVey, quoted in Wittelsbach, *Isis and Beyond,* 47.

5. William Seabrook, "The Witch and Her Doll," in *Witchcraft: Its Power in the World Today* (London: Harrap, 1941), 20.

6. Burton H. Wolfe, *The Devil's Avenger* (New York: Pyramid Books, 1974), 70.

7. Cecil Nixon, quoted in Wittelsbach, *Isis and Beyond,* 44–45.

8. Orrin E. Klapp, "The Dialectical Process of Selection," in *Symbolic Leaders: Public Dramas and Public Men* (New York: Routledge, 2017), 31, e-book.

9. W. Somerset Maugham, *The Summing Up* (London: Mandarin, 1990).

10. W. Somerset Maugham, *A Writer's Notebook* (Harmondsworth, UK: Penguin, 1967).

CHAPTER 5 BEWITCHED, BOTHERED, AND BEWILDERED

1. Anton LaVey, "Letters from the Devil," in the *Exploiter,* March 14, 1971, reprinted in *Letters from the Devil* (Baltimore: Underworld Amusements, 2010).

2. Quote from the film *Anton LaVey: A Drink with the Devil,* available on the streaming service Amazon Prime since 2018. This material was shot by Adam Parfrey and Nick Bougas and constitutes outtakes from their film *Speak of the Devil.*

3. Anton LaVey, quoted in Burton H. Wolfe, "Interview with Anton LaVey," *Fling,* July 1978, 60.

4. LaVey, quoted in Burton H. Wolfe, "Interview with Anton LaVey," *Fling,* 56.

5. Anton LaVey, interviewed by Dick Russell, "The Satanist Who Wants to Rule the World," *Argosy* 281, no. 6 (1975): 43.

6. Anton LaVey, "The Nine Satanic Statements," in *The Satanic Bible* (New York: Avon Books, 1969), 25.

7. Anton LaVey, *The Satanic Witch* (Los Angeles: Feral House, 1989), 140.

8. LaVey, *The Satanic Witch,* 154.

9. LaVey, quoted in Burton H. Wolfe, "Interview with Anton LaVey," *Fling,* 58.

10. Orrin E. Klapp, "Hero Stuff," in *Symbolic Leaders: Public Dramas and Public Men* (New York: Routledge, 2017), 214, e-book.

CHAPTER 6. MAYBE WE SHOULD
WATCH A MOVIE NOW?

1. Blanche Barton, *The Church of Satan* (New York: Hell's Kitchen Productions, 1990), 157.
2. Isaac Bonewits, "My Satanic Adventure," neopagan.net (website), retrieved August 14, 2020.
3. Anton LaVey, in *Satanis: The Devil's Mass,* produced and directed by Ray Laurent, 1969.
4. Anton LaVey, in *Witchcraft 70,* directed by Luigi Scattini, 1969.
5. As told to this author in *Reasonances* (London: Scarlet Imprint, 2014), 141.
6. Jack Stevenson, "Freaks—The Movie and the Myth Reconsidered," in *Shock: The Essential Guide to Exploitation Cinema,* ed. Stefan Jaworzyn (London: Titan Books, 1996).
7. Diane Arbus, letter to Doon Arbus, reprinted in *Diane Arbus: A Chronology,* eds. Elisabeth Sussman and Doon Arbus (New York: Aperture, 2011), 33–34.
8. Johnny Eck, autobiographical notes published in Jack Stevenson's *Pandemonium,* no. 3, (1989), 160.
9. Anton LaVey quoted in Daniel P. Mannix, *Freaks: We Who Are Not as Others* (New York: Pocket Books, 1976), 151.

ACKNOWLEDGMENTS

1. Robert Barbour Johnson, "The Headless Girl," in *Mike Shayne Mystery Magazine* 11, no. 4 (1962): 125.

INDEX

Numbers in *italics* preceded by *pl.* refer to insert plate numbers.

BOOKS OF RELATED INTEREST

Occulture
The Unseen Forces That Drive Culture Forward
by Carl Abrahamsson
Foreword by Gary Lachman

Sex Magicians
The Lives and Spiritual Practices of Paschal Beverly Randolph,
Aleister Crowley, Jack Parsons, Marjorie Cameron,
Anton LaVey, and Others
by Michael William West
Foreword by Hannah Haddix

Aleister Crowley in America
Art, Espionage, and Sex Magick in the New World
by Tobias Churton

Aleister Crowley: The Beast in Berlin
Art, Sex, and Magick in the Weimar Republic
by Tobias Churton

The Miracle Club
How Thoughts Become Reality
by Mitch Horowitz

John Dee and the Empire of Angels
Enochian Magick and the Occult Roots of the Modern World
by Jason Louv

Lords of the Left-Hand Path
Forbidden Practices and Spiritual Heresies
by Stephen E. Flowers, Ph.D.

Energy Magick of the Vampyre
Secret Techniques for Personal Power and Manifestation
by Don Webb

INNER TRADITIONS • BEAR & COMPANY
P.O. Box 388
Rochester, VT 05767
1-800-246-8648
www.InnerTraditions.com

Or contact your local bookseller